Black Panther in Exile

UNIVERSITY PRESS OF FLORIDA

Florida A&M University, Tallahassee
Florida Atlantic University, Boca Raton
Florida Gulf Coast University, Ft. Myers
Florida International University, Miami
Florida State University, Tallahassee
New College of Florida, Sarasota
University of Central Florida, Orlando
University of Florida, Gainesville
University of North Florida, Jacksonville
University of South Florida, Tampa
University of West Florida, Pensacola

BLACK PANTHER IN EXILE

The Pete O'Neal Story

Paul J. Magnarella

University Press of Florida

Gainesville · Tallahassee · Tampa · Boca Raton · Pensacola

Orlando · Miami · Jacksonville · Ft. Myers · Sarasota

25 24 23 22 21 20   6 5 4 3 2 1

Library of Congress Cataloging-in-Publication Data
Names: Magnarella, Paul J., author.
Title: Black Panther in exile : the Pete O'Neal story / Paul J. Magnarella.
Description: Gainesville : University Press of Florida, 2020. | Includes
    bibliographical references and index.
Identifiers: LCCN 2019052091 (print) | LCCN 2019052092 (ebook) |
    ISBN 9780813066394 (hardback) | ISBN 9780813057491 (pdf)
Subjects: LCSH: O'Neal, Pete. | Black Panther Party—History. | African
    American political activists—Biography. | African Americans—Civil
    rights—History—20th century—Biography. |
    Americans—Tanzania—Biography.
Classification: LCC E185.97.O54 M34 2020 (print) | LCC E185.97.O54
    (ebook) | DDC 322.4/20973—dc23
LC record available at https://lccn.loc.gov/2019052091
LC ebook record available at https://lccn.loc.gov/2019052092

The University Press of Florida is the scholarly publishing agency for the State University
System of Florida, comprising Florida A&M University, Florida Atlantic University, Florida
Gulf Coast University, Florida International University, Florida State University, New College
of Florida, University of Central Florida, University of Florida, University of North Florida,
University of South Florida, and University of West Florida.

University Press of Florida
2046 NE Waldo Road
Suite 2100
Gainesville, FL 32609
http://upress.ufl.edu

For Pete and Charlotte O'Neal,
and for all who contribute to racial equality and social justice

Contents

Figures

Preface

Felix "Pete" O'Neal grew up in a country that disadvantaged its black inhabitants, first as slaves and then as citizens. Pete spent his youth and young adult years in an impoverished, racially segregated section of Kansas City, Missouri. Growing up during the height of America's civil rights era, he experienced and witnessed the kind of police brutality that was reserved for the underprivileged. He was fourteen years old when the US Supreme Court finally held that racial discrimination in public schools was unconstitutional (*Brown v. Board of Education*, 1954). When he was fifteen the Supreme Court called for an end, with all deliberate speed, to racial discriminatory admissions to public schools (*Brown v. Board of Education*, 1955). He was twenty-seven years old when the Supreme Court finally invalidated apartheid laws that criminalized interracial marriages (*Loving v. Virginia*, 1967). That was followed in 1968 by the assassination of the civil rights leader Martin Luther King by a white racist. One year later, O'Neal joined the Black Panther Party, becoming deputy chairman of the Kansas City Chapter. He soon became a victim of the government's unconstitutional electronic surveillance and a target of Alcohol, Tobacco, and Firearms agents, local police, and the FBI's COINTELPRO (Counter Intelligence Program), which was designed to destroy the Black Panther Party. On October 30, 1969, ATF agents arrested O'Neal, accusing him of having transported a shotgun across the Kansas City, Kansas–Kansas City, Missouri, state line some nine months earlier.

After being convicted in a trial that involved judicial errors and serious constitutional rights violations, and fearing for his life, Pete and his wife, Charlotte, fled to Algeria, joining Eldridge and Kathleen Cleaver and other Black Panthers already there. They were not alone in their flight from injustice. During those same years thousands of white, middle-class American males were fleeing the United States to evade the draft and military service in Vietnam. Fortunately for them, President Jimmy Carter's executive order of January 21, 1977, granted a full pardon to approximately 10,000 of these Vietnam-era draft evaders. Earlier, President Gerald Ford had offered nearly 70,000 Vietnam-era military deserters clemency. These two presidents, one a Democrat and one a Republican, wisely forgave so that the country might heal.

Many hundreds of Americans have called for O'Neal's free return to the United States. His lawyer, the present writer, has filed petitions with the US District Court in Kansas documenting the constitutional irregularities in his original trial and requesting a new, fair trial. Yet, O'Neal remains in Tanzania, unable to return to his country of birth, without going to prison for a wrongful conviction. He is one of the last Black Panthers in exile. This is Pete O'Neal's story.

Acknowledgments

Many people contributed to this book. Pete and Charlotte O'Neal graciously hosted me in their Tanzanian home and shared their life stories with me. Austin F. Shute, Pete's defense attorney in Kansas and Missouri during the late 1960s and 1970, assisted me in the 1990s and 2001 as I represented Pete before the US District Court for the District of Kansas. Austin also turned over to me his accumulated legal and newspaper files on Pete and the Kansas City, Missouri, Black Panther Party. My wife, Sharlene, typed up the many hours of recorded interviews I had conducted with Pete and Charlotte in Tanzania. Sharlene also proofread my court petitions and the manuscript chapters for this book. Sian Hunter, a senior editor at the University Press of Florida, and freelance editor Stan Ivester offered valuable advice and assistance during various stages of my writing. Professor Mary Adkins of the University of Florida College of Law was especially helpful with the legal chapters. Professor Kwasi Densu of Florida A&M University, Professor Mark Gibney of the University of North Carolina, and Professor Rhonda Williams of Vanderbilt University also made positive contributions. Others who contributed in one way or the other include: US House Representative Emanuel Cleaver II, journalists Harry Jones and Steve Penn, attorneys Kurt D. Marquart and Kevin L. Jamison, Federal Public Defender Dave Phillips, Assistant US Attorney Leon Patton, former Kansas City Detective Thomas Saunders, Court Operations Supervisor Heather Wilkerson, Mickey Dean, Christine Magnarella-Ray, David Ray, Professor Haig Der-Houssikian, and Ben Dyal. To them and others whom I have met and conversed with over the years in connection with my legal work for Pete, I express my sincere thanks.

Introduction

Deep unrest marked the 1960s and 1970s in the United States. Resentment against the US involvement in Vietnam fueled riots in major cities and protests at universities. The civil rights movement grew in intensity as African Americans, American Indians, Mexican Americans, and women demanded equal rights and better economic opportunities. Blacks and many other minorities expressed fear and resentment of municipal police departments, few of which had more than a token number of minority officers. On August 28, 1963, over 200,000 people, mostly blacks, marched on Washington, DC, to hear Martin Luther King's "I Have a Dream" oration at the Lincoln Memorial. Despite King's popularity, militant blacks challenged his nonviolent, Gandhian approach to attaining civil rights. In August 1965, the National Guard was called out to help quell six days of protests and riots in Watts, a large black section of Los Angeles. The very popular black leader Malcolm X was murdered in 1965, and the following year forty-three American cities—including Washington, DC; Baltimore; Atlanta; and Detroit—experienced race riots in which over 3,500 persons were arrested and 7 killed.

Within this context of social and political unrest, Huey P. Newton and Bobby Seale founded the Black Panther Party for Self-Defense (BPP) in Oakland, California, in October 1966.[1] They appropriated the black panther symbol from Alabama's Lowndes County Freedom Organization[2] and composed the Black Panther Party Platform and Program (BPP), entitled "What We Want; What We Believe."[3]

With few exceptions, the wants stated in the BPP Ten Point Program were universal in nature. All people want (1) freedom, (2) full employment, (3) an end to their exploitation, (4) decent housing, (5) a true history of themselves, (7) an end to police brutality, (9) trial by a jury of peers, (10) land, bread, housing, education, clothing, justice, and peace. Point 6, the exemption of all black people from military service, and point 8, freedom of all black men held in prison and jails, were specific to African Americans, who believed that their historic experience of slavery and the injustices in the American criminal justice system justified their claims that involuntary military service and imprisonment were unfairly oppressive.[4]

The Black Panther Party became part of the American black power movement, formed by black citizens who rejected their subordinate positions in society and wanted to self-determine their lives, control economic resources, gain political power, and achieve better living conditions.[5] Because they regarded the police and white racists as enemies of the people, they insisted on the right to arm themselves for self-protection. By so doing, the BPP joined the long history of African American individuals and organizations who engaged in armed self-defense.[6] The Panthers organized watches to prevent police from engaging in callous or brutal behavior toward black inner-city residents.

The iconic image most Americans associate with the Panthers is militant: Huey Newton sitting in a large, throne-like cane chair, wearing a black beret, black turtleneck and leather jacket with a bandoleer across his chest. He holds a rifle in one hand and an African spear in the other. In an interview Newton downplayed the weaponry and pointed out the shield at the foot of the chair, maintaining that it better symbolized the purpose of the BPP: "to shield our people from the brutalities visited upon them by the police and other racist institutions in the society."[7]

The Panthers' stress on self-defense and service to the black community captured the imaginations of young blacks across the United States. Soon BPP chapters cropped up in many major cities. Similar to other African American individuals and organizations (for example, Father Divine, Garveyites, Nation of Islam), the Panthers organized "survival programs" that included free breakfast for schoolchildren, free health clinics, rent strikes against slumlords, and clothing drives for those in need.

In addition to focusing on domestic issues, the party developed a strong international orientation, allying with anti-colonial movements and peoples subjected to oppressively, discriminatory governments.[8] They supported all peoples' struggles for freedom from repression.

Evolving Panther Ideologies

In December 1966 Eldridge Cleaver was released from Folsom Prison and paroled in San Francisco. He joined the BPP and became its minister of information and one of the party's most eloquent spokespersons. He wrote that "the ideology of the Black Panther Party is the historical experience of Black people . . . interpreted through the prism of the Marxist-Leninist analysis by our Minister of Defense, Huey P. Newton. . . . One of the great contributions of Huey P. Newton is that he gave the Black Panther Party a firm ideological foundation that frees us from ideological flunkeyism and opens up the path to the future—a future to which we must provide new ideological formulations to fit our ever changing situation."[9]

This is not to imply that everyone in the party followed Newton's instructions or agreed fully with his pronouncements. There were often sharp differences between the West Coast Panthers, headquartered in Oakland, California, and the East Coast Panthers in New York. As Eldridge Cleaver writes, "The Panthers were never a tightly run, cohesive national body. Metropolitan groups would spring up, using our name . . . but their operations were often vague and their motivations puzzling. Discipline was constantly a hassle and enforcement a real challenge for people running the party."[10]

Newton wrote that, "when we started in October 1966, we were what one would call black nationalists."[11] Influenced by the early writings of Malcolm X, Garveyites, and the W. E. B. DuBois Club of America, Newton then believed that the suffering at the hands of others would end when African Americans established a nation-state of their own.[12] He advocated taking land from the United States to create a separate state for American blacks. Later he realized that was impractical. He considered a movement of American blacks to Africa, but concluded that Africa was too foreign a place for people who had been deprived of their African language and culture. Since all of the earth's livable land surface was already claimed, establishing a new nation-state required the power necessary to take land from others. Realizing that the BPP and African

Americans alone would be incapable of doing this, and believing that class not race was critical, in 1969 he changed the party's identity and goals from those of black nationalism or separatist nationalism to revolutionary nationalism.[13]

Revolutionary Nationalism

Part of the reason for the rejection of cultural nationalism may have been the Panthers' confrontations with other black nationalist groups. Early in its history, the BPP clashed violently with Maulana Karenga (aka Ron Everett, b. 1941), a self-described cultural nationalist and leader of US (United Slaves) Organization, who advocated for a separate state for blacks and the adoption of African culture. In the late 1960s, the US Organization and the Panthers vied for control of the African studies program at UCLA. In their confrontation, two US members shot and killed two Panthers.[14]

David Hilliard, one of the BPP's first members and its chief of staff, commented on the party's new self-identity as follows: "We call our position 'revolutionary nationalism,' as opposed to 'cultural nationalism,' which limits the struggle for self-determination to appearances—dashikis, African names, talk about 'new nationhood' and the black nation. . . . We won't free ourselves through steeping ourselves in an African past and folklore but by aligning ourselves with other liberation fighters."[15]

Newton reasoned that white racists are able to oppress black people because they control the means of production and profit from maintaining a black underclass.[16] To effect real change, the reigning economic system of capitalism had to be replaced with socialism. Newton realized that capitalists exploited people regardless of color and that many whites (communists and socialists) who opposed capitalist exploitation were also genuinely concerned about racism. Furthermore, Newton saw that black capitalists exploited poor blacks, just as white capitalists did. Consequently, he changed Point 3 in the Panthers' Ten Point Program to read: "We want an end to the robbery by the capitalists of our black community." The original version had read "robbery by the white man."[17] Newton contrasted revolutionary nationalism to the reactionary nationalism of the cultural nationalists, who viewed whites as the oppressors, whereas he regarded the capitalist class as the oppressor.

The revolutionary element of the BPP was heavily influenced by international liberation literature, particularly works by Frantz Fanon, Mao Zedong, and Che Guevara.[18] The goal of the BPP was to overthrow the capitalists and put the people in power, and since the party was primarily concerned with black Americans, it called for black power. Given his Marxist ideology, Newton was willing to ally the BPP with largely white groups, such as the white communist Peace and Freedom Party, Students for a Democratic Society (SDS), and the Gay Liberation Front. Eldridge Cleaver and several other BPP members ran for political office as Peace and Freedom candidates.

Newton also believed it was important for the Panthers to ally with the peace movement that was campaigning against the war in Vietnam. He saw the military-industrial complex as part of the system of class exploitation. "At one time I thought that only Blacks were colonized. But I think . . . the whole American people have been colonized, if you view exploitation as a colonized effect. Seventy-one companies have exploited everyone."[19]

These alliances cost the BPP support of black nationalists, who detested any political associations with whites. However, alliances with sympathetic whites proved very beneficial, in terms of money and propaganda, to the Panthers who were orchestrating a "Free Huey Campaign" nationally. In September 1968, Newton had been convicted of manslaughter and sentenced to two–fifteen years in prison for allegedly shooting a police officer. Newton continued to guide the party from his cell. Eldridge Cleaver appreciated that white liberals gave the party significant amounts of money to help with Newton's legal defense fund and bail for himself.

While Newton was in prison, Stokely Carmichael visited him and advised Newton that the only way he could get out was by "armed rebellion, culminating in a race war."[20] Newton disagreed with him and explained: "While I acknowledged the pervasiveness of racism, the larger problem should be seen in terms of class exploitation and the capitalist system. In analyzing what was happening in the country, I said that we would have to accept many alliances and form solidarity with any people fighting the common oppressor."[21] Carmichael objected to the Panthers' alliance with the Peace and Freedom Party and warned that white radicals would destroy the movement and alienate black people. Newton later reflected on Carmichael's prophecy and conceded that Carmichael's warning had some validity, although he was wrong in principle. "As a result of coalitions," Newton wrote, "the Black Panthers were brought into the free speech movement, the psychedelic fad, and the advocacy of drugs. . . . All these causes were irrelevant to our work."[22]

Revolutionary Internationalism

While imprisoned, Newton had added a strong international dimension to revolutionary nationalism. He viewed Western capitalism or the Western bourgeois ruling class as being the exploiters of peoples around the world. Evidence of this existed in the colonizing of Third World peoples, economic imperialism, and the United States' opposition to Castro, communist China, North Korea, and North Vietnam. He believed all the exploited peoples of the world had to unite to overthrow the international ruling bourgeois class. "We said that we joined with all of the other people in the world struggling for decolonization and nationhood, and called ourselves a 'dispersed colony' because we did not have the geographical concentration that other so-called colonies had."[23]

Newton's views concerning colonialism came primarily from Frantz Fanon's *The Wretched of the Earth*. Bobby Seale claims that he had read that book six times before introducing it to Newton, who immediately became enthralled with it.[24] They made the book part of the BPP's assigned reading. Frantz Fanon (1925–1961) had been born on the Caribbean island of Martinique into a mixed lineage that included African slaves. He became one of the preeminent thinkers on the issue of decolonization and the psychopathology of colonialism. His works inspired anti-colonial liberation leaders such as Ali Shariati in Iran, Steve Biko in South Africa, and Ernesto Che Guevara in Cuba as well as other peoples seeking self-determination such as the Palestinians, the Tamils, and the Catholic Irish.

David Hilliard expressed the BPP's international position in his November 15, 1969, speech in San Francisco: "Black people should not be forced to fight in the military to defend a racist government that does not protect us. We will not fight to kill other people of color in the world, who like Black people are victims of US imperialism on an international level."[25] Hilliard prefaced his remarks with the following slogans: "All power to the people. Black power to Black people, Brown power to Brown people, Red power to Red people, and Yellow power to Ho Chi Minh, and Comrade Kim Il Sung the courageous leader of 40,000,000 Korean people."[26]

In July 1969, Eldridge Cleaver, then a fugitive from American courts, arrived in Algeria as a guest of the Algerian government to attend a pan-African cultural festival. There he made contacts with numerous African, communist, and other Third World leaders. In 1970, the Algerian government gave the BPP International Section, based in Algiers, quasi-diplomatic status with the right to obtain entrance and exit visas for members and guests, a monthly stipend, and official identity cards.[27] The BPP International Section in Algiers functioned until 1972. During this period, Newton, Cleaver, and other Panthers visited by official invitation a number of African and communist countries, including Cuba, North Vietnam, China, and North Korea.

While in Algiers, Eldridge Cleaver explained the following to an interviewer: "We [BPP] are a Marxist-Leninist Party, and implicit in Marxist-Leninism is proletarian internationalism, and solidarity with all people who are struggling, and this, of course, includes white people."[28] Cleaver maintained that suffering is color-blind and that oppressed people need unity based on revolutionary principles rather than skin color.

Revolutionary Intercommunalism

In May 1970, the California Appeals Court, citing an error in juror instructions, reversed the voluntary manslaughter sentence of Huey Newton's 1968 conviction; he was released August 5 on $50,000 bail, and during a speech delivered on November 18 at Boston College, Newton explained the final shift in BPP ideology. He explained that revolutionary internationalism would not work because the United States, the world's dominant military and economic power, was not a nation-state, but rather an imperial empire that coerced or bribed the governments of other states to serve its interests. Hence, most states consisted of communities of peoples who were exploited by the international capitalist class. He explained that "the world today is a dispersed collection of communities. A community is different from a nation. A community is a small unit with a comprehensive collection of institutions that exists to serve a small group of people. . . . The struggle in the world today is between the small circle that administers and profits from the empire of the United States and the peoples of the world who want to determine their own destinies."[29]

In his 1974 speech entitled "Who Makes U.S. Foreign Policy," Newton explained: "The strategic agencies of foreign policy—the State Department, the CIA, the Pentagon, and the Treasury, as well as the key ambassadorial posts—have all been dominated by representatives and rulers of America's principal corporate financial empires."[30] He further asserted that the corporate ideology prevails in the United States because corporations control the communication media and indoctrinate people into believing that the corporate interest is the national interest to be pursued domestically and internationally.

Newton had originally conceptualized black Americans as being a colony within the American empire. Now, he admitted he was mistaken. Because black Americans originated in Africa, have lived in the United States for generations, and have lost their African heritage through slavery and exploitation, they could not be considered a colony subjugated by others. They are, Newton reasoned, an oppressed community within the boundaries of the United States.[31] The oppressed communities of the world needed to unite in the common cause of destroying capitalism, making socialism a reality, and bringing the power of local control to communities. Each community should be able to govern and police itself and control the means of production so that it can have the economic resources necessary to enjoy a humane living standard. "Our ultimate goal," Newton wrote, "is to have various ethnic communities co-operating in a spirit of mutual aid, rather than competing. In this way, all communities would be allied in a common purpose."[32]

The Panthers on Race and Class

The Panthers recognized the existence of racism, but refused to become reverse racists. They allied themselves with a number of predominantly white liberal and radical groups, and they believed that black policemen could be just as fascist as white policemen. Cleaver wrote: "My mother had taught all her children that there were whites you could count on, for they were good and just, and that there were blacks you should avoid, for they were unkind and dishonest. Our family was not fed racism. I argued this position night and day within the Panthers. . . . we were against police brutality; and some of them were black."[33]

The lawyer the Panthers relied on and trusted most was a white man, Charles Garry. None of the Panther leaders ever claimed racial superiority. Instead, they recognized that many ethnic communities wanted respect and dignity just as they did. Newton wrote that BPP programs had one goal: "complete control of the institutions in the community. Every ethnic group has particular needs that they know and understand better than anybody else, each group is the best judge of how its institutions ought to affect the lives of its members."[34]

Newton explained racism in terms of material profitability: "The white racist oppresses Black people [because] it is economically profitable to do so. Black people must develop the political power to make it unprofitable. . . . This racist United States operates with the motive of profit; he lifts the gun and escalates war for profit. We will make him lower his guns because they will no longer serve his profit motive."[35]

David Hilliard quoted Bobby Seale as saying: "We don't see ourselves as a national unit for racist reasons. . . . We don't fight racism with racism. We fight racism with solidarity."[36] During the question-answer period following a talk Newton gave on intercommunalism in February 1971, someone commented that the ideology of intercommunalism and the restriction of BPP membership to blacks appeared to be a contradiction. Newton agreed, but explained that it was a contradiction the party was trying to resolve. The party's first goal, he said, was to help the black community. The Panthers have to meet the people on the grounds that they can relate to best. Because blacks relate best to other blacks, the party was being pragmatic to get the job done. "When that job is done, the Black Panther Party will no longer be the Black Panther Party."[37]

Regarding class perspectives, Panther ideology differed from conventional Marxism by regarding the lumpenproletariat as the vanguard revolutionary force that could eliminate capitalism and racism in the United States. As Eldridge Cleaver explained in his article "On the Ideology of the Black Panther Party," American blacks had to develop their own version of Marxism applicable to their unique historic experience. Cleaver credits Newton: "what Huey did was to provide the ideology and the methodology for organizing . . . [and transforming] the Black lumpenproletariat from the forgotten people at the bottom of society into the vanguard of the proletariat."[38] Cleaver maintained that there were major differences between the white proletariat and lumpenproletariat on the one hand and the black proletariat and lumpenproletariat on the other. Each had different historic experiences and related to society and the means of production differently. Eldridge Cleaver described the black lumpen as

all those who have no secure relationship or vested interest in the means of production and the institutions of capitalist society. That part of the "Industrial Reserve Army" held perpetually in reserve;

who have never worked and never will; who can't find a job; who are unskilled and unfit; who have been displaced by machines, automation, and cybernation, and were never "retained or invested with new skills"; all those on Welfare or receiving State Aid. Also, the so-called "Criminal Element," those who live by their wits, existing off that which they rip off, who stick guns in the faces of businessmen and say "stick 'em up," or "give it up"! Those who don't even want a job, who hate to work and can't relate to punching some pig's time clock, who would rather punch a pig in the mouth and rob him than punch that same pig's time clock and work for him, those whom Huey P. Newton calls "the illegitimate capitalists." In short, all those who simply have been locked out of the economy and robbed of their rightful social heritage.[39]

Cleaver argued that the very conditions of life of the lumpen dictate spontaneous and extreme reactions against the system as a whole. Because the lumpen have been bypassed by the labor unions and even the communist parties, they are forced to create their own forms of rebellion. "The streets belong to the Lumpen," Cleaver declared, and "it is in the streets that Lumpen will make their rebellion. . . . [They are] the true revolutionaries in the urban centers."[40]

As Bobby Seale recalls: "Huey wanted brothers off the block—brothers who had been out there robbing banks, brothers who had been pimping, brothers who had been peddling dope, brothers who ain't going to take no shit, brothers who had been fighting pigs—because he knew once they get themselves together in the area of political education (. . . the ten-point platform and program), Huey P. Newton knew that . . . once you organize those brothers, . . . you get black men, you get revolutionaries that are too much."[41] Some scholars argue that Newton's reliance on the lumpen weakened the Panthers' potential for effective change.[42] Newton himself eventually appears to agree. In a 1971 speech, Newton acknowledged that successful revolutions of the past were led by people with bourgeois skills. "They are people who have gone through the established institutions, rejected them, and then applied their skills to the community."[43] He acknowledged that the BPP "is not so blessed. . . . We see that administrators of our Party are victims who have not received that bourgeois training. . . . We have now what we call the Ideological Institute, where we are teaching these skills, and we also invite those

people who have received a bourgeois education to come and help us."[44]
"In the past," Newton wrote, "the Black Panther Party took a counter-revolutionary position with our blanket condemnation of Black capitalism. Our strategy should have been to analyze the positive and negative qualities of this phenomenon before making any condemnation."[45]

Black Panther Finale

Throughout the relatively short history of the BPP, Newton and his followers displayed a fair degree of intellectual flexibility in their conceptualization of socioeconomic-political relationships and the place of black Americans within the domestic and global contexts. They moved from being black nationalists to revolutionary nationalists, to revolutionary internationalists, and finally to revolutionary intercommunalists. In terms of tactics, they also changed; originally they stressed self-defense, guns, and police patrols, but eventually party leaders realized that shoot-outs with the police not only reduced their numbers, they also caused many in the black community to fear the Panthers. Consequently, Newton dropped "Self-Defense" from the party name and focused more on "survival programs" that involved serving the community by providing breakfasts for children and medical care and clothing for families. By 1971, Newton had also reconsidered the roles that the lumpenproletariat, bourgeois education, and black capitalism could play in the struggle. On the issue of racism they remained consistent in their determination that it should be eliminated in all of its forms.

By the mid-1970s, however, the BPP was in shambles. Newton and Cleaver had split the party into rival factions that were at each other's throats; many Panthers had been killed by the police, and many others were in prison. J. Edgar Hoover's COINTELPRO division of the FBI was unrelenting in its determination to destroy the party by means of misinformation campaigns, the planting of agent provocateurs among the Panthers, and other illegal tactics.

Eldridge Cleaver would return to the United States from exile abroad to become a conservative Republican and a born-again Christian. He died in 1998. Huey Newton would become a drug addict. On August 22, 1989, he was murdered on the streets of Oakland in a drug dispute. What, for Newton, had begun with high idealism ended in tragedy.

The Ghettoized City: An American Tragedy

The inner-city environment that Pete O'Neal and many other blacks grew up in was socially, economically, and spatially segregated, lacking in decent jobs, housing, and human security resources. People in such urban cores vented their anger and frustration in the form of summer protests and riots, which rocked many American cities in the 1960s. In response, President Lyndon B. Johnson authorized a blue-ribbon commission to investigate the causes of the urban upheavals and to offer recommendations. The resulting March 1968 report of the National Advisory Commission on Civil Disorders, known as the Kerner Commission, concluded that the country was "moving toward two societies, one black, one white—separate and unequal." Unless conditions were remedied, the commission warned, the country faced a system of apartheid in its major cities. The Kerner Commission urged legislation to promote racial integration and to enrich inner cities, primarily through job creation, job-training programs, and decent housing. President Johnson, unfortunately, rejected the recommendations.

Kansas City, Missouri, in the 1960s resembled the apartheid situation depicted by the Kerner Report: "two societies, one black, one white, separate and unequal." In 1968 most blacks lived in segregated sections of the city. Integration at any level was rare. Neither the prestigious 1,500-member Kansas City Club nor the 600-member University Club had a single black member in 1968.[46] A Missouri school-redistricting plan designed to equalize the wide differences in tax base supporting each student died under a wave of white opposition. The Kansas City local 1,200-member Iron Workers Union and the 177-man Elevator Contractors were totally white. The percentages of blacks employed by local insurance carriers were 1.6 percent; Kansas City, Missouri's Police Department 6.3 and Trans World Airlines 3.4 percent. The 1,365-member International Brotherhood of Electrical Workers along with the local plumbers and pipefitters unions with over 1,700 total members did not accept their first black apprentices until 1968. In general, black workers in all of the local crafts unions amounted to only about 4 percent. In 1966, blacks made up only 2.1 percent of white-collar workers, but 19.9 percent of common laborers and 32 percent of low-paid service workers. Two major local hospitals—Baptist Memorial and St. Luke's—had a total of 796 doctors on staff, of whom only 3 were blacks. According to the Equal Opportunity Employment Commission, black males on average earned 20 percent less than their white counterparts, while black women earned 15 percent less than white women. A study conducted by the University of Missouri's business research center concluded that the average family income for blacks with a high-school education was about $5,000; for whites, nearly $8,000. About 20 percent of blacks with an elementary-school education were unemployed, as compared to fewer than 10 percent of similarly educated whites.

According to the Kerner Report, "The abrasive relationship between the police and the minority communities has been a major and explosive source of grievance, tension and disorder. . . . To some Negros, police have come to symbolize white power, white racism, and white repression." Attitudes toward the police in Kansas City, Missouri, reflected the report's findings. The racial inequalities in urban housing, education, and employment were paralleled by racial inequalities in arrests, incarceration rates, and deaths due to enforcement actions termed "legal intervention." In 1968 blacks made up about 23 percent of the Kansas City, Missouri, population but 43 percent of all arrests for non-traffic offenses.

When poor, disadvantaged people break the law out of economic desperation, comfortable middle-class society often faults them for "making bad choices." In reality, these people had too few "right choices." Owing to structural racism, the number of realistic opportunities available to many of the underprivileged fell grossly short of their needs.

The King Assassination and the Reactions of Two Kansas Cities

On April 4, 1968, Martin Luther King was murdered in Memphis, Tennessee, where he had gone to support a sanitation workers' strike. Over one hundred American cities experienced protests after the event; while tension reigned in both Kansas City, Missouri, and Kansas City, Kansas, these two neighboring cities handled the situation differently, with dramatically different results. Approximately forty years later, the Reverend David K. Fly, who in 1968 was a twenty-four-year-old newly ordained minister, described events as he witnessed and interpreted them. The following is based on his description.[47]

The morning after King's murder, a number of students in Kansas City, Kansas, walked out of school saying they wanted to march downtown. The school superintendent met them, voiced his approval, and volunteered to march with them. He then phoned the chief of police and asked that the most senior black law-enforcement officer join the march. The students, the superintendent, and the black officer then walked together to the city center. After a few speeches, the superintendent invited everyone back to the school for a memorial service. The group returned to the school and attended the service. Essentially the crisis was over.

On Monday, newscasters announced that Dr. King's funeral would be televised the next day. The Kansas City, Kansas, School District canceled classes for Tuesday so that students could stay home and watch the funeral. The situation in Kansas City, Missouri, was very different. Dr. James Hazlett, the superintendent of schools, had decided he would not cancel school classes under any circumstances and left town Sunday afternoon on a business trip. On Tuesday large numbers of black students at Lincoln, Manual, and Central high schools requested that they be allowed to go home to watch Dr. King's funeral on television. Dr. Hazlett was out of touch, and no one in the city had the authority to cancel classes. When school authorities rejected the students' request, the young people wanted to march to city hall to protest. Some students vented their anger and frustration by running through the hallways, kicking over trash cans. The school authorities called the police. Some responding officers sprayed mace on students. Large numbers of students poured out of the schools, intent on marching downtown to protest.

The local NAACP representative asked the clergy who were gathered for the King memorial service at Grace and Holy Trinity Cathedral to go immediately to the scene to organize the march and keep things cool. A number of clergy, including Reverend Fly and Father Ed Warner, a black Episcopal priest, joined a crowd of students at Nineteenth Street and Prospect Avenue. They locked arms and led the march.

At each cross street, police, many wearing gas masks and riot gear, positioned themselves to block the marchers from staying their course. Although isolated incidents of violence occurred—student stone throwing and police use of mace on students—the march was relatively peaceful until it reached a line of police at Truman Road and Paseo, a couple of miles from city hall. At the time, Reverend Fly and other marchers did not know that Police Chief Clarence Kelley had ordered his officers to prevent the student marchers from proceeding past that intersection. The students, shouting angrily, pushed toward the police blockade. The police, anticipating trouble, were fully dressed in riot gear. Many were armed with rifles; some had police dogs, straining at their leashes and growling fiercely. The police deterred Mayor Ilus Davis's attempt to ease tensions by joining the marchers and continuing down Paseo. The confrontation revealed the inadequacy of city government to deal with the crisis. The school board was an entity unto itself, and the Police Department was governed by a commission appointed by Governor Warren E. Hearnes, a man who had accepted the title of "honorary Georgian cracker" given by Georgia Governor and staunch segregationist Lester Maddox.

Students forced their way through police lines and ran down I-70 toward downtown. The march became a wild run down the center stripe of the highway against oncoming traffic. Fly, Warner, and others tried to run ahead to wave down traffic. About four to five hundred students reached city hall a little after noon. They crowded together on the plaza between city hall and the county courthouse. Soon a large number of police, sheriff's deputies, and state patrol officers, many in full riot gear, surrounded the crowd. Fly and Warner spoke to some of the officers about removing the dogs and putting their guns out of sight to ease tensions.

Students and others took turns addressing the crowd with a bullhorn. As the demonstration was winding down, a local disc jockey announced that the students were invited to Holy Name Catholic Church for a dance. Buses were arranged to transport students to the church. Then, suddenly, a spark of indeterminate origin transformed the relatively peaceful scene into a frenzy. Frantic students tried to escape the plaza as the police charged into the crowd with tear gas, mace, dogs, and clubs. Fly and Warner also tried to escape, but were flattened by police clubs. Five young black men helped carry them to a WDAF News Station van which transported them to Holy Name Catholic Church.

As many as four hundred students made it back to the church, where the dance was being held in the basement. Police units surrounded the church and blocked the wooden basement doorways, so no one could exit. Police then threw tear gas through the small basement windows. Trapped inside, the youngsters began screaming. Eventually they were allowed to leave.

When students returned to their neighborhoods and told others what had happened, anger against the police spread. Burning and looting occurred in some parts of the city. A seven o'clock curfew was declared, and police arrested many blacks who violated it. The jails were filled to overflowing. In four days, five blacks died at the hands of police and many more were injured. Reverend Fly himself was treated at Saint Luke's Hospital for cracked ribs resulting from police clubbing on the day of King's funeral.

Pete O'Neal's Story

Against this backdrop of the turbulent 1960s and early 1970s, Pete O'Neal tells his own story about the conditions and ideals that led him to join the Black Panther Party and become one of its leaders both in the Midwest and abroad. In the vein of Judson L. Jeffries's book *Comrades* (2007), which describes the unique circumstances, challenges, and ground-level actions of seven city chapters of the Black Panther Party, Pete reveals the circumstances that gave rise to the Panther chapter in Kansas City, Missouri, as well as the day-to-day activities, organizational structure, and differing personalities of those who created it.

In chapters 1 through 4, Pete describes his life growing up in that city. For some young black men in Pete's segregated black neighborhood the admirable models of manhood were the pimps with their flashy cars, flamboyant clothes, and easy money. Pete describes his ordeal in the Navy, his first marriage, and his unsuccessful attempt to live what he called a middle-America lifestyle. Pete achieves his false ambition by becoming a pimp, only to find that the spiritual emptiness and immorality of that lucrative profession ruin his marriage and drive him to a mental breakdown, followed by remorse and a search for meaning.

Pete finds inspiration in the Black Panther Party's commitment to protecting and uplifting the black community. He enters into a "revolutionary marriage" with fellow Panther Charlotte Hill, and together they commit themselves fully to Black Panther community survival programs. In chapters 5 and 6, Pete discusses his arrest, defective trial, and decision to flee the United States and join Eldridge and Kathleen Cleaver and other fellow Panthers in Algiers. In chapters 7 and 8, Pete tells how he and Charlotte leave Algeria for Tanzania and embark on a new, Black Panther–inspired life of commitment to native Africans and African Americans back in Missouri. At different points in these chapters Charlotte offers her perspectives.

Throughout the chapters of Part I, I have honored the spoken words of Pete and Charlotte, transcribing their vivid speech, intelligence, and humor. I complement their stories to a limited extent by offering supplemental information about described events as well as additional context where needed. My additions usually appear in italics and brackets.

In 1997 I became Pete's attorney of record and began submitting a series of petitions to the US District Court of Kansas in Kansas City, which had sentenced him to four years in prison for allegedly transporting a firearm across a state line. In Part II, which comprises chapters 9 through 13, I describe the legal issues and deficiencies, even constitutional violations, in Pete's 1970 trial and my attempts to convince two federal judges to reexamine Pete's original trial, recognize the significance of its legal errors, and grant Pete a new trial.

The final part and concluding chapters describe Pete and Charlotte's lives in Tanzania. Despite the injustices afflicted on Pete by an American federal court that refuses to recognize its own errors and its mockery of justice, Pete and Charlotte have called on the spirit of the Panther to record enormous achievements for the people of Tanzania and for non-Tanzanians whose lives they have touched. This book weaves personal, historical, and legal stories together to show how the human spirit, even after being assaulted by the state establishment, can survive and flourish.

PART I

1

Growing Up

Family Life

I [*Pete O'Neal*] want to tell you about growing up in Kansas City, Missouri.[1] First of all I don't remember a great deal of my childhood. I do remember it being very unpleasant. My earliest remembrances are when my father was in the war and my mother and I lived with my grandmother. So to this day, because of living with my grandmother, I call my mother by her name and my father by his name. My mother is Florene to me, and my father is Buddy, because that's what my grandmother called them. And they, in turn, called my grandmother "Mama." So I called her Mama as well.

One of my early remembrances is in 1945, when the war ended. I was five years old and we lived on the third floor of an apartment building. Common toilet, common bath for everyone. These little two-room apartments, really little dinky impoverished things, and they had this shotgun corridor that went the whole length of the building. At the front of the building there was a window with a screen. I would press my head against that window and look out all the time, looking at the people on the street. I remember at the end of the war horns blowing and guns firing, and I honestly believed this was to bring my father home. I said, "Boy, they're bringing Buddy home! That's why they're shooting all these guns." Of course, they were celebrating the end of the war.

When I speak of my grandmother, I'm speaking of my maternal grandmother. My paternal grandmother was Miss O'Neal. She was a very large, very strong black woman. And do you know, I could read before I went to school. She would take me to visit her sister every summer to Booneville, Missouri. Her sister worked for Kemper Military Academy. And from all these little rich white kids she would get boxes and boxes of comic books. Things that no one in the black community could afford to buy. Little luxuries. So every summer I would go there. I was about four years old. I would crawl under her bed with the comic books, and I would try to decipher. I'd get out, I'd run to my grandmother or to her sister and ask, "What do these words mean?" They'd say, that means this, this means that. Then, I'd go back down under the bed. And this was day in and day out.

My father's mother, Miss O'Neal, demanded respect from everyone. She married a mulatto when she was fourteen years old. He came out of prison for double murder. His name was Rosco. He was a very red man. They were living in Kansas City. This was before I was born. The L. P. Price man would sell blankets and things to poor blacks. They paid like fifty cents a week to take care of it. And so the L. P. Price man came to Miss O'Neal. She was a very young woman then. She didn't have the fifty cents and so the man began to abuse her. He said, "Bitch girl, damn it, you'd better get my damn money and I mean, you'd better get it."

Now here's the thing you got to understand. This man was white. Whites could deal with blacks in that manner in those days, because often times blacks wouldn't respond. He said, "I'm coming back this evening, and I want my money." Rosco came home and Miss O'Neal told him what happened. He said, "Okay, don't say nothing. Just sit here." The L. P. Price man came and knocked on the door. Rosco opened the door, shot him in the forehead and killed him dead. Rosco turned around and said, "Well, baby, it's time to go. I got to go now." He took off and went to Texas.

Rosco was a very, *very* notorious man. He and all of my father's people were originally from Texas. They tell the story of how a lynch mob had Rosco tied up in a wagon and were preparing to lynch him for something he had done. They said, "He's one of them half-black, half-white niggers, and he's uppity." Rosco told them, "You know, before I die, can you untie me so that I can pray so that I'll be with my Savior this night in heaven." They said, "Let the nigger pray." And they untied his hands. Rosco jumped off that wagon, ran through the woods and escaped.

Ironically, I honestly would have to say we were impoverished. But, I probably had greater opportunities than many people in our community, because of the will of my mother. She was a strong-willed woman. She worked hard to keep me clothed and clean. She was not a physically strong person. She was a very shy person. My mother's mother, my grandmother, Miss Pennington, or Mama, also was a very shy mild-mannered person, but a devoutly religious person. I mean, religion was her life. Her entire existence was based on her belief in Christianity and her belief in her God.

We lived at 1211 Woodland, in two rooms: a kitchen and a small living room. I had two brothers and three sisters. For the first thirteen years of my life, I slept in a little narrow kitchen on a roll-away bed. I remember we had a Roper gas stove in there and not much room to move around. I was the first of six children. So at the end, shortly before we moved out, eight of us were living in these two very small rooms.

My First Arrest

In the summer of 1951, I was eleven years old and my buddy Otis was twelve. We planned to steal cigarettes from a local supermarket. We figured we'll sell the cigarettes later for 75 cents a carton. Because the supermarket was usually busy with customers, we thought we could snatch several cartons of cigarettes off the shelf, tuck them under our jackets, and then squeeze through the crowded checkout line and out of the store without being noticed. All but the last part of our plan worked.

"Hold on there!" yelled the store manager as he gripped each of us by the arm. He pulled us into a small office at the back of the store, where he yanked open our jackets, popping buttons in the process and grabbing the hidden cigarette cartons. "I knew you two were up to no good," he said. "Now I caught you stealing."

I knew I was busted. I became nervous as a white patrol car pulled up to the front of the supermarket. But still there was an air of excitement about the situation. I had seen hustlers off the block get busted. It seemed like they took it all in stride. They did it like it wasn't a big deal. So I put on my tough guy face and stared straight ahead.

A policeman loaded us into the back of the patrol car and drove to the station, where he took us to the booking desk. The white officer in charge ordered us: "All right you niggers, put your black asses up against that wall until I call you over here. And keep your mouth shut!" I felt helpless surrounded by white men in blue uniforms. Next, a big officer appeared in the doorway and ordered me and Otis to come with him. He took us down a long hallway to a room marked "juveniles," then motioned us inside.

"Okay boys," he said. "We got the goods on you. Now we ain't too worried about these cigarettes you stole. I want to talk to you about all those pocketbooks you've been snatching."

I was stunned. Otis, who had been sobbing, let out a wail. "What pocketbooks?" I yelled out. "I ain't snatched nothing from nobody!"

"Now," the officer said, "don't start that lying to me boy. I'm trying to help you. Don't you know they send people to the penitentiary for twenty years for crimes like this."

The police officer got up from the desk and walked toward the door. He called another officer and told him to take the "cry baby" Otis over to juvenile detention. "Leave this one to me," he said, pointing to me. In desperation I cried out, "I ain't done nothing to nobody!"

"Oh yeah?" the big officer said. "You know, if there's anything I hate, it's a smart-ass nigger. I see I'm gonna have to teach you the facts of life."

The officer continued his tirade as I stared at the floor. Then he ordered me to stand and forced me to hold my arms out in front palms up. He then took a big telephone book from the desk and placed it on my palms. "You better hold this up, because if it drops an inch, I'm going to kick your smart black ass," he threatened. I was determined, out of fear, to hold up the heavy book.

Then the policeman continued questioning me: "How many pocketbooks have you snatched all together? Tell me!"

"I ain't snatched nothing from nobody," I shouted. "All I did was take some cigarettes."

The policeman walked behind me and booted me hard in my behind. "You're lying to me nigger; tell me the truth."

"I'm telling you the truth," I answered.

The officer then backhanded me in the face so hard that it knocked me and the telephone book to the floor. He said, "Ain't no nigger going to tell me no damn lie." The officer stood over me, his face flushed with rage and his fists clenched. A knock on the door interrupted his fury. "Get your ass up from there," he ordered. "Fast!"

Another officer stuck his head in the door. "That the O'Neal boy?" he asked. "Yeah," the big officer responded.

"Well, the parent of the boy just called. The juvenile authorities have the other boy. Now they're wondering what's happened to this one. I believe we should get his ass over to juvenile right now."

I was eventually released into my mother's custody. But I could never forget the brutal, racist treatment inflicted on me by the white police officer that day.

Pete Describes Buddy, His Father

My father worked his fingers to the bone as a laborer with the Kansas City Water Department. My father also drank. That was his way of dealing with the horrible, horrific situation. On payday my father and his friends would go behind the Community Laundry and sit in the back on a parking ramp with their bottles and they'd drink there. And my mother would say, "You go down there and tell Buddy I said to come home with his paycheck right now, or give the paycheck to you to bring home." And I would go down there and my father would grumble, but he would get up and bring his money home. The next morning after his drinking he would get up and go to work. Reflecting on that now, looking back as I've grown older and perhaps a little wiser, I think about my father's drinking, and I say, good God, who in the hell wouldn't drink living under circumstances like that. Who in the hell wouldn't drink and use anything to try to ease the pain that he must have endured in trying to take care of his family and having to live in situations like that. It was really, really bad.

My father was a fighter. He would have his drinks, then he'd go on Twelfth Street and get in fistfights. He'd whip everybody. If I showed you a picture of my father you'd be very shocked. He looks like a white man. So they called him Red Onion. He came from down around Waco, Texas. When I went down there in the sixties I'd find these old southern white folks, they're sitting there and I'd strike up a conversation and say, "Yeah, my family came from here." And they'd ask, "Who is your family?" I say, "My father's name is Buddy O'Neal." "Buddy O'Neal, that's the meanest black man ever lived on the face of the earth!" Well, that was the kind of reputation he had in Texas, and that was the kind of reputation he had in Kansas City. He was a fighter—not a hustler, just a fighter. So everybody on Twelfth Street knew my father and respected him in that sense.

You know one thing I didn't say and I've never said this to anybody. I was absolutely terrified of my father. I mean my father would come home after drinking, we lived in absolute terror. When he wasn't drinking he was the nicest person in the world, but when he'd come home drinking he'd want to fight. He'd start a fight with my mother. My mother was a very scary kind of woman, though. She would run, "Mama, call the police!" My father was so bad that the police would come up there, five or six of them. He would back himself up into the room and say, "Come on." And they would all come with their night sticks swinging. I mean they would have the fight of their lives. They would ultimately get him, of course. And off he would go, and he would end up getting like thirty days in jail. Each time he would come out, he'd go right back to work, and bring his paycheck home, taking care of his family. He never left. So many African American men, and I suppose a lot of men under those circumstances, just say, "I can't deal with it anymore," and get up and leave. He stayed. But, boy, there was a price to pay in his staying. I was terrified of him.

I used to box. I boxed in the Golden Gloves. I think I boxed, not because I wanted to, but because my father thought it was a good thing. I got good and they started putting it in the paper, calling me Young Hurricane Jackson, because I'd fight in flurries. And my father, even after I was grown, would say, "You know this boy could've been a contender if he had just stuck. His problem is he doesn't stick with things."

I remember one of the first jobs I had. I was around thirteen, when a farmer came around in the black community. He couldn't sell his eggs, so he was going around, making contracts left and right with young black kids. He'd tell them, "I'll give you so many eggs, you sell them, you get a huge percentage. You get 50 to 60 percent." He brought me a crate of three hundred and some odd eggs. I felt so industrious. It probably wouldn't have worked, but I had a plan to sell these eggs. My father came home drunk, three o'clock in the morning. He saw this crate of eggs. He ordered my mother, "Get that boy down here." He asked me, "What in the hell are you doing with these damn eggs?" I said, "Well, I'm going to sell them." "That shit, I'm tired of. . . ." He lifted up the crate of eggs in the kitchen and dashed three hundred eggs on the kitchen floor. And then looked at my mother and said, "Now clean this God damn mess up!"

Now he has changed so drastically. And it's amazing, the man who drank to excess stopped drinking years and years ago. This man developed into the kind of person who follows the lead of my mother. If she said, "We're going to do this." He'd say, "Okay, okay, well, let's go ahead and do it." My mother told me one time, and this just hurts me to my heart, she said, "Buddy's greatest fear is that you will remember. He just hopes and prays that you, as the oldest, don't remember all of the stuff that he took us through." But I do. [*Buddy passed away on December 9, 1999, while Pete was still in exile.*]

Pete Describes Florene, His Mother

My mother had a vision of getting out of our death trap. And ultimately she did it when they built the T. B. Watkins Housing Project in Kansas City, Missouri. My mother was a go-getter, boy. She put in applications when they announced they were going to build it. And we were absolutely the first to move into these projects. Our pictures were in the paper. We're all there with my mother, a little skinny thing standing with her six kids. We moved into 1300 Woodland, just one block, literally, one block from where we had lived. And I thought we were in paradise. I said, "If heaven is any better than this I don't want to go because it would probably scare me to death." I thought that was just the absolute end-all, be-all. I had a room to myself for the first time, man! It was a big change in our lives!

So I remember living at 1300 Woodland projects. We never had enough to eat. I was hungry all of my life. I cannot ever remember a day in my life not being hungry. I have an obsession to this day. You've been with me when I buy food [*in Tanzania*]. I buy food in huge quantities. I think this is a result of my childhood. We never had enough food. And my mother to stretch it couldn't have me eating it all up. She'd put locks on the refrigerator and on the cabinets.

I learned that if you take the pin out of the hinges you can open the doors. If you ask her about this now, she'll laugh and say, "I never could figure out how he was getting in there. I'd go in there in the morning and the food is gone!"

Just as my mother was struggling to get us out of that early death trap, my thing was to get out of the constraints of our family structure so that I could pursue what I perceived as a path to freedom. For me Twelfth Street was it.

Twelfth Street

Oftentimes you'll hear me speak about Twelfth Street and the influence it had on my life. But it wasn't so much by choice at first. I was terrified of Twelfth Street. It was an extremely violent environment. All of the big-name musicians were there: Big Joe Turner, Charlie Parker, Count Basie. It was a party kind of town. I can remember Twelfth Street between Paseo and Woodland being so packed with cars that you couldn't move down the street. If you see any of these old movies that talk about African American jumping cities in the forties, Kansas City was like that. But at the same time it was an extremely violent, extremely frightening environment to be in. The only way I knew to deal with that fear was to expose myself to it. And so I did. My mother's position was always, "Stay away from that, don't get involved in that." But, my way of dealing with that fear was to continually expose myself and to try to become as much a part of it as I possibly could.

When I begin to think about my aspirations in life, my goals, all of that was formed by the experiences I had on Twelfth Street. I saw people on Twelfth Street who were respected, who were comparatively wealthy, people that stood out in the community—these were the hustlers. These were the pimps. They had money, women, fine clothes, and expensive cars. This was when African American doctors and lawyers in that particular community were far and few between. I can remember the Bell brothers. People talked about them for years. The Bell brothers ended up having—this was in the forties—a shoot-out with the police. I think two or three of them got killed and four or five of the police got killed. These brothers were heroes in the African American community, and I was very, very much affected by that. Twelfth Street for me was a path to get out of there. At twelve years old, I kept pocket money by running errands for people in the neighborhood. Prostitutes who worked the Lincoln Hotel would stick their heads out the window and call out to me, "Hey sweet baby, run to the liquor store and get me a half pint of Jack Daniels, a pack of Luckies, and two rubbers. Here's five dollars. Keep the change, but get your ass back here as fast as you can."

I started working at fourteen or fifteen at Nance's Café. I worked in restaurants a lot in Kansas City. Doing busboy, washing dishes. I moved out from my mother's house when I was fifteen years old. I had a job making twenty-four dollars a week. I got a room, for like seven dollars a week. I bought me a little smoking jacket, a half-pint of whisky, trying to look grown. I'd sit there in the evening, fifteen years old, and smoke cigarettes. Then I started hanging out with people much older than myself. I started getting into little petty crimes. It was at that point that I dropped out of school.

School Experiences

I never did well in school at all. They tested me and they said, "This boy's eyes are very bad. He can't see." So they gave me glasses. Okay, I could see a little better. Might've improved a little bit, but school just wasn't interesting to me. So when I was in the eighth grade, they said, "We're going to take this boy downtown." They gave me a battery of tests. I did extremely well on the tests in everything except math. They said, "Oh, the work is too slow for him." So then they said, "Let's take him out of the eighth grade and put him in the tenth." So I skipped the ninth and went into the tenth grade. This was just when they were desegregating schools. Man, they put me in this integrated school, and I just couldn't function. It was just too alien. I started fighting, and eventually they kicked me out of there. That was my last time going to school. I was sixteen.

Joining the Navy

I continued to get into trouble, fighting and things like that. I remember going before a juvenile judge. He said, "I'm going to give you an opportunity. I am so tempted to send you to reform school, but I'm going to tell you if you join the military service I am going to let this go." So now I wanted to go into the Navy. My father took me to Kansas City, Kansas. I used my grandmother's address over there to join. So on my seventeenth birthday I joined the United States Navy.

The Navy put a group of us on a plane and took us to California. We got off the plane, and they took us to a restaurant in Los Angeles. A naval officer said, "Okay, before we head on to San Diego for boot camp, we're going to stop here for dinner." I looked in the restaurant, saw all these white people, and I said, "I'm not hungry." I had never been in a situation that was not segregated in terms of restaurants and things like that, in my life. I was so experienced in other things, but I had never been around anything like that. I said, "I'm not hungry." The officer said, "Just come in and have some water." I said, "I'll just wait out here, I'll be fine. You go ahead." I stood out there and waited while they all went in there and ate. Eventually we went on.

I got into a situation on a ship. I had left the ship without permission. So the Navy said, "We're going to give you a court-martial." And they sentenced me to thirty days in the brig. At the time of sentencing I got very angry and said, "Ah, to hell with it!" And I walked off the ship again. The MPs came up, grabbed me and took me back to the brig. That got me seven more days.

I was sent to Guam, and finally it's time to be transferred to Stockton, California. Now I'm about nineteen years old. I met this young girl named Sylvia and just fell head over heels with her. It was kind of refreshing, because it was something that I had never experienced before. You'll notice today when everybody was out on the dance floor, I never dance out there—never. I do not dance with my wife; I do not dance with anybody under any circumstances. One of the reasons is Sylvia told me, "Felix, you know when you dance you just go around in circles." That just broke my heart. So I've been off the dance floor ever since and probably never will get on there again.

Trouble with the Law

There was this guy in the Navy named Dallas, from Chicago. We would all go and drink and smoke marijuana. We were in Sylvia's house one time, and he got into an argument with Sylvia and called her a bitch. And I said, "Whoa. No, that's not going to happen!" He said, "What the hell are you going to do? Come outside." He was a big fellow. I got up to walk outdoors with him, and as I was walking through the kitchen, I saw a butcher knife on the table. I picked it up. We got out and he said, "So what are you going to do?" I took this butcher knife and stabbed him in the chest. Of course, the police came, took me to jail, and I'm awaiting trial.

People from the Navy came out. They said, "Look, this is a losing proposition. You don't like us and we don't like you. Should we end it right now?" I said, "Yes, let's do." "Sign on the dotted line." I signed. I was given an undesirable discharge while I was in jail.

I go to trial. The judge listened to this whole case and testimony. And the judge said, "Clearly, there's no way I can say that this wasn't, in a sense, self-defense. But you know what, I just cannot condone people stabbing people with butcher knives. I just cannot. I'm going to sentence you to six months in jail." After I served six months and got out of the county jail, Sylvia was long gone.

I drifted back into the streets of Stockton, California. One sunny day this street guy comes up, "Pete, I got a radio. If you can sell it for me, I'll give you a cut." I'm out of money, so I take it and walk to the pawn shop. I pawned it for so little money you wouldn't believe it. And the guy gave me three or four dollars. Now this guy was a burglar, but I didn't know it. He was arrested later. The next thing, I'm arrested for receiving stolen property and sentenced to nine months.

They sent me to the farm where you're in a yard, but in the daytime you go out and work. It's nicer than just sitting in a cell. While there I got in trouble for fighting with a big redneck from Mississippi. The hearing was set for the next couple of days. They threatened to send me back to the jail. A guy named Smitty and I decided to break out. The jail compound was surrounded by two fences with dogs running around in between them. But whenever it rained the dogs would get under the shelter of the office. We waited until a rainy night which, luckily, was before my hearing. Smitty and I threw blankets over the barbed wire, jumped over the fences and were gone.

We traveled on trains, like hobos, to Oakland. From there I bussed to my parents' home in Kansas City, Missouri. I'm afraid my mother, Florene, will call the police. My younger sister, Pat, told me to go to the basement, where she gave me some food. One day my mother walks in the basement, sees me and bursts into tears.

She says, "Oh, my God! You're going to kill me! What have you done now?" I said, "I know what I'm doing. I've got it all worked out. I can get a job if you don't say anything. All this California business is over. Nobody will ever know anything about that." "Okay," she says, "Are you sure?" "Yes." "Okay."

I got a job with a man who catered food to Ford employees. I worked there for three or four months. I had a little girlfriend. Things were going real nice, but my mother—at some point called the police and had it set up where I would be arrested at the house. I was in complete shock. The police said, "We have a fugitive warrant for you from the State of California." They took me to the county jail. They went through all the extradition procedures and sent me back to California.

Later I asked my mother about this, and she said, "Well, you know, Pete, I did what I thought was absolutely the best thing to do. I had to make a decision. I had to do it." Now, viewing that from the vantage point of maturity, I would have to say that she was very, very right. I can't imagine what would have happened eventually, had she not done that. It could have developed into something tragic. I certainly didn't feel that way then.

Soledad Prison

So I went back to the County Jail in Stockton, California. I was taken to Superior Court in California, charged with escape. I probably pled guilty. The judge announced that he was handing me over to the California Youth Authority and that I would be sent to an institution of their choosing. I was furious. Quite frankly, I thought they might drop the whole thing. I jumped up in the courtroom and burst out verbally at the judge, demanding that he send me straight to the penitentiary without any Youth Authority attachment. The judge looked at me and said, "Well, son, I'll tell you what. When you get to the Youth Authority, you make your feelings known to them and I'm sure they will accommodate you. Case closed." Bam!

Eventually, I was transferred to Soledad Prison. Soledad is made up of three parts. There's the Barracks, there's Central, and there's North Facility. They're all one huge compound, but separated by guards, gates, and fences from each other. In North Facility, you have regular prisoners; that's where all of the Youth Authority prisoners are. Central is your more hard-core murderers, and things of that ilk. Barracks, of course, would be the choice, because prisoners there have the opportunity of working outdoors, fighting fires, and things like that. I was in North Facility for about a year. While there, I said, boy I'm going to take advantage of this time. And I did, I'm rather proud of that. The first thing I did was I enrolled in school.

They give you tests to determine where they should put you. I was put in the final year of high school for biology and psychology. On math, they put me in the fifth grade. So I was in math classes with people that could barely read—if they could read at all. I joined Toastmasters International. I remember they were having a tri-facility speaking contest. All of the three facilities—Central, North Facility, and Barracks. Now, they got some brains in prison and, I mean, some brains in there. I'm twenty years old. So I signed up for the contest and wrote my speech. They chose me to speak and represent North Facility. I can remember the day we went there. This was a big hall in Central, well over a hundred people in there, people from outside with suits and ties. Inmates were part of the judging procedure. Everyone made their speeches. Mine was "Religion and You," some anti-religion something. I remember my turn came. I was very nervous. I got up and said to myself, "Deal with this, deal with this, deal with this." Once I got into it I saw that I could do it. Finally they had the judging. They said, "And the third place winner is. . . ." I said, "If I get anything, it would be third." And they said, "So and so from Central." And I said, "Oh, my God." And they said, "And the second place winner is so and so from Barracks." And I said, "That's it, I gave it my best shot." And they said, "And the first place winner is, the very dynamic young man, Felix O'Neal from North Facility." In all the things that have been written about me good, bad, and indifferent, nothing in my life has given me as much pleasure as that. Next day the prison newspaper described the contest and said, "A cold wind blew in from North Facility in the form of Felix O'Neal." That was a proud moment for me.

I began to feel comfortable in there. Funny. Of course, I wanted out as everyone else did, and that's all you thought about. I can remember going to the parole board. They said, "You have done very, very well. And quite frankly we view most of your crimes as youthful transgressions. We are willing to work with you. Are you willing to work with us?" I said, "I certainly am." They said, "We're giving you a parole date." I'm going to say it was March of '62. Oh, I was happy. I was looking forward to getting out, but at the same time, I had started to do well in there. I had adjusted; I was going to school. I found something that I had a talent for, and I was doing it well. I met some of the sharpest people that I have ever met in my life in prison. You talk about pimps and hustlers, I mean, good God. People who took that whole thing to a level beyond belief. Finally, the day came for me to get out. They had a policeman—a plainclothes policeman—because I was going out of state, meet me outside the gates.

2

Life's Transitions to the Black Panther Party

Pete's First Marriage

I returned to Kansas City and ended up getting a job with this old white man. He had a little general delivery service somewhere on the west side of Kansas City. He hired me to drive his truck, make deliveries, pick up and do odd jobs. I hated this thing, but it was something to keep me going. I hired my younger brother, Gary, who was only fifteen, or sixteen. Maybe that's why Gary and I don't get along so much, because he worked for me. I taught him to drive, and we would go do these little odd jobs together—both of us hating it.

I met two sisters and moved in with them. I remember I'd talk to both of them every evening about matters psychological. I even wanted to study hypnotism. I got a lot of books on hypnotism. Both of the sisters were practical nurses. One day they brought one of their coworkers, Tilly, to the house. Well, Tilly and I were smitten with each other and started going together, much to the displeasure of the two sisters. So Tilly and I were married in June of 1963. Tilly was a deeply religious woman, and I remember distinctly one of the women from her church said that our marriage was doomed to failure. "You cannot combine the clean and the unclean," she said.

In 1963, I got a job with Ford Motor Company, which at that time was an *extremely* good, well-paying job, a much sought-after job. With a lot of overtime, you could make up to two hundred dollars a week. Oh, I was overwhelmed. With that job, Tilly and I were able to move out of our small, cheap apartment and move into a small subdivision called Parade Park. We got a nice house there. We were able to buy a new Ford, getting Ford's discount. In 1965 my son, Patrick, was born.

But that old thing that had dogged me and had nagged me for as long as I could remember, the pull of the street started to just grab hold of me, and I started to just despise Ford Motor Company. Going there for me was like walking into a prison cell. Just a horrible experience. So I started hanging out in the streets more and more. This started to impact very negatively on my marriage. And I could really see my marriage starting to fall apart, but I really didn't care, because I said, "No, this is the time for me to really go ahead and put to the test what I've always wanted to do." So as I was saying, the streets started to pull on me. I stopped going to Ford Motor Company. But I didn't quit. I got sick leave. At one point my wife was just at the end of her rope with this. I told her, "Look, the best thing for you to do is to go back to Kansas City [*Kansas*]. Go back there, I've got to deal with this within me." I said, "Let me deal with it, and let me get this straight in my mind and I'll come back." "You coming back?" "I'm coming back, I promise you I am." So she left, she went back to Kansas City. She's gone, taken the kids, our son and Nakita, my step-daughter. I had the house, and good God, I felt like I was free now to try what I wanted to do. [*For about a year, Pete became a pimp with three young women and a Lincoln Continental. He realized his youthful ambition by becoming the kind of figure some people of Twelfth Street admired.*]

Breakdown

I made money as a pimp, but I was becoming more and more dissatisfied. It started to weigh heavily on my mind. A seed was being planted; it was sending out roots. It was just becoming bigger and bigger in my mind. What in the world am I doing? This got so heavy, so bad in my mind, that it started to get unreal to me. I just had—to put it shortly—a nervous breakdown. My mind shut down. One of my girls ended up calling Tilly. She came and said, "You're sick. You need to be in the hospital." When I was admitted, the doctor asked me if I knew where I was. I said, "No, but I know where I've been: in hell!"

One of the things I wanted to say that is so very important to me. I was profoundly affected by what I had done with these young women. To this day, in the wee hours of the morning—in the hours when the demons come out—that still can give me problems. It's not something I like to dwell on. I suppose everybody wishes for an opportunity to go back and either undo or make amends for the things that they've done, that they know were not right. Well for me I had an opportunity for that, and that was with Raneissa [*a high-school student who went to Tanzania in 1994 to participate in Pete and Charlotte's Heal the Community Program*]. When Jim Dougherty [*then executive director of Kansas City's De LaSalle Education Center, an alternative school for troubled teens*] told me there was a seventeen-year-old coming out here who needed help with her life, that was heavy for me. I'm telling you it really was. As part of the Heal the Community Program, together we climb up Mt. Kilimanjaro to build confidence. I had to cajole and plead "Come on Raneissa, you can do this, come on. Try harder. Reach down deep. You can do it. Come on, Raneissa." Finally got her up to the top of that mountain. And to look at her expression, just so pleased and so proud with herself. It lifted my spirits. And when we were coming down, I started crying. I mean, not sobbing, but actually I was crying. I was trying to keep my head averted so she wouldn't see it. Finally, I told her, "Raneissa, I got much more out of this experience than you did." She said, "What are you talking about? No. See, because I did this." She didn't understand, and of course, I wouldn't tell her. But for me, brother, that was my opportunity to make amends.

So, back in Missouri late sixties now, I was in the hospital. If you've ever seen the movie *One Flew Over the Cuckoo's Nest,* let me tell you that was my experience in there. I'm probably the only person in the world to be kicked out of a mental institution. Anything that was wrong, I got into it. Dr. Sanders tried so hard to work with me. He said, "You know. You're very smart; you should see that you associate money with love. When you want these women to give you money, what do you think you're really asking for?"

Back with Tilly

Shortly after that I got out of the hospital and went back to living with Tilly. We bought a very small, very cheap house in Kansas City, Kansas, and I started fixing it up. I started plastering walls and putting boilers in the basement. I always enjoyed those kinds of things, they're relaxing to me. I even went back to work at Ford Motor Company. I was working on the assembly line. That is the most mindless activity known to man. You stand there and you screw in a bolt and you wait for the next one and you screw in a bolt and then you screw in two bolts, and it goes on and on like that. I couldn't do it. I tried, but then things started to fall apart.

Tilly wanted to be a part of middle America. I had really tried with all my heart and soul, but that was not for me. It seemed so pretentious; it had really nothing significant to say about the real situation of African Americans. I couldn't buy into the superficiality of middle-class African American life. I could not do it. Many of the black middle class had adopted a "head in the sand" attitude and as long as their personal situation was secure they were content with the status quo! I can vividly recall how many middle- and upper-class blacks referred to Martin Luther King as a troublemaker. Tilly and I separated. It was just an inability for me to adjust to the kind of life that she wanted. Kansas is so quiet, almost country. It was just depressing being away from the city and city life. So finally, I left. I moved to Kansas City, Missouri.

Forming the Black Vigilantes

After Pete's separation from Tilly, he stayed at his parents' home until he had the wherewithal to get an apartment with brother Gary. Some months later, in November 1968, he went with a local group called the "Black Youth of America" to a meeting of the United Campaign Fund, hoping to get money for the black community. At this meeting Pete got into a verbal altercation with Judy Brockoff, a white police officer's wife. Pete formally charged her with verbal assault, claiming she hurled racial slurs at him. A subsequent trial exonerated her. Enraged by Pete's interactions with his wife, officer Larry Brockoff cornered and threatened

Gary O'Neal and, through him, Pete. Gary described the encounter to me as follows:

> Sometime in November of 1968 I was shopping in a local grocery store. When I exited the store, I was confronted by police officer Larry Brockoff of the Kansas City, Missouri, Police Department. He was in civilian clothes, but armed, and apparently was moonlighting as a security guard at the store. He pushed me up against the wall and vented his anger at me because Pete and I had accused his wife, Judy, of cursing and making racial remarks against us and other Afro-American civil rights activists who were attending a United Campaign meeting some days earlier. He kept shoving me and yelling at me. He yanked a handkerchief out of my breast pocket and threw it on the wet ground in an attempt to provoke me into fighting back. He threatened, "I'm going to kill all of you O'Neal brothers! I'll get you, you son-of-a-bitch!" An on-duty police officer talked Brockoff into stopping. He advised Brockoff that it was not wise for him to carry on like this in a public place. Later, we called police headquarters to complain about what had happened, but nothing was ever done. In fact, the police continued to harass us and threaten us. We realized that we could not rely on the local police to protect us from their own members.

To protect themselves and the black community from police aggressions, twenty-eight-year-old Pete formed the Black Vigilantes with Bill Whitfield, Keith Hench, and others who would later form the nucleus of the Kansas City Black Panther Party. Meanwhile, Gary O'Neal, then twenty-three, became leader of the Catholic University of America–affiliated group called Soul, Inc. Rev. Timothy Gibbons, a white Catholic priest, served as Soul's advisor.

Pete explained that the focus of the Black Vigilantes was on police interactions with members of the black community:

> We emulated what the Black Panther Party was doing in California. We followed the police. When they stopped people, we would get out and tell people their rights; they did not have to respond; they did not have to answer questions. A lot of people thought—and justifiably so—that the police represented a potential terror. So when the police stopped someone and said, "What are you doing? Where are

you going? Why was this? And how was this?" People started answering immediately, even when it was to their own detriment. And
so we would say, "Wait a minute, brother. You don't have to answer
these. You can have a lawyer present before you answer anything.
You can refuse to answer."

As Pete read and learned more about the Black Panther Party and other
black power organizations, his revolutionary dedication to help the black
community strengthened. He likened it to a born-again Christian con-
version. Pete explains:

African Americans were looking for inspiration, and the Black Panther Party was inspiring. We read about their very defiant revolutionary stances, how they defied the police and said, "We're going
to stand up for what we believe." For a lot of people the nonviolent
civil rights movement worked. But for a lot of people it didn't. It
was very courageous, but a lot of people could not go that route. I
was one of them, and most of the people that I knew were not of
that mind-set. And so when people found an organization whose
policy was: we will try to find a peaceful way of resolving contradictions, but if you come for war, you're going to find war. That was so
inspiring.

Forming the Kansas City Chapter of the Black Panther Party

Pete made several trips to Oakland, California, to talk with BPP chief
of staff David Hilliard and party chairman and co-founder Bobby Seale.
Pete remembered: "I spoke very persuasively with David Hilliard about
starting the Kansas City Chapter of the Black Panther Party." Pete told
Hilliard about the Black Vigilantes. He sat in on political theory classes
and constructive criticism sessions. "I began to learn the terminology
of Marxism that was so much in use throughout the whole movement
back then—not just the Black Panther Party. The capitalists, the oppressor, the proletariat, and so on and so forth and on it went." When Pete
admitted that he was from the street and not a political theorist, the
Panthers responded: "Hey, brother, most of our folks do come from the
street. That's their background. We want to mobilize and revolutionize
the lumpenproletariat, the nonworking part of the proletariat." Pete
loved living communally with Panther members:

We lived, worked, and did everything together from selling news-papers to organizing, to me talking about Kansas City, the kind of work that we would be doing. People would critique some of the things I said. I would explain about the Brockoff affair and about challenging the police; people would offer constructive criticism: "Well, brother, maybe you should have done this. Maybe it would have been better if you had waited. Maybe you shouldn't have done it exactly that way." And just brainstorming together, trying to fig-ure out the best—and learning in the process.

The Panthers authorized Pete to set up a party chapter in Kansas City, Missouri. As deputy chairman of the Kansas City Black Panther Party (KC BPP), Pete was to report to Party Chairman Bobby Seale. Pete real-ized the importance of information dissemination, but thought head-quarters put too much emphasis on selling *The Black Panther* newspaper. "You've got to get these papers out, you've got to get these papers out, we need the funds, and so on." "Hey man," Pete responded, "we'll sell the papers, but that's not all we're going to do."

Pete returned to Kansas City and officially announced the formation of the Kansas City Chapter of the Black Panther Party on January 30, 1969. The reputation of the party was a big pulling point. So it never was a question of persuading people in Kansas City to become a part of it. Pete explained:

When we announced the party, people started beating a path to our door. Some came with all the sincerity that you can find in a human being. A lot of people came for the most trivial reasons. Some simply wanted to wear a black jacket and a beret. There was turnover, but that wasn't bad. There were always people coming in to take the place of those who left.

As deputy chairman I held overall command authority. My job was to coordinate the deputy ministers, who formed the central committee. At different times, Bill Whitfield and Andre Weatherby served as deputy minister of information. My second wife, Char-lotte, held two posts. At one time she served as the deputy minister of finance; at another, as the deputy minister of culture. Tommy Robinson was deputy minister of labor, and Charles Knox served as deputy minister of education. There was no deputy minister of defense; Huey Newton stood alone in that position. Other key mem-bers were Billy Robinson, Keith Hench, Brian O'Neal—my younger brother—and Alonzo Ashe. Below the ministers were the captains, who coordinated the rank and file. The central committee met with the deputy chairman to discuss policy and objectives. Once these were agreed upon, they would be passed down to the captains, who would see that they were implemented with the rank and file.

The rank and file were broken up into squads. Squad leaders were responsible for the five to seven individuals in their squad. There was a duty officer who slept in the office and an officer of the day in charge of the office during working hours. Someone was always in the office. We were much more regimented than other chapters. National headquarters was much more laissez-faire. Ours was run almost like a very tight-knit military vessel—like a ship at sea. We had a very strong chain of command, and enforced it. Even when I went to Algiers in 1970 and joined Panthers there from other chapters, they were a little taken aback at how structured I wanted to make things. Their attitude was very different from what we had experienced and had implemented in Kansas City.

Let me tell you about a few of the members. Keith Hench by today's standards probably would be considered a nerd. No, that's a little too strong for him, but he certainly had no street background. He was a college graduate. Very, very bright young fellow. He ended up a professor somewhere. Keith Hench wore glasses, average height, fair complexion in his early twenties. Keith may have been five or six years younger than me. He had a scholarly look about himself, very slender fellow. He was married and had a daughter. He had a very strong desire to be a part of the Black Panther Party. So we welcomed him and knew that we could take advantage of his brightness for the betterment and uplifting of the party. He began as our minister of education.

There was Bill Whitfield, probably the most important person in the party initially. The man who really helped me put it altogether. Bill Whitfield was married and had a daughter. He never had a street kind of background. He had always been a working man; he took care of his family and home. He was very loyal. He served as the deputy minister of information. Bill Whitfield was called Chubby, because he had plump cheeks. Practically everybody who met him commented on his resemblance to Che Guevara. Bill was of average height and in his twenties. He wore the big natural Afro hair styles, as did all the brothers. Bill had a tendency to be wild. One of my main jobs was trying to keep Bill cool. "Mudholing" [*stomping on someone*] seemed as though it was made for Bill. He'd say, "My brothers we got to have a meeting. This brother committed this infraction and we've got to discipline him, mudhole him."

Speaking of height, Henry Findley, who was a captain in the Kansas City Chapter of the Party, was six foot, six inches tall. Turned out that he was a paid informant who aided the House of Representatives investigation into the Kansas City Chapter. Henry Findley was their secret witness. He worked with this guy, Shaw [*US House Committee investigator*]. Findley went into the hearing masked, and in his private testimony, he said very negative things about the Kansas City Chapter. So when he came back to Kansas City a bunch of young brothers from Twelfth Street gave him a severe beating.

The investigation Pete refers to was conducted by the US House of Representatives Committee on Internal Security and devoted to the Black Panther Party of Kansas City. Richard A. Shaw was an investigator for this committee, which was chaired by Richard H. Ichord, Republican representative of Missouri.[1] During its 1970 hearings, Ichord stated, "If we are to believe some of those press reports, I think we would be justified in concluding that the BPP is more interested in realizing the objectives of the international communist movement rather than to solve some of the ills and deficiencies that we have in our society."[2]

Pete's Pride in the Chapter's Work Ethic

When we worked on our Breakfast for School Children Program, everybody got in the kitchen. Bill Whitfield, our deputy minister of information, served breakfast. I, the deputy chairman, scrambled eggs. *Everybody* worked. You heard Charlotte mention how this work ethic is so inculcated into her thinking that when she's not working she feels guilty. And I am the same way. If I'm not doing something or at least planning to do something, I feel like something is wrong. This I learned in the Black Panther Party. This policy enabled us to weed out those who could not hang with the work policy. I remember a time when a farmer came in and donated 150 live chickens to us. He drove his truck up and said, "Where do you want me to put them?" Most Panthers had never seen a live chicken in their lives. We got about thirty people running around chasing chickens. We tried to get those who had lived on farms to give us instruction. We had a whole day of chaos, but when that day was over, we had cleaned the chickens, and the next morning we had fried chicken for our Breakfast for School Children Program.

One might ask where did this work ethic come from? In our enthusiasm to build, we had nothing. When we started the Black Vigilantes, we had nothing. No funding, no support whatsoever. We knew anything we were going to create we would have to create with our hands. When the Inner City Parish [*a Methodist Parish run by Rev. Phil Lawson and Rev. John Presipes*] donated the house on Twenty-Second Street for our first office, we had to repair everything with our own hands. Nothing worked in it. We didn't have money to hire people. When people came to join the Black Panther Party because they were so impressed with the berets and the black leather jackets, we'd tell them not to worry about leather jackets. They needed to understand that we work and we don't tolerate people who can't work with us. When they saw the extent to which we stressed our work projects, many of them would leave.

Our headquarters was open seven days a week, from about seven in the morning to something like seven at night. But, someone was always in the office. Someone even slept there. It's interesting now that I think about it, how our operation here in Tanzania mirrors what we did in Kansas City. Someone's always in our Community Center.

Pete especially respected Rev. Phil Lawson, pastor of the Methodist Inner City Parish in Kansas City, Missouri, and a committed follower of Martin Luther King Jr. Lawson had a profound commitment to nonviolence, beginning when he joined the Fellowship of Reconciliation, a pacifist organization, when he was only fifteen. As a teenager, he joined in nonviolent direct actions to integrate stores, movie theaters, and swimming pools in Washington, DC.[3] His older brother, Rev. James Lawson, was one of the most important nonviolent trainers for the freedom movement. He had traveled to India, studied Gandhi's nonviolent campaigns, and then taught Gandhian nonviolence to members of the Southern Christian Leadership Conference.

Pete said that "Reverend Phil felt we could find a nonviolent way to resolve contradictions. I did not agree with that, but he said, "this disagreement does not nullify our ability to work together and try to seek answers together." He was under tremendous pressure from his church, from many of his parishioners, white and black, to break his ties with us. But he stayed loyal to us and his ideals. I'm very impressed with him."

Apparently, Rev. Phillip Lawson's association with the BPP and certain other black organizations caused the United Methodist Missouri Western Conference, comprised predominantly of white ministers, to vote by a two-thirds majority to cut off funding to Lawson's Inner City Parish. The cutoff amounted to $50,000 or two-thirds of the parish's annual budget. Among the delegates' complaints was Lawson's visit to Hanoi, during which he recorded a message to African American servicemen in Vietnam, advising them to disobey orders and not to kill women and children. Lawson told the white delegates that they wanted to drop him in favor of blacks more acceptable to themselves.[4]

The KC BPP had a policy of nondiscrimination toward women. But, Pete admits, that was in theory. "The sisters were our other halves, but somehow the sisters remained in the kitchen and the brothers were not. So there was a lot, a lot of sexism there." Charlotte Hill, who joined the KC BPP shortly after graduating high school and soon thereafter became Pete's wife, complained insistently to the deputy chairman about sexual discrimination in the party.

The Panthers rented two apartments in a complex on Purcell Street in Kansas City, Missouri. Pete lived in one; the other served as party headquarters. Jean Young, a white woman, managed the complex. Her husband, a black man named Harold Young, later told Pete that on several occasions Jean had let FBI agents into the Panther apartments to plant listening devices. In 1998, during this conversation I asked Pete if he knew about the wiretapping. He said, "Yes we assumed that was the case, because we stopped paying the phone bill, and we were never cut off."

Pete and Charlotte Meet

Pete narrates:

> I want to tell you how Charlotte and I met. But before I begin I'd
> like to tell you that the party had very strong anti–hard drug policy.
> Absolutely, we did not tolerate its use. Marijuana was smoked by
> everybody. Most young people that I knew from all walks of life in
> the sixties, smoked marijuana to some degree. Our policy regarding

marijuana was that you could not smoke it during office hours and you could never smoke it to the point of being nonfunctional.

I first met Charlotte when I was coming back from a speaking tour in Omaha. I walked up to our Panther house on Thirty-Ninth Street and saw these young people, some of them in the party, Brian [*also called Charlie*], my younger brother was there. Oh boy, they're just having a good time! It was obvious all of them were high. I went into a rage. They said, "Here comes brother chairman!" And they're terrified. I started blessing them out. And this young woman, little skinny woman, so high she could barely stand, comes up to me. She's slurring her words, exclaiming, "Brother Chairman. Brother Chairman, I want to make a complaint. I don't feel that women are being treated equal and I don't think it's right." I said, "What are you talking about?" "We were in the kitchen working and the brothers were not helping. I just don't think it's fair." I said, "Who are you, first of all?" "My name is Charlotte Hill." I said, "Look sister, you don't bring this to me. I don't know who you are. You are supposed to take this through the chain of command. You talk to your squad leader, he'll take it to the captain, the captain will bring it to some-one; if he can't resolve it, *he'll* bring it to me. But don't *you* bring it to me." She continued, "But I think I have rights." I said, "Shut up." She said, "You can't tell me to shut up." I said, "Shut up, now. Don't say another damn word." I told somebody, "Get this girl out of my face. I can't stand this little girl!" I was outraged. As punishment, I had the group doing all sorts of rigorous exercises. Some of them were carrying others on their backs, they're running around the house and they're stumbling and falling, and their eyes are rolling back in their heads. I remember, I took them all down to the basement and locked them in a huge cabinet. I said, "You stay in there until you all come down."

Later I heard that Charlotte could write well, and I needed someone to do my writing. I hate writing with a passion. So I said to Charlotte, "Listen, why don't you come on and just help me out." And she started helping me. We got a little bit closer and obviously the dislike changed so this is the woman I've been with now for all these years. But, boy, when I met her I did not like that woman, and I was probably thinking of ways to get her out of the party.

Charlotte's Recollections

On a sunny day in June 1998, Charlotte O'Neal (also known as Mama C.) and I sat together at a table outside her home in Embaseni Village in Tanzania. I asked her to talk about how she met Pete, why she joined the Black Panther Party, and gender roles in the party. She explained:

Compared to a lot of the brothers and sisters in the Black Panther Party, I had an idyllic childhood, a very blessed childhood. I grew up without much want of things and no want of love from my parents and family members. But I felt the needs of other people in the community. I was always interested in black history and African history from junior high on up to high school. I was a militant student, but I did very well in school. I loved school. In high school I started reading and seeing news on TV about the Black Panther Party nearly every day. I even cut out a picture of Pete.

I lived in Kansas City, Kansas; the Black Panther Party headquarters was in Kansas City, Missouri. I began going there ("over town" we called it), but it was a couple of months before I met Pete. To me the party stood for self-defense. It was exciting. It made me feel good to see black men, particularly young black men, really standing up for our community. I wanted to be a part of that. I attended political education classes, learning about Chairman Mao, which was sometimes boring I must say. Even though, it still taught me to relate troubles globally. Before that I had looked at it more as a national struggle of African Americans. But then, when we started learning about Chairman Mao and the different countries in Africa that were seeking liberation it broadened my way of thinking.

I graduated high school in June and signed the papers to join the party in July. I didn't meet Pete until August. The first time I met Pete he disciplined me because of drug use. I remember the scene vividly. Some other young party members and I were partying outside of party headquarters, high on drugs. Pete came on the scene very sternly telling us, "Oh, you shouldn't do this. This is against party rules." In my confused state I couldn't understand why he was chastising us, so I talked back to him. I was always one to demand, "Give me my rights!" This was the time not only of the black liberation struggle, but women's liberation struggle. Pete was angry. He disciplined us with physical exercises in front of the community.

A few days after our unfriendly first meeting, we started really relating with each other. Within a few weeks we were living together in Kansas City, Missouri. I can remember so well carrying my toothbrush up to his apartment. That was like some kind of transition; it represented another level of our relationship. I can remember going home and collecting all my clothes and my father just crying, crying, crying, "Charlotte, please change your mind." Because all my parents knew of Pete and the party was what was on TV and in the news. Later, after they met Pete, they really liked him. I remember Daddy always wanted to participate in party activities. He even got a black leather jacket. Years later, when Kathleen Cleaver came to Kansas City, he was one of her bodyguards, and she stayed at his house.

On gender roles, it's really funny because, even though brothers and sisters worked side by side in the community and in the Breakfast for School Children Program, in our health clinic; even though we were all required to sell papers, and that was a big deal; even though brothers and sisters would get busted almost equally, almost on a daily basis; even though we were supposed to be equal in our work, there still was inequality. You would see pictures of Kathleen Cleaver with the guns, but it all boiled down to mostly the sisters were relegated more to traditional roles: secretary, cooking, and stuff like that. I had worked on newspapers, both in junior high and high school. So, I was recruited, of course, to write articles for the Black Panther paper. If there was some kind of crisis situation everyone was expected to take up arms. Sisters did, all across the country. I remember we used to have weapons training. I never had an affinity for guns. One day in Kansas City we expected a police raid on our offices in Kansas City and I wasn't sure if my gun was loaded, but I was too embarrassed to check. The brothers had a protective thing with the sisters. They didn't want us being out on the front lines. Nothing bad about that, but women during that era wanted to be perceived as warriors too. In reality, we were warriors on typewriters.

Years later I asked Pete to describe the major factors that caused him to transform his life from a factory worker to a pimp to a Black Panther totally committed to community involvement. He replied:

I would like to think that somewhere deep inside my psyche there was a seedling-like understanding of right and wrong and that somehow the former emerged from the depths of my being and changed my life. The real moment for me came when I joined the Panthers. I can't say this enough. The Black Panther Party saved my life. Before that I was a useless piece of shit. I thought I was smart, but my common sense must have been sorely lacking to follow that misguided dream of becoming a street hustler. I was on the edge of an abyss. The party just turned my life around. I am in debt to its revolutionary concept. I live that concept. I need that belief structure to survive.

In a similar vein, Charlotte may have been on the edge of an abyss in the sixties before she joined the party. She explained to me:

I grew up in the sixties with drug experimentation. I was going through that phase. But the Black Panther Party's strict discipline really turned my life around. If I hadn't had that experience, if I hadn't had Pete, if I hadn't been in that disciplined militaristic atmosphere, I think the sixties and that whole atmosphere would have gotten me. The party really saved my life. Meeting Pete transformed my life. Even today, in times of crisis, we call on the spirit of the Panther. Pete and I say to each other: "You're a Panther. Be strong." The party still plays an important, positive role in my life. That's why when I hear people say negative things about the party's history, it really upsets me. These people just don't know how it helped not only me, but young people all across the country. Like the Nation of Islam, it has transformed drug addicts, thieves, and thugs and uplifted them.

Pete and Charlotte's Revolutionary Marriage

Pete narrates:

In late 1969, Charlotte and I slipped off to California. This was just so counterrevolutionary! This was her first time on a plane. We went to a big hotel in San Francisco, sneaking off on a honeymoon. Got us a nice room and then called David Hilliard. Told him that I wanted to come over and that I had a sister I wanted to marry. He laughed, "Brother, you're supposed to be struggling for the people." I said, "I am, but we're going to struggle together." So we went over. "Brother, we want you to sanction our relationship." Hilliard asked,

"Do you all care for each other in a revolutionary manner?" We replied, "We do!" "Well alright then, nothing else needs to be said. You are man and wife." "Thank you, brother." So that was it. I've never felt, to this day, that I need the state to justify my relationship with my wife.

Pete on Security and Internal Discipline

If someone did something that jeopardized our security, that was serious in the extreme. We were terrified that the police were going to come in and kill us. We were convinced they would either come in and kill us or they would come in and poison us. We had no doubts that government policy was to wipe us out at all cost. We believed this, and this was true in every chapter across America. So we had to be extra cautious to try to ward this off as much as possible.

I also worried about the security of Tilly, my first wife. She had been receiving threatening phone calls at home and on her job at AT&T. Callers threatened to kill me and her. So I bought a shotgun [*in Kansas City, Kansas*] and took it to her house [*also in Kansas City, Kansas*]. I didn't want her to be completely defenseless there. I tried to show her how to work it, and told her that I was going to leave it there. [*In 1970 Pete would be wrongfully convicted of transporting this shotgun across a state line.*]

The penalty for disobeying a serious order could be mudholing. Violation of the drug policy was a problem, because a lot of people came to the party from a drug-using background. We had people coming in who were trying to shoot heroin. Hard drugs were prohibited. And, there was no smoking of dope during office hours. So we had to wait until after five—after the sun was over the yardarm. Another problem was unauthorized robberies. A lot of people tried to use the Black Panther Party as a staging ground to do their own robberies. There were people going around to business establishments, claiming they were Panthers, asking for donations, trying to get things in the name of the Black Panther Party. All of these things were met with severe discipline.

The national headquarters sent us to Omaha to straighten out the wayward chapter, the pretenders, up there. And we did. We got them straightened out, after some severe disciplining. We got them clear on what party policy was, what you could do, what you could not do, what our goals and aspirations were.

More on Party Structure

Our central committee had authority over every aspect of the Kansas City chapter, but we were subordinate to the dictates of national headquarters. And that power was misused a great deal. They would arbitrarily make decisions. For example, we are from the Midwest. There is a certain mindset that exists here. Some of the things that took place in California and in New York and in Chicago just couldn't happen here. You would turn off everybody in the community.

We had an altercation with an all-white church in the middle of the black community. While it was my decision to confront the church, making demands for resources to help the community, national headquarters was urging us on, "You've got to move hard on this. Don't be soft." Pushing hard lost us community support. You don't attack churches in Missouri. It was a horrible mistake. If there had not been the push from national headquarters, I would have been a bit more cautious. Not being from the Midwest, national headquarters could not sufficiently understand the particular conditions of our area.

When we entered the party, National was a bit more structured. It began to fall apart in terms of direction toward the end. And more and more all we heard was, "We need money, we need money. You've got to sell more newspapers." The national was under a hell of a lot of pressure. David Hilliard was out there running things—not doing a very good job in some areas, but running it nonetheless. Bobby Seale was in jail. Eldridge [*Cleaver*] was in Algiers. As we started getting less direction from Oakland, we began making more and more really basic decisions on our own. We started pulling away from national's influence. This ultimately led to the split within the party. It was exacerbated when Charles Gary [*the Black Panther's lawyer*] refused to help me in my federal case. Instead, he said I could be more help to the party in prison!

Our deputy minister of information was in charge of the political education of the chapter. Also coordinating activities between schools and developing means to interact with the Kansas City public education system. We wanted school kids to know what we were about, what we believed, and what we felt was a proper course of action. We wanted to enlist their participation. Initially, Bill Whitfield, a very sharp fellow, was in charge of that, but we wanted somebody who had a very firm background in political education. And that's how we hooked up with Brother Charles Knox from Des Moines, Iowa. Very, very sharp political thinker and a strict teacher. We loved him with all our heart and soul. We'd see his car pull in—he'd be coming in from Des Moines, "Oh my God, here comes Charles!" We knew we had some very strict lessons in store for us.

The minister of finance organized the meager finances of the Black Panther Party. I can remember the first time we went and opened a bank account. I think Charlotte was the minister of finance at the time. The job required bringing in funds through donations or what have you and organizing them into some kind of financial structure, bank accounts and things like that.

The weekly *Black Panther* newspaper cost twenty-five cents. We sold hundreds. It was a big thing, especially for the rank and file, to sell papers and not come back with unsold papers. You want to talk about people being disciplined—"you came back with the papers and didn't sell your paper! Sell them. You've got to get this information out!" Much of the money from newspaper sales we'd send to Oakland. Also, there were the avaricious businessmen who come into our communities in the morning, do business, and leave with community money. Their profits did our community no good. So there were people robbing them—people not necessarily in the party, but associated with the party. Suffice it to say that a lot of the money that we raised, even from donations, went to headquarters. "We got a problem, brother," this is national headquarters talking, "We've got a problem, we're trying to get this thing for Huey, but we don't have the money." I would say, "Man, look, we've got some money, but this is earmarked for this certain project; maybe we could send out a thousand dollars." "Send it out, brother. Tell you what you do. Send it out by telegraphic transfer and we'll have it in an hour." So we were taking money from our programs and sending it to Oakland. Now I wonder, how much of that money was, in fact, for the drug parties that they're now talking about.

When I think of how hard we worked for money to run our community programs. . . . Charlotte and I would be in our office until late at night preparing for the Breakfast for School Children Program. We'd skip dinner because we didn't have time, because we were so busy trying to keep all these things going. And when I juxtapose that with people in Oakland taking our money and using it for drugs, man that's very, very disappointing to say the least.

The minister of labor was supposed to coordinate with labor groups in places like the Ford Motor Company and General Motors. If there was a strike or a planned strike, we were supposed to go out there, speak and try to inject some sort of revolutionary philosophy into the activity that was taking place.

The Underground

We sincerely believed that the revolution was imminent and we were preparing for it. We knew that when the day came, boy, when the clarion call was made, we would have to have an underground in place prepared to start fighting. The underground was very, very, flexible. They could be in Kansas City one week; they'd be in New York at another time; they'd be in Oklahoma; they'd be in Des Moines; they'd be in Omaha, or wherever. There were people from the Kansas City Chapter who formed the Kansas City underground, but they were not always in Kansas City. One guy got so hot he had to go to Mexico. I never heard another thing about this brother. Geronimo Pratt was the field marshal in charge of the underground nationally. Geronimo was well-liked in the party. But Huey would go into a tailspin when he thought someone was getting the kind of attention or admiration or power that he had. So, he disliked Geronimo.

3

Black Panther Party—Community Relations

Community Support Programs

Pete narrates:

> We take great pride in the fact that for a brief moment [1969–1970] in history we fed up to seven hundred children a day in churches and community centers. We had three or four operations going. Kids were coming from all the projects to get this free meal. We didn't propagandize to the same extent that others did. We told them about Huey Newton. We told them about the Black Panther Party, but we weren't into the "off the pig" kind of thing with these children.
>
> In 1990, when Charlotte first returned to the States after twenty years in Tanzania, she was at my mother's house. My father was being taken to the hospital by a medical service van. The guy driving this van recognized Charlotte from her picture in the paper. He told her, "I just want to thank you and your husband. I was fed at your Breakfast for School Children Program, and oftentimes that would be my only meal for the day." Boy, that made me feel so good!
>
> We had food distribution programs. White farmers would bring in crops and tell us, "Here take this. I know how the government can be. I see what they're doing to my life. Here, take this if it helps you, good for you. Don't like what you're doing with those guns, but still

take it." One farmer brought us a hundred and fifty live chickens. We were the only chapter in America that had sirloin steaks for our children and for part of our free distribution program. These came about from the Mafia families that were supplying us from their meatpacking firms. For Thanksgiving or Christmas and New Years we would have turkeys. McDonald's, *McDonald's,* would give us sides of beef. Would you believe that McDonald's would donate a side of beef to the Black Panther Party school program? They most certainly did. Shoot, we had a dealership give us an old car. Another one, we had no credit rating whatsoever, let us take a brand new Volkswagen bus and said, "Pay it off as you can." We had a lot of support, man. That was our crowning glory. It was.

Noted American journalist Alexander Nazaryan has written: "Nothing the Black Panther Party for Self-Defense did may have been as genuinely revolutionary as offering free breakfast to public-school children in Oakland, California, where the group was founded. . . . Yes, there were powerful rebukes to institutional racism, and there were the famous black leather jackets and guns, but it was the Free Breakfast for School Children Program that posed what FBI director J. Edgar Hoover called "the greatest threat to his effort of depicting the Panthers as violent hoods."[1]

Pete continues:

We even had counseling services. People wanted jobs, and we'd tell them how to get them. If they were having marital problems, some of the sisters would talk to them. A woman came to us and said her landlord was abusing her. "If I don't have the money to pay the rent, this man comes and curses me." She let us sit in her living room. She's talking to the landlord through the door. And this man is using the foulest language you can imagine. "God damn it, if you don't pay your rent I'll kick your ass!" He didn't know we were in there. So we came out of that apartment and kicked his ass. We perhaps did not always use the wisest ways, but our goals and our aspirations were to serve the community.

We also had a free clothing distribution program. All of the Panthers, all of their clothes, came from a lot of good people, a lot of women's groups. A lot of white liberal organizations would drive by our offices and they would bring big bundles of clothes and say,

"Can you use this? We hear that you're helping poor people." So in effect, we became something like Goodwill. We distributed clothes to anybody who had a need.

We had a big professional ironer that someone donated to the party. This big electric, *huge* professional ironing machine, you put stuff in between the rollers and it comes out pressed. So all the Panthers were very sharp.

We had an unprecedented level of support even if we jumped the gun, like we did perhaps with the health clinic. There was a pharmacist, a white guy, who had some huge rooms on the second floor above his pharmacy. He donated those to us, and he donated a lot of medicines as well. We had a nurse, a black woman, named Ellie, who worked with us. She tried to help me get a girl named Norma off drugs. Ellie got the services of a doctor, but that's all we had. We didn't have the proper medical equipment, and so I think we worked for only two or three weeks. We hadn't really thought through what would be involved. Still community support was there. [*The August 16, 1969, issue of the* Black Panther *newspaper announced the opening of the Bobby Hutton Community Clinic over John's Pharmacy in Kansas City, Missouri. The clinic is "for the benefit of the poor and oppressed masses, whose needs the government does not recognize as being imperative."*]

People would come to the office with the weirdest stories. Some people would come for rent money. Of course, we couldn't give it to them. Some people needed to pay their electric bill. We couldn't. But we wouldn't turn them away without talking with them. "Okay, we can't help you. First of all, we don't have any money for your electric bill." Then sister Andrea might get on the telephone and call the power and light company and say, "I'm trying to help Mrs. Johnson who is having difficulty with her bill. She's fearful that her electricity is going to be cut off. Can we work something out?" She might get Mrs. Johnson an extension of two weeks, or something like that. Sometimes we were successful and sometimes not. But this is how our office day unfolded, trying to deal with problems that people in the community had. People would come in with forlorn lost-love stories and sisters would take time, sit down and talk to them. Lot of people wanted to be close to the Black Panther Party.

I take a great deal of pride in the fact that the Kansas City

Chapter of the Black Panther Party turned the lives of many people around. We had a lot of people who were used to drinking heavily or using a lot of drugs, etc. And following the example of the Nation of Islam we began to work with them and in some instances people's lives improved. Certainly, not to the same extent that the Nation of Islam had, but we did have some successes. So when we speak about our programs, the fact that people who had been prostitutes and pimps and hustlers of all kinds, alcoholics, drug users, and drug addicts, and the fact that we turned some of these people's lives around, that really warms my heart.

Trash, Jail, and Electricity Protests

The Panthers (headed by Pete O'Neal), Soul Inc. (headed by Gary O'Neal), the Black Youth of America (led by Lee Bohannon), and a representative of Students for a Democratic Society joined forces to protest the city's imposition of a May 1, 1969, no-burn ordinance coupled with its failure to conduct regular garbage pickups in the black sections of Kansas City, Missouri. The approximately fifty protesters gathered in front of city hall and boisterously criticized the mayor and city government for ignoring the unsanitary trash situation that exposed black citizens to unhealthy and dangerous conditions. The police arrested the two O'Neal brothers and charged them with using profanity in public.[2] Judge Richard Sprinkle fined Pete O'Neal twenty-five dollars, and dismissed the charge against Gary.[3]

In January 1970, the Panthers joined with Soul, Inc., and radio station KPRS to campaign for reform of the Jackson County Jail. The two black civil rights organizations, headed by Pete O'Neal and Melvin Bowie, respectively, gave KPRS the signed statements of over one hundred jail inmates attesting to racial discrimination, brutality, and poor jail conditions. The jail housed young prisoners with hardened criminals and tolerated a "key man" system of social control in which the strongest, most brutal inmates, rather than sheriff's deputies, policed jail tanks.[4] An unsigned editorial in the *Kansas City Times* described conditions in the jail as intolerably overcrowded, understaffed, and grossly underbudgeted.[5] The jail critics called for the creation of a citizens' commission comprised of penologists, criminologists, and psychologists to study jail conditions and make recommendations for reform.[6]

The September 27, 1969, issue of the *Black Panther* carried an article by Kansas City Panther Andre Weatherby entitled "Confrontation with Kansas City Light Company." In it, the author states that the Kansas City Panthers had marched with the residents of the Wayne Minor Housing Project who had been without power for twenty-two hours.

The Pageant Fracas

Pete narrates:

> After Melvin Bowie took over Soul Inc., that group and the Kansas City Black Panthers were able to work even more closely than we had before. I remember, there was a white guy who came into the black community. He was organizing a beauty contest that involved about a hundred young black girls. He had all these girls lined up in their finery. We got word that this man was a con artist; he comes into these communities from city to city, takes advantage of some of these young girls, molests some of them, he rips off their money, and things like that. We, Melvin Bouie, Soul Inc., and the Panthers together burst into the auditorium with all of these girls, more than a hundred girls. And we yell out, "It's over! If you don't leave town, you're dead!" [*The events described here took place on June 8, 1969. The pageant involved black girls aged thirteen to fifteen.*] The con man was terrified, he's running down the aisle, girls were screaming. Melvin Bouie and I were arrested for that. We were put in jail overnight, and I was convinced they were going to formulate some heavy charge against us for assault or threatening. They took it to the DA while we're in jail, and I'm waiting for them to move us from the city jail to the county jail. The next morning the jailers came and said, "The DA decided not to prosecute." The con man refused to testify for one thing—but it came out that he was wanted; he was some kind of crook.[7]

The Kansas City Chapter's Place in the Midwest

Pete narrates:

> Kansas City was not a big gang town then, as such. You had people in areas and groups on certain streets. You had groups on Twelfth Street, Eighteenth Street, Twenty-Third Street, and

Twenty-Seventh. People from these various neighborhoods were turf conscious. But the Panthers enjoyed respect almost throughout the city. We had difficulty at times with some of the street people who were into things like drugs. We had a hard drug policy. One of the most dangerous guys in Kansas City was a guy named Richardson that I grew up with. There was a girl involved with him that tried to jump out a window. I remember he came down, not to talk to me, but to talk to the nurse, Ellie, who had helped me with that girl for awhile. He said, "Listen, you ought to tell Pete, don't push too hard on my business. I don't bother his thing. Tell him, don't push me too hard when it comes to my business." He was a pimp and a hustler and a gangster. And I mean a real one. He was arrested shortly thereafter, and I remember Charlotte and I went down to the courtroom. He was given a million years to life or some such ridiculous sentence.

We didn't have the nationalist confrontations that they had in the bigger cities. Nationalist groups that did exist in Kansas City, like Black Youth of America, wanted to work with us, to share in some of the respect we had in the community. So whatever they were trying to do, they didn't want to do it in opposition to us; they wanted to do with us. We had an unusually high level of community support. That started to change when we attacked the white church.

When you talk about the Kansas City, Missouri Chapter, you have to imagine it being the hub of a midwestern wheel. The spokes would branch out from Kansas City, Missouri, to Oklahoma City to Des Moines, Iowa, to Omaha, Nebraska, and even with some influence to St. Louis and southern Illinois. These satellites of Kansas City had little to no contact with national headquarters. They were dealing directly with Kansas City, Missouri. There was no chapter in Kansas, but there were a lot of people from Kansas who belonged to the Black Panther Party.

Kansas City, Missouri, is a well-known "big city." It was so easy for people to drive over from Des Moines, Iowa, and to us and say, "What are you about? Can we be a part of it?" People from Omaha, Nebraska, people from Oklahoma City, people from Southern Illinois, from St. Louis and, of course, Kansas City, Kansas. When the people came down, we didn't treat them as though we were the Panthers and they were the subordinates. We said, "What talents do you have?" When Charles Knox came down, he said, "I know politics.

I can teach politics." We said, "you'll work with our minister of education and take over the PE [*political education*] classes for all the people we deal with." When he came, *all* of Des Moines came with him. When national sent us up to straighten out a group in Omaha that wasn't really a chapter, we went up there and gave them a good mudholing, a good straightening out, and then told them, "Come down and work with us." People joined us because of our location, but perhaps more importantly because of the manner in which we dealt with them. We didn't try to present ourselves as being something special, being something above and beyond. We said, "Hey, we're here trying to get a job done. If you've got something that you can seriously contribute, come on in." And they did so.

Shortly after we joined the Black Panther Party, national head-quarters started clamping down on opening new chapters, in large part because they were afraid of infiltration. Also, they were beginning to be afraid that they were losing control—the reins of power could more easily be pulled away by the larger number of chapters. Because of this concern over control, they called me to national headquarters. They had a policy that you not testify before a grand jury. I had been subpoenaed to go before a grand jury. I can't remember what it was about. Now, I could refuse to testify and go to jail. I chose what is the smartest, logical course. I took the Fifth Amendment: "I refuse to answer on the grounds that it may incriminate me." They said, "you're excused." I get up, I walk out. End of story. It was on the news that I had been called before the grand jury.

And so, David Hilliard calls me. He wants to know why I appeared before a grand jury. I tried to explain over the telephone. And he said, "No, we want to talk to you face-to-face about this, because we have a strong policy." He's adamant about my coming out there to California. So I spend some of our scarce money to fly there. I get out there at noon and he's still in bed. May have had a hard night working for the people, struggling for the people. "Oh hey, Pete, how you doing?" "I'm fine," I said, "but I'm here to talk about what you insisted on seeing me about." And he said, "Oh, that's right, Pete. Listen, man, we have a strong policy, we do not under any circumstances testify in front of grand juries. Our position is we. . . ." I said, "Wait a minute, David. Listen man, first you have to understand some of the peculiarities of the area from which I come. First of all, we have a lot of support from the community. And it's because we're highlighting how the system is dealing with us inaccurately. But if I very foolishly refuse to testify and go to jail, that's dumb. And it would be viewed as just dumb. So what I did I went in, I took the Fifth Amendment and that was the end of it." "Oh, that's different man." I said, "That's it?" He said, "Yeah, I just wanted to get it straight. I said, "But I told you that on the phone." "Oh yeah but you know, man, but it's good if we discuss these things face-to-face." So then I went back to Kansas City. This added to the disillusionment that I was feeling.

Clash with a White Inner City Church

The Panthers targeted the Linwood United Methodist Church, a white church in the heart of the black community. They resented the periodic presence of apparently rich white people in, but socially divorced from, the black inner-city community. Pete and the Panthers drew up a list of demands which they presented to the church congregation on March 31, 1970. The list included demands that the church turn over a significant portion of its income to the black community, that the church open its facilities to community functions, such as the Panthers' Breakfast for Children program, that it denounce police departments across the country for their inhumane treatment of the poor and oppressed, and that it take a stand against the United States' "genocidal war" in Vietnam.[8] The Panthers returned to the church on April 7, 1970, to learn that church leaders would be willing to discuss the demands, but would not immediately agree to them. Consequently, Pete and his followers (now members of the Sons of Malcolm, rather than Black Panthers) returned to the church on May 31 with the intention of joining the church and insisting on their demands. They interrupted the minister's sermon. The outraged congregation confronted them and bedlam ensued. Pete describes the chaotic scene:

We had a confrontation with a white Methodist Church in the black community. When white flight took place, they could not take their church with them, a big beautiful edifice. They had to come back to worship there on Sundays. We confronted the church, making demands for resources to help the community. Initially, they refused. The people from the church and our group had a physical battle on the altar there, a physical knock-down, drag-out battle.

There were TV cameras there showing us fighting white church members, and the pastor, and the deacon, and all of them on the altar and a big brouhaha. The police came in there in an absolute fury. Attacking the white church! They were *outraged*. They started jumping across pews. We ran out of the building. African Americans on the street were running; it became chaotic. The police started arresting people off the street at random. One poor woman was screaming, "My babies are at home! I was going to the store to buy milk." [*The Reverend Robert L. Beech, director of the Mid-West Training Network, publicly complained that eight of the persons arrested at the Linwood Methodist Church on May 31 were religion trainees, who played no part in any disturbance.*[9] *Several Kansas City church ministers met with Chief Clarence Kelley to complain that the police indiscriminately arrested black people who were not involved in the Linwood Church disturbance.*][10]

People were running everywhere. Charlotte and I ran into a hospital; we ran out of the hospital and jumped into a cab. A lot of other African Americans jumped into the same cab. This poor white driver thought he was being kidnapped and robbed. He drove off. Police cars swerved in and blocked him down. The police took us all to jail. First time Charlotte had ever been in jail in her life; she wasn't charged with anything. They charged me with disturbing a religious service. I was ultimately convicted of a misdemeanor, not a felony. Interestingly enough, the church people who had initially brought charges tried everything they could to drop the charges, but the prosecution would not allow them to do so.

Good did come out of this; we and the church started working together on common programs. We began to discuss what we could do in terms of food distribution. They wanted to help us with some of our other programs, making it very clear that they didn't want to be involved in anything revolutionary, not at all. But any community service, they said, "We're willing to talk with you, and we're willing to work with you."

The confrontation was plastered all over the newspapers. I think it went across the country. In the black community in Kansas City you can disagree with the church. You don't have to believe, but you should respect the church. To go into a church and involve yourself in a knock-down, drag-out brawl, no-no, that shouldn't happen. So, shortly after that we started to see a cooling of our black community support. My declaration of embracing Marxism didn't work well either.

In retrospect, Pete regretted attacking the Linwood United Methodist Church and Pastor Ralph Roland, because it demonstrated unnecessary disrespect for a people's religion.[11] After the May 31 melee, Pete was arrested. He was tried in a magistrate court on June 25 and found guilty of disturbing a religious assembly. Magistrate Harry S. Davis gave Pete the maximum penalty of six months in jail and a fine of $500.[12] In pertinent part, the subject Missouri Statute 562.250 states that "Every person who shall willfully . . . disquiet or disturb . . . an assembly met for religious worship . . . by making a noise, or by rude . . . or profane discourse . . . shall be deemed guilty of a misdemeanor."

Prior to trial, Pastor Roland and other leaders of the Linwood Church signed sworn affidavits asking the prosecutor to dismiss all charges against Pete O'Neal and others arrested and charged. However, prosecutor Joseph P. Teasdale refused to dismiss the charges and warned that, if the church members who originally filed complaints did not appear at trial to testify, he would subpoena them to do so.

Pete had maintained that he went to the Linwood Church in order to become a member and was frustrated by his inability to do so. He stated that his group wanted to join the church to make it more relevant to the black community. During the trial, defense attorney Austin Shute[13] was able to establish through cross-examination of prosecution witnesses that the church service on May 31 departed from the usual in that the customary invitational hymn was not sung and the pastor did not invite guests who wished to join the church to come forward. In the absence of the customary invitation to join, O'Neal took one of the microphones and announced, "I am going to join this church and the first thing I am going to do is put Dr. Roland out of a job."

During the trial, Shute argued that O'Neal was a member of a black Methodist Church. He called three ministers (two black and one white) to offer testimony that O'Neal's actions of going forward and debating the pastor were expected behavior in a black church. However, each time Shute asked a minister a question about the appropriate patterns of behavior in black congregations, the prosecutor objected that the testimony was immaterial, and Magistrate Davis agreed by sustaining the objection. One of the defense witnesses, whose testimony was denied, was the Rev. Tex Sample, a white Methodist minister with a doctorate

in the sociology of religion. Magistrate Davis told Shute, "If you're going to bring in sociology professors and any of that stuff, I don't want
to hear it because it doesn't have any bearing." Before announcing sentence, Magistrate Davis, acting more like a witness for the prosecution
than a neutral judge, stated, "I've never known O'Neal as a very active
churchman."[14]

Prior to the trial, three groups had been formed to deal with the root
causes of the conflict. The Missouri West Annual Conference of the
United Methodist Church created a reconciliation group to mediate between the Linwood Church (represented by the Linwood Church administrative board) and the black community (represented by various black
organizations and headed by Pete O'Neal). The latter two groups agreed
to meet faithfully with the reconciliation group to work on the larger
issues of concern to the black community and the Linwood Church ministry. Derrell Cuningham, lay leader of the Linwood Church, stated, "The
Linwood administrative board entered into this agreement in the attempt to make the Gospel applicable to the needs of the community and
in the interests of better human relations. We believe in brotherhood,
goodwill and love, and hope to have the opportunity to prove it."[15] In
reaction to this Christian show of goodwill, Magistrate Davis "chided the
Linwood Church Board for holding discussions with the Blacks, saying
that this encouraged them in their effort at what he called extortion."[16]

Attorney Austin Shute planned to appeal the guilty verdict to the Sixteenth Judicial Circuit Court of Missouri. In his "Suggestions" to that
court, Shute complained that the charge ("Information") against O'Neal
(that is, "making a noise" and "rude behavior") was too vague. He argued
that the Information fails to state what type of noise and to describe the
rude behavior in specific terms so that the defendant can make a proper
defense to the charge. In his application to the Circuit Court for a con-
tinuance, Shute made the disturbing observation that

A fair trial is . . . unlikely for defendant in that black people are
systematically excluded as jurors during the preemptory challenges
exercised by the prosecuting attorney in the trial of criminal actions where the defendant is a black person; that this has been the
general practice and custom of the prosecuting attorney's office
of Jackson County, Missouri, and results in the final analysis to a
racial imbalance on juries in the trial of black persons for criminal
charges; that such a method is inherently unfair to both black and

white citizens, since it assumes a black juror cannot fairly and impartially sit as a juror in the trial of a black person for a criminal offense, whereas it assumes that a white person is superior enough to be able to fairly and impartially sit as a juror in the trial of a white person for a criminal offense; that in fact, the present practice is merely an extension of racism into the administration of justice, and as such denies the defendant of due process of law in violation of the Fourteenth Amendment of the Constitution of the United States, and further denies him a fair trial by a jury of his peers.

It wasn't until 1989 that the US Supreme Court in the case of *Batson v. Kentucky*[17] fully agreed with Shute by ruling that the use of peremptory challenges to remove potential jurors from the jury pool based on race violates the Equal Protection Clause of the Fourteenth Amendment to the Constitution. Because Pete O'Neal would flee the country in November 1970, Attorney Shute was never able to present his appeal to the Circuit Court.

4

Police and US Government Relations

Once Pete announced the formation of the Kansas City Chapter of the Black Panther Party, the Kansas City, Missouri, Police Department formed a special unit to monitor it twenty-four/seven and follow its members' movements. This frequently resulted in hostile confrontations that produced numerous traffic citations and charges of disorderly conduct, disturbing the peace, interfering with police duties, profanity in public places, and so forth. Local police and federal agents pursued a strategy of eliminating the BPP by tying its members up in court, jail, or prison and depleting their finances through frequent fines and the necessity of bail bonds.

Harry Jones, a white journalist with the *Kansas City Times* and a keen observer of racial relations, wrote that police stopped and questioned almost everyone who visited the local Black Panther headquarters.[1] "Police officials privately acknowledge that an effort has been made to move the racially biased officers out of sensitive positions in which their prejudices might be vented."[2] Ironically, the governor's Advisory Commission on Human Rights, to which citizens could air their grievances against the police, met at the discretion of the police board, whose chairman, Joseph Kelly, opposed it.[3]

The following affidavit by detective Thomas Saunders evinces the hostility local police held toward the Panthers and Pete O'Neal.

Saunders Affidavit

Comes now Thomas Saunders, of lawful age, and first being duly sworn, upon his oath states voluntarily as follows:

My name is Thomas Saunders. During the time that the Black Panther Party existed in Kansas City I was a detective in the Intelligence Unit of the Kansas City Police Department. I worked in this capacity for approximately seven years. My role in the unit was to monitor the actions of groups deemed subversive by the Department. The Black Panther Party was one of the groups that I monitored. Pete O'Neal was the leader of the local Panther Party. There was a fear on the police force that the Black Panthers were aggressors. Many officers felt that they would do harm to people. I didn't necessarily agree with this perspective. There was a lot of verbal posturing by the Panthers but I didn't feel that they were much of a threat to public safety. I knew the guys. I had no major problems with them. They talked a lot about protecting the neighborhood.
If Pete had been caught alone by white officers I believe that he would have been in danger. There is no doubt in my mind about this. The message on the force was that he was armed and dangerous. Sometimes I would hear officers talk about what they would do if they caught him. However they wouldn't talk much around me. There were rumors that some police officers at the time belonged to the Ku Klux Klan and the Minutemen.
At times officers would attempt to bait Pete and taunt him. For example there would be unwarranted car checks. It was common knowledge that the climate on the force was hostile toward Pete and the Panther Party.

Signed: Thomas Sanders
May 23, 2000 (notarized by Michelle A. Greer. Notary Public, Jackson County, Missouri)[4]

Carl T. Rowan, former US ambassador to Finland, former director of the US Information Agency, and award-winning journalist, wrote in his 1969 opinion column that the "white law-enforcement machinery has moved against the Panthers with a zeal and ruthlessness that they never deployed against the Ku Klux Klan, the Minutemen, or any of the white groups that have armed heavily and resorted to violence and intimidation. . . . The Klan's record of murders, lynching and beatings makes the Panthers look like a non-violent, loud-talking gun club."[5]

The Dacy Affair

A highly inflammatory and damaging article written by Kansas City Black Panther Andre Weatherby and unfortunately endorsed by Deputy Chairman Pete O'Neal appeared in the August 2, 1969, issue of the *Black Panther* newspaper. The article insensitively celebrated the murder of Kansas City policeman John Dacy and threatened other police officers with assassination. The circumstance of the murder was as follows: Three men, none of whom were Panthers, were robbing a local loan company when off-duty patrolman Dacy entered. One of the robbers ordered Dacy to a back room, where they exchanged gunfire and Dacy was mortally wounded. The Weatherby article, reproduced in part below, was headlined "Kansas City Fascist Pig Performing His Final Duty":

> The people of Kansas City are in an ecstatic state today following the execution of a pig. Three (3) un-known heroic brothers had the pleasure of "offing a pig." The late pig, John Edward Dacy, 31 year old slum lord, was shot by three black brothers in the same area where he owns property. Dacy was a well-known pig and well known exploiter of black people. The brothers were in the process of getting back what was theirs from Jo-Art Loan Company. . . . Let all the oppressors of the people beware. Dacy was an off-duty pig: the next pig may be on-duty. . . . the pig may well be sitting at a counter drinking a cup of coffee and come up missing. The brothers are ready and they will deal with the fascist pig.[6]

As expected, fellow police officers vented outrage, and many local black leaders voiced disapproval. Over the years, Pete has repeatedly expressed regret for the article. On January 5, 1999, he put the article in historic perspective with the following open letter:

> Through the hindsight and wisdom of many years, I will readily admit NOW that the 1969 article (in the Black Panther Party national newspaper) was sadly, insensitive. . . . I NOW could not make light of or applaud the death of any human being, however the fact remains that that was a reflection of the hostility and hatred that existed between segments of the Black Community and the Police

Department, and while it was a feeling that I and many other young Blacks shared, it was also an attitude that was shared and expressed by law enforcement agencies across the country. I am sure that most folks have read accounts of how policemen and FBI agents "toasted" the assassination, also in 1969, of Fred Hampton, the Deputy Chairman of the Chicago Chapter of the Black Panther Party . . . an assassination I might add that was later proved in a Federal court of law to have been carried out by the Chicago Police and the FBI. So, it should be clear to any reasonable person that a climate of hatred existed in the sixties, a climate of hatred that has yet to be completely eradicated. It is my sincere and heartfelt belief that as we approach the new Millennium, a symbolic time of new beginnings, we have a profound opportunity to bring about a change in attitude that will allow all Americans to begin to create the kind of egalitarian society that thus far has not moved much beyond a dream. I am convinced that a first step in this creation effort is a letting go of the racial, political and social animosities that we have held so close to our hearts for so many years. In this regard, I have no hesitation in stepping forward and extending my hand in love and reconciliation to all good people. To all the relatives of those who suffered and died, including the family of Officer Dacy, and to all the survivors of the turmoil of the sixties, I say this. . . . I make a commitment to you here and now to work my fingers to the bone to insure that the kind of just and fair society that we all desire has a fighting chance to come into being. . . . It WILL come to be if we join hands and work together to make it so!

    Sincerely,

    Pete O'Neal

    Embaseni Village

    Arusha, Tanzania, East Africa[7]

The chief of the Kansas City, Missouri, Police Department during the Black Panther years was Clarence Kelley. He had been born in Kansas City, Missouri, earned an LLB from the University of Kansas City in 1940, and was later admitted to the Missouri Bar. Kelley served as an FBI special agent from 1940 to 1961. Thereafter he became chief of police in Kansas City, Missouri, where his predecessor and four senior departmental officers had been indicted on corruption charges. The most controversial event of Kelley's years as police chief occurred after the assassination of the Rev. Martin Luther King Jr. on April 4, 1968, when six blacks were killed in demonstrations in Kansas City. Critics faulted the supervision of the police who quelled the disturbances. Kansas City blacks regarded Kelley with suspicion and complained that blacks found it difficult to rise in the ranks of the Police Department. Kelley later directed the FBI from 1973 to 1978.[8]

Pete's Views of the Kansas City, Missouri Police

I was opposed to Police Chief Clarence Kelley and what he stood for. He represented a very oppressive kind of system, a police department that was corrupt and racist to the core. I opposed the manner in which policemen treated members of the African American community. And I was right in that opposition. But having said that, I also have to say Clarence Kelley was not dumb. He was very smart. You could not push button A and get a response from him. You take the other police chiefs like Parker in Los Angeles, police chiefs in Chicago and places like that. You could provoke them. And, yes, in a war you provoke your enemy. They try to provoke us, we try to provoke them. It was so easy to do in these other cities. Kelley was a little smarter. He would counsel his policemen, "No, don't do that. No, don't do this. No, don't respond this way." And he even said one time that they would have classes so that his policemen would avoid being provoked and falling into situations that would paint them in a bad light, which is, of course, what we wanted to do.

The police had a plan in the works to raid the Black Panther office. Harry Jones of the *Kansas City Star* and some other news people came and said, "Pete, we got word that the police are coming to your place. They're going to storm it and people are going to get killed." I said, "Well, if they come in, yes people are going to be killed," because we had the policy—so very foolishly I think now—of defending our threshold. It was so ridiculous; you put yourself in a little narrow room with four, five, or six guns and say we will fight to the death if anybody comes. Not a very guerrilla-like tactic, I don't think, but that was our policy nonetheless. And so we said, "If they come we will fight." Then Harry Jones and some others said, "We've got to stop this." They contacted African American community leaders. They all came. We invited them into the Panther house, and nothing more ever came of that threat.

We had particular bad feelings with two black policemen, Winston and DeGraffenreid. These were patrol-car policemen. Winston was a big fellow. He had shot and killed a fourteen-year-old black girl at a skating rink. He claimed she had a weapon, when she did not. Nothing ever came about as a result of this girl being killed. We played it up in the *Black Panther* paper as much as we possibly could. And boy they hated us and we hated them. I really despised them, particularly DeGraffenreid. They would see me in a store and start making little snide remarks, and we'd make snide remarks back. Once in a liquor store, I was buying cigarettes and had my car keys on the counter. DeGraffenreid literally picked up my car keys. I said, "Man this is silly now, I mean this is getting almost childish." And we get into a scuffle that ends up in blows being exchanged outside. Both of them grab me and put handcuffs on me, but never took me to jail, because it would have looked so ridiculously bad for them. I'm sitting there with a bloody lip.

So now we come to Sergeant Parker. Sergeant Parker for me was the epitome of Uncle Tom. It is almost as though that phrase was invented for him. He had that kind of personality. While I disliked Winston and DeGraffenreid and thought they were horrible examples of what policemen were supposed to be—servants of the people—at the very least, they tried to conduct themselves in some sort of dignified manner. Sergeant Parker was not like that. He would do anything that he could to ingratiate himself with his superiors. He would tell blatant lies, and he would make accusations. He came to me several times, "Will you let me help you, Pete? Pete, will you let me help you?" And then he actually had the nerve to sit there and start crying and wiping his eyes, "They're going to kill you, boy, if you don't let me help you. I'm trying to save your life. I know, I know what you're doing, but you're going about it wrong, you're going about it wrong." And then immediately he would go off, and his whole persona would change, and you would hear him say, "Yes, we're going to deal with these Panthers. We're not going to take any stuff from them."

We would see Parker outside one of our breakfast program sites with a very stern posture, trying to see what's going on. And if we fed three hundred children in one location that day, this man would go *swear* to the news media that he saw fifteen straggle in. He really did that a great deal. He tried everything in his power to dissuade parents from allowing their children to come to our Breakfast for School Children Program. He would tell them that we were trying to propagandize their children and that it could be very dangerous, because you never knew what could happen. Perhaps a shooting incident could occur or something like that.

One day, my brother Charlie [*also called Brian*] and some Panthers were outside the Panther house. Police claimed Charlie spit on them, which is ridiculous. Then they claimed that Panthers came on the porch with guns. The Panthers on one side, DeGraffenreid and Winston on the other began hurling names back and forth. And then the police opened the trunk of their cars and started taking out shotguns. Now when they did this the Panthers started getting guns from in the house. Charlie gets a gun and gets up on the roof. I'm on the porch standing there—general-like, I like to think—and Panthers are around with guns. More police cars come and everybody got guns. This was a most tense moment; things are hectic, and we're saying, "This is it. It's getting ready to go down!" Then, Henry Findley, who later would prove to be an informer, says, "I'll be right back. I got to go change my pants," or something ridiculous like that! Next thing I know, he's gone. Next, one of the Channel 4 news wagons drives up with cameras. Suddenly, things start to cool down. The policemen start to put their guns back in their trunks. Next day, there was a lot in the paper about the shoot-out that almost came about.

Kansas City Panthers' Charges against Police Chief Kelley

Pete believed the Panthers had evidence implicating Chief of Police Clarence Kelley in the sale of confiscated weapons to right-wing organizations, such as the Minutemen. Pete describes his attempt to convey that information to a US Senate Investigating Committee on October 12, 1969:

We went to Washington, DC, to try to burst in on the hearing regarding Clarence Kelley and the illegal transfer of guns. There were three of us: Bill Whitfield, Keith Hench, myself. We sat in the back of the hearing room. I waited until Clarence Kelley started to testify. I stood up and I began to shout out, "Yes, we have evidence that he has been transferring guns illegally." And we went on and on about this. Boy, did they ever trick us. They sent a guy back to us. He was so slick. He's got us quieted down. He said, "This is important information. We have to have this information. Come with me to the office." He got us out of the Senate chambers, took us down to an office and then told us, "Wait a minute, we're going to have people come down here shortly." We sat there, and we sat there, and we sat there, and before you know it the hearings were over. But we had made our point. And again it was on the news, broadcast across the country.

The Senate hearings Pete refers to were conducted by the Senate Government Operations Committee's Permanent Subcommittee on Investigations, with Abraham A. Ribicoff (Democrat, Connecticut) as acting chairman. One of its foci was the illegal activities of Major General Carl C. Turner. Philip R. Manuel, a subcommittee investigator, testified that Turner had obtained at no cost hundreds of weapons from the Chicago and Kansas City, Missouri, police departments and later sold some of them to a gun dealer for his own profit. According to the 1970 *Congressional Quarterly*, Kansas City Police officials said they had given Turner 113 guns under the impression he would use them in training courses, Boy Scouts and civic group lectures, and for the Army museum at Fort Gordon, Georgia.[9] On April 9, 1971, Turner pleaded guilty in federal district court to unlawfully soliciting 136 firearms from the Chicago police and keeping them for his own use.[10] Kansas City Police Chief Kelley was not implicated in any illegal activity.

Determined to pursue their allegations against Kelley, the Kansas City Panthers attempted to attend a press conference on December 5, 1969, at police headquarters. Kelley had ordered his officers to prevent the Panthers from attending. Pete describes the incident:

One of our major confrontations between the Kansas City Chapter and the Police Department happened when Police Chief Clarence Kelley was holding a press conference to respond to charges that we had leveled against him about supplying confiscated weapons to right-wing organizations. The press had picked up on it. Several of us went there—myself, Tommy Robinson, one of the Rawlins brothers, and Johnnie Jacobs. We went into the police station up to the second floor, to the hallway leading to Clarence Kelley's office. There were four policemen there. And so we told them, "We're here to attend the press conference." We had on badges indicating that we were members of the press. We had on our cards indicating that we were representatives of the Black Panther Party newspaper. They said, "You're not going in there." And we said, "Oh, yes, we're going in." They said, "Oh, no you're not." We made a charge for the door, and they attempted to repulse us.

A big melee, a big scuffle breaks out and they're blowing whistles, and before you know it, other policemen are coming. We are sharply overwhelmed after a fierce battle. Tommy Robinson fought so hard they took night sticks and repeatedly hit him as hard as they possibly could on his head; blood was going everywhere. They had me down, handcuffed me and then took their foot and stomped on the handcuffs to tighten them even more. I had a problem with that wrist for years after. So we are bloodied and beaten, but unbowed. We're dragged off and put into cells. The first person that came to see me was journalist Harry Jones of the *Kansas City Star*. He saw us all sitting there bloodied and beaten. He just looked at us, shook his head, and said, "Man, I'm telling you, you're not going to last like this." I always had the feeling that Harry Jones empathized with our efforts. He never said it. In my youth and inexperience, when I would lean toward a tendency to exaggerate things, he would say, "Man, you maybe ought to be careful with things like that, because that brings your credibility into question; when you've got something *really* important to say, no one will pay any attention." So that was food for thought, and something I bore in mind a great deal.

Footage of police beating us was broadcast on national news, and it didn't look good. We were trying to attend a press conference. The news reported we were beaten and bloodied. The police fractured Tommy Robinson's skull with their night sticks. He needed eighteen stitches to have his skull sewn back up. He was severely injured and never recovered. Never was the same. His condition continued to deteriorate, his mind, his thinking wasn't as clear and sharp as it had been. He started to become more and more erratic. He did eventually die. I am convinced in my mind and in my heart that that beating played a major part, if not the reason for his young death. [*The Panthers' brawl with police outside of Chief Kelley's office occurred on December 5, 1969. In addition to multiple stitches needed to close his head wounds, Tommy Robinson suffered a concussion and a sprained left arm.*][11]

Black and White Citizens Express Concern

Concerned and alarmed with the police's brutal beating of the four un-
armed Panthers at the police station and the general hostility between
the police and the Panthers both in Kansas City and nationwide, a group
of over forty citizens, mostly black leaders, sent an open letter on December 12, 1969, to Police Chief Kelley and the Board of Police Commissioners asking them to consider four recommendations: (1) that any police searches be carried out during daylight hours; (2) that the Panther
leaders will accept any legal police searches if their attorney and some
members of the black community who have signed this statement ac-
company the police; (3) that if police want to serve an arrest warrant or
speak with any member of the Black Panthers, party leaders will agree to
present that person if the police first contact the Panthers' attorney; (4)
that the police stop the provocative harassment and the killing of young
black leaders.[12]

On the very next day, a wide-ranging group of white religious, welfare, and legal leaders endorsed the above recommendations in their
own statement of concern which they sent to the Missouri governor,
lieutenant governor, senators, congressional representative, chief of police, police commissioners, mayor, and other governmental, civic, and
religious leaders.

Despite the broad expression of concern by black and white citizens,
the board of police commissioners, chaired by Joseph Kelly, rejected the
recommendations.[13]

Arrests without Convictions

The following arrest case evinces the extent to which prejudice against
black civil rights activists extended to the judiciary. According to the arrest report filed by patrolman Pruitt[14] at 12:45 p.m. on January 2, 1970,
he received a call about a robbery at Twenty-Ninth Street and Prospect
in Kansas City, Missouri. Officer Pruitt went to the site and reported
that David Nelson said he had been robbed of a watch and sixty-five dollars by a "negro male," who acted as though he had a gun. Nelson said
the robber then ran northward on Prospect Street. Officer Pruitt wrote
that he also questioned George Murphy, who reportedly witnessed the
robbery. Then, at approximately 12:55 [only ten minutes after the initial
call] the robbery victim reportedly spotted the alleged robber walking

southbound on Prospect Street. Officer Pruitt then arrested Melvin Bowie, the alleged robber, who possessed a watch similar to the stolen one. Bowie, however, did not have a gun or sixty-five dollars. At the time of the arrest, Pete O'Neal arrived on the scene. Officer Pruitt reported that he arrested O'Neal after allegedly witnessing him striking both the victim and the witness. At the police station, Bowie was booked for robbery and O'Neal for assault.

The very next day, Detective F. Smith reported that the victim (Nelson) and alleged witness (Murphy) went to the prosecutor's office and said they did not want charges filed against Bowie and O'Neal.[15] The alleged witness said that he did not witness the robbery and Pete O'Neal did not fight with him. He said he was only playing with O'Neal. When asked, both the victim and the alleged witness denied that they had been contacted or threatened by anyone since the robbery report. Despite Nelson's and Murphy's statements, the prosecutor filed charges against suspects Bowie and O'Neal, and issued a subpoena against Nelson to appear in Magistrate's Court on January 8, 1980.

According to the *Kansas City Times*,[16] the Kansas City Police asked the FBI to enter the case and investigate O'Neal for possible violation of a witness's civil rights. The FBI reportedly stated that it would cooperate with the Kansas City Police in connection with its policy of keeping track of Panther activities and would consult with FBI headquarters for possible action. Apparently, none was taken in this case.

At trial, Nelson denied that Bowie was the person who robbed him or that O'Neal struck him. Nelson said the watch taken from Bowie was not his; it lacked a personal inscription found on his own watch. He said he had identified Bowie as the robber when he was emotionally upset, and he had signed police statements against Bowie and O'Neal without reading them. Given Nelson's testimony, Magistrate Robert W. Berry III had no option but to dismiss all charges. However, the magistrate showed his hostility and bias toward the defendants by telling O'Neal in open court that he was a "parasite on the community and his people" and lecturing the defendants that, if they had been tried "in countries whose governments they seek to install here, they would have been convicted and sent to the penitentiary."[17]

US House Hearings on the Black Panther Party of Kansas City

The Committee on Internal Security (CIS) was authorized to investigate the objectives and activities of foreign or domestic organizations that seek to establish, or assist in the establishment of, a totalitarian dictatorship within the United States.[18] A House Resolution adopted on October 8, 1969, called on the CIS to investigate the origin, character, objectives, activities, and other facts relating to the Black Panther Party. Representative Richard H. Ichord (Republican, Missouri) chaired the hearings. Others present included Representative William J. Scherle of Iowa, Chief Counsel Donald G. Sanders, and investigator Richard A. Shaw. In addition, the committee subpoenaed a number of witnesses to appear before it. Chief Counsel Sanders was a former FBI agent who had once served under Clarence Kelley in the FBI office in Birmingham, Alabama.[19]

Richard A. Shaw's primary assignment was to investigate the Kansas City BPP. He stated that he is a member of the same race as the Panthers. The committee had subpoenaed the June–December 1969 records of two of the telephones used by the Kansas City BPP as well as the party's bank records. The March 10, 1969, balance was $101.08. Shaw testified that he had obtained the list of all deposits and withdrawals associated with the account as well as the names of all persons and organizations whose checks were deposited into the account. He reported that Pete O'Neal was receiving about three thousand *Black Panther* newspapers per month at a cost of 12.5 cents each.

Shaw related his February 10, 1970, interview with Reverend Preciphs, the assistant director of the Methodist Inner City Parish. Preciphs reportedly stated that "the Panthers are the best thing that ever happened to the Negro community, that their philosophy has given the Negro community something to be proud of. It has given the Negro momentum." Preciphs claimed that the Panthers had done more for the black community than either the NAACP or the Urban League. Preciphs said violence for the Panthers meant only self-defense.

Shaw's recounting of a case involving a Kansas City Panther whose gun charge was dismissed alarmed the committee chair. The case, which was heard in the US District Court of the Western District of Missouri, involved William Whitfield, who had purchased a firearm from a Kansas City, Kansas, gun shop and had stated on a government form that he was legally allowed to do so despite knowing that he had a 1961 felony conviction for burglary. The Gun Control Act of 1968 prohibits convicted felons from receiving a firearm in interstate commerce. However, defense attorney Austin Shute had argued to the court that, in 1961, Whitfield was convicted and sentenced under the terms of the Youth Correction Act, Title 18, Section 5010(a). Thereafter, Whitfield satisfactorily completed his term of probation, which, by law, automatically set aside (expunged) his 1961 felony conviction, thereby making him ineligible for conviction under the Gun Control Act. Consequently, the presiding federal judge dismissed Whitfield's indictment.

Committee Chair Ichord disagreed with the ruling, saying, "Obviously, there is a deficiency in the Federal Gun Control Act." Ichord asked for the name of the presiding judge and ordered that the case documents be sent to the Judiciary Committee, because "this should be brought to their attention."[20]

Some of the questioning of the first committee witness, Rev. Phillip C. Lawson, executive director of the Methodist Inner City Parish, KCM, went as follows:

> CHIEF COUNSEL SANDERS: "Does the Black Panther Party of Kansas City believe in racial equality?"
>
> REVEREND LAWSON: "My understanding is that they talk in terms of equality, period, and not in terms of racial, white-black, but simply equality; they speak, in terms of class differences rather than racial differences."
>
> SANDERS: "You don't regard them [the BPP of Kansas City] as the black counterpart, let's say, of the Ku Klux Klan?"
>
> LAWSON: "No, I do not. My understanding is very clearly it is not a separatist kind of ground in terms of race."

Another witness to appear was African American Walter Parker, a Mississippi native and a sergeant in the tactical unit of the Kansas City, Missouri, Police Department. He testified that the BPP of Kansas City was first organized in February 1969, and its breakfast programs were inaugurated in the early summer of 1969 at Paseo Baptist and St. Stephen. During a week in February he conducted a surveillance of the Wayne Miner Housing Project and the St. Stephen Baptist Church breakfast programs and observed a total of 262 children at Wayne Miller and 72 at St. Stephen.

Parker stated that the local police were monitoring BPP phone calls. He noted that there had been a deterioration in inner-city police relations in cities around the country, including Kansas City, Missouri, and agreed that many people attribute these relations to police brutality. Most inner-city residents were black. In the August 2, 1969, issue of their own *Black Panther* newspaper, the panthers claimed that "Members of the Kansas City Chapter, Black Panther Party, have been subjected to repeated acts of brutality, trumped-up charges, resulting in unjust arrests, and harassments" by the police. Officer Parker admitted that no Kansas City Panther had ever killed a policeman and that there had never been a shoot-out between the Kansas City Panthers and the police. Because the police and federal agents had killed a number of Panthers during the execution of search warrants on Panthers homes in the early hours of the morning (for example, in Chicago and Los Angeles), the words "search warrant" had become synonymous with a "warrant of death."

Another witness was Captain William Ponessa, commander of the tactical unit of the Kansas City, Missouri, Police Department. Ponessa estimated the population of Kansas City, Missouri, to be 616,000, with blacks comprising 18 to 21 percent of the total. In 1970 (according to Ponessa) there were 963 members of the Kansas City, Missouri, Police Department, including 46 captains. These totals included 57 black patrolmen and only 1 black captain. From Ponessa's testimony it appeared that that city's police were oriented to the BPP through newspaper articles about the national BPP, not specifically about the Kansas City BPP. Hence, their impressions about the militancy of the locals were exaggerated.

Witness Paul E. Levitt, a Kansas City, Missouri, food merchant, testified that he donated breakfast food to the BPP children's breakfast program and that Pete and Gary O'Neal never demanded money of him and that "they were very easy for me to talk to because I watched them grow up."

Herman A. Johnson, a local retailer and black member of the Missouri House of Representatives for the Thirteenth District, testified that, "Just as the extravagant rhetoric of the Black Panthers has frequently beclouded the issue, so has overreaction and over-defensiveness by the police reduced their stature in the eyes of the black citizens. Poor police image can only lead to poor law enforcement and less respect for authority." According to journalist Harry Jones, Johnson's charge of police overreaction brought a sharp rebuttal from Representative Scherle, who criticized the "leniency" of the law and the "permissiveness" of society.[21] Giving an example of overreaction, Johnson said that, after the Panthers established their headquarters on Lydia Avenue, near his home, he and the neighbors were kept awake at night by police surveillance helicopters. He claimed that people were scared to death there was going to be a confrontation.[22]

The committee also included in its report *The Black Panther Party Staff Study*, which contains a compilation of quotes and other information. A statement of political philosophy written by the BPP national office for publication in 1970 went as follows:

> The Black Panther Party stands for revolutionary solidarity with all people fighting against the forces of imperialism, capitalism, racism and fascism. Our solidarity is extended to those people who are fighting these evils at home and abroad. Because we understand that our struggle for our liberation is part of a worldwide struggle being waged by the poor and oppressed against imperialism and the world's chief imperialist, the United States of America, we— the Black Panther Party—understand that the most effective way that we can aid our Vietnamese brothers and sisters is to destroy imperialism from the inside, attack it where it breeds. In the words of the party's chairman, Bobby Seale, we will not fight capitalism with black capitalism; we will not fight imperialism with black imperialism; we will not fight racism with black racism. Rather we will take our turn against these evils with a solidarity derived from a proletarian internationalism born of socialist realism.

The staff report went on to state that "Four specific programs have been emphasized by the Panthers: free breakfast for children, free health clinics, liberation schools and the petition campaigns for community control of police. Every branch was required to implement at least the breakfast program and the police petitions."

The staff study estimated the BPP membership at 1,200 to 1,500 at its highest and about 1,000 in 1970, spread over twenty-five to thirty branches in cities across the United States. The staff study also lists the BPP's Ten Point Program and platform, which refer positively to two basic American political documents. Point 9 calls for black people to be tried by their peers in accordance with the Sixth Amendment of the US Constitution, and point 10 demands a United Nations–supervised plebiscite so that black people can determine their own destiny. This demand is justified by a lengthy quotation of the Declaration of Independence.

5

Arrest, Trial, Escape

Pete's Arrest

On October 30, 1969, about eighteen days after Pete had gone to Washington, DC, and attempted to intervene in Police Chief Kelley's Senate hearing, ATF agents arrested Pete in Kansas City, Missouri, and charged him with violations of the Federal Gun Control Act of 1968. Pete describes his arrest:

> I remember the day that Alcohol, Tobacco, and Firearms agents
> arrested me. I had been in a cafe a couple of doors from our head-
> quarters. I was there with one of the Rollins brothers. We walked
> out and police swarmed us with guns drawn. Policemen were on the
> roofs; they were everywhere. Before I even knew what happened,
> I was in custody. The agents put me in a car and drove me to the
> federal building. Two agents took me in and started making note of
> all my tattoos. They photographed me. They were very blasé about it.
> "You're being charged with violating the Gun Control Act. Yeah, you
> think you're something. We got you now. We've been watching you.
> We listen to you. We know what you really do." Talking about me
> smoking dope and making other silly remarks. They said I could call
> my lawyer and my bondsman. And I did. We had an ongoing thing
> with Bruno Bonding Company as a result of the Civella family in
> Kansas City. And so immediately I called them. Bam, they and Shute
> come, and I'm out on bond. [AFT agents arrested Pete in Kansas City,
> Missouri, but rather than having him tried in the federal court there,

they took him out of state to Kansas where he would be indicted for al-
leged violations of the 1968 Gun Control Act. Defense attorney Austin
Shute had earlier freed a Panther in the Kansas City, Missouri, federal
court of almost identical charges. It appears that the ATF agents inten-
tionally avoided the Missouri federal court, hoping to get a pro-prosecu-
tion judge in Kansas. They got such a judge in Arthur J. Stanley.]

Austin Shute made all the arrangements for my court appearance. There were three charges, and each one carried five years. I'm
getting worried. They could really put me away. Shute had done a lot
for us. He had represented us a great deal, and not one cent came his
way. But I thought it would be good to get Charles Garry's opinion
and advice. [*US District Court Judge Arthur J. Stanley issued an order*
allowing Pete to travel to California on February 23, 1970, and return on
February 25, 1970, for the purpose of conferring with attorney Charles
Garry,[1] the regular defense attorney for the Black Panthers there.
Instead of offering to help defend Pete, Garry told Pete he could do more
good for the party inside prison.]

Leaving the Black Panther Party

After I left California, after speaking with Garry and finding out
there was not going to be support for my case, I decided to leave
the Black Panther Party and form the Sons of Malcolm. When I
addressed the brothers and sisters, you could see their fallen faces.
The Black Panther Party had become a very important part of our
lives. But all of us had had a common complaint. And that was that
our activities were being stifled by national headquarters, in part by
their dictatorial practices without any consideration for our particular situation and the particular mindset and values of the midwestern community. So, it was a very hard sell. No one wanted to give
the party up. But I told them, "If we leave, we can build something
and do some really good community work here in the Midwest.
Brothers started coming down from Des Moines. Charles Knox and
Poindexter came down from Omaha. People came from Kansas. We
explained that we felt we could be more effective and that, if they
stayed with us, we could really build something very special. Most
of them said, "Okay, let's do it. Let's go ahead." Man, we felt so good
about that.

I called out to headquarters and told David Hilliard our decision. He said, "Wait a minute, man, don't do this, don't do this. Let me talk to Huey; let me get back to you." I said, "No, brother, we've done it. You can talk to Huey, but this is it. We're adamant about this; this is the way it's going to be." I told him we cannot work within the party. I said if we left the party we could focus specifically on issues that were very important to our folks in the Midwest. I also told him that we would love to have strong fraternal ties with the Black Panther Party. He reacted, "No, you can't do this. Hold off, hold off. I'll get back to you."

A couple of weeks later, here comes a phone call from David. "Brother," he says, "listen, June [*June Hilliard, David's brother*] is coming out there tonight. He's bringing another brother with him. We've got an important message for you, man, from Huey." I said, "Okay. When are they coming in? Somebody will meet them."

Now, put the Midwest in context, guns are so easily available. Everybody in the party had guns *legally*. All of them had their papers and receipts to own rifles and shotguns with sniper scopes, semiautomatics, and all of these things. They look like they came straight out of the Vietnam War. Nothing illegal about this whatsoever. June comes out with this other Panther. We had a brother who really looked menacing pick them up at the airport. His name was Che, after Che Guevara. And he had his beret down on the side. He wasn't a big guy, but he just looked dangerous. He had a semiautomatic weapon. We took June and the other guy into our headquarters. You could see that June was extremely uncomfortable. He said, "Man, here we got a tape for you. We'll leave and you can listen to it." I said, "No, stay we'll listen to it together." "No, we got to get out of here. We're going back to the airport." They're nervous. So we had some brothers take them back. Huey Newton had sent me this tape from jail. On it he said, "Now, I want to deal with this Pete E'Neal (he called me Pete E'Neal). I know what this brother's trying to do. He's trying to set up a private empire. He's trying to become a kingpin in that Midwest out there. So I want him to know that, if he continues with this line of action and if he wants war, he can have war. But if he wants to come back to the fold, he can come back to the fold." And so the brothers and I listened to that and I asked them, "Brothers, are we going to stay strong now? Are we going to continue?" Everybody said, "We're going strong." I said, "Okay."

In its May 8, 1970, issue, the *Call*, a Kansas City–based African American weekly, carried an article entitled, "Black Panthers Become Sons of Malcolm." The article reports on a press conference held at the former headquarters of the Black Panther Party where Pete O'Neal announced the reorganization of the party into the Sons of Malcolm. O'Neal stated that the new organization had two hundred members across a four-state area in the Midwest. Twenty-four members attended the press conference.

Another Call from David Hilliard

About a week after we received the tape, I get a phone call from David Hilliard. He's talking very congenially; alarms go off in my head. He said, "Brother, listen I want you to do something for me." I said, "What's that, David." He says, "I want you to meet me in New York. We need to talk. I'm thinking about you taking over the New York chapter." Now, that wouldn't make sense to a drunk man, I mean, to a damn fool! New York was a very strong chapter with very strong brothers and sisters up there. There is no rhyme or reason why anyone could even entertain the idea of my going up there to take over the New York chapter. I believe the river up there is the Hudson River. I think had I gone I would have ended up floating in that river. This conversation with David Hilliard was my last direct contact with national headquarters in California. [*Within two years Newton would expel the New York Chapter.*]

Sons of Malcolm

Let me tell you why we called ourselves the Sons of Malcolm. You know, the Black Panther Party, in large part, is based upon the philosophy of Malcolm X. And the philosophy of Malcolm X puts, as I understand it, a tremendous emphasis upon community control. After his trip to Mecca, Malcolm's position, even after his new thinking, was that integration was secondary; it was not anything of major influence. What was extremely important was the development of the black community—to develop the economy, to develop the politics, and develop our social lives. And when we have ourselves together and have developed a degree of power, then we can go to the table with the larger society. Then we sit down and begin to talk about what's the best path to follow. Do we choose an integrated path? Or do we follow another? What do our people really want? What's best for all concerned? But you do not do this from a position of extreme weakness where you have nothing whatsoever to put upon the table. That in a nutshell was Malcolm X's philosophy. Not to mention the fact that he always stressed—while we will strive to find reasonable ways to resolve contradictions—we certainly are not turning the other cheek. If we can reason together, let us do so. But if you hit me, I'm hitting back. So that really is just a continuation of what the Black Panther Party was supposed to be about before we made the side trip into Marxism which, I think may have been a really big mistake.

We were having difficulty reviving our programs as Sons of Malcolm. It all boiled down to financial support. After we left the party, there was a little slackening off of donations. We put out a few issues of our own newspaper on a weekly basis. I found a printer who would do it, and we were able to scrape up some money. But boy, that was hurting us; we never made money on the thing. We re-started our community work and continued our Breakfast for School Children Program. We had a lot of people who had court cases. Money was being spent, and there wasn't much money coming in.

Pete's Trial

Pete O'Neal faced a three-count indictment in the US District Court of Kansas. Count one alleged that, without a proper license, Pete transported a firearm from Kansas to Missouri in violation of 18 U.S.C. 922(a)(3). Count two alleged that, when he purchased the firearm from a licensed dealer, Pete made false statements in violation of 18 U.S.C. 922(a)(6). Count three alleged that Pete, having previously been convicted of a crime punishable by imprisonment for a term exceeding one year, transported a firearm across a state line in violation of 18 U.S.C. 922(g)(1). At trial Pete was convicted of count three only.

As my trial date draws near, I'm becoming more and more concerned. I remember going to [defense attorney] Shute's office on several occasions, to his home once or twice. I remember taking Charlotte there during a tornado watch one night. I remember Shute being excited about one of the charges that he said won't hold. It had something to do with the California Youth Authority. He was going to make a motion about this before the trial started. Well, sometime later, he said the judge denied it. So that one fell through. [*The legal argument that Shute had successfully used in a similar case in the Missouri Federal Court was rejected in the Kansas Federal Court by Judge Arthur J. Stanley.*]

The Sons of Malcolm began mobilizing support in the community. We had posters printed with my picture: "Keep Pete O'Neal free." We wrote articles in our newspaper about the upcoming trial and how it was part and parcel of a national program to eliminate militant black leaders. We talked about how the police had tried to kill Huey and how they killed Fred Hampton in Chicago. The community started to respond, and we started to hear people talking: "Yes, we're going to be there. Don't you worry. We will be there." But we were putting so much focus, time, and energy on this legal effort that our community work started to slow down drastically. Quite frankly, I think the powers that be knew this would be the case. My case and the other legal problems we had consumed a great deal of our time.

I remember the first day of trial. Shute was *adamant* about this. He said, "Pete, I'm representing you. I'm getting nothing for this. But I want you to be very, very clear about one thing. I'm withdrawing immediately if there are any outbursts or if there is any attempt to disrupt the court. I really believe we can win this, and we can do it within the system. Now what you do after the trial, that's your business. Can we get an agreement on that?" I said, "You got it." So I told everybody in our organization, "What we're going to do is go to court and be very cool and calm. We're going to just let this thing proceed and see what happens playing by the rules in this one instance." And so we did. We went in there and everybody was really straightforward. There was a good community turnout. Nobody caused any problems.

But it seemed as though the police wanted some trouble. They would shout at people lined up trying to get into the court house, "You can't stand here. Move here." People not protesting, not marching, just waiting to get in. The police would start pushing people and just being excessively rough with people. They were discouraging, even stopping people from coming in. Why that was, I don't know, because all the seats were not filled. On a couple occasions when I was going into the courtroom, policemen would make snide remarks. "You know, prison is our turf. You know that." Then laughing, "You're not going to be out here long. We can deal with you in prison. Ha-ha-ha." Laughing, but if anyone came around, they would wipe the grins off and put a serious expression on their faces.

The court police had metal detectors that people had to go through to enter the court. They also looked in bags. This may have been the first time for metal detectors in Kansas City. [*Intensive screening was not common at the time. Presiding Judge Arthur J. Stanley had issued a special "Standing Order" for Pete's trial, which stated that "No person carrying a bag or parcel shall be permitted to enter or remain in any courtroom or in any hall, corridor, entry-way or stairway on or connected with the first floor of the United State Courthouse, without first submitting such bag or parcel to the Marshall or Deputy Marshall for inspection."*]

I went into the court the same way everyone did. Remember, I showed up on my own. I would come in, be searched for weapons with these detectors. I always wore a black leather jacket with slacks and a sweater on under that. We would take hats off in the courtroom, so the beret would be off. I always wore dark glasses. I don't recall anyone asking me to take them off. Had they asked me to I would have. It certainly wouldn't have posed a problem.

I can remember the judge sitting there with white hair. I thought, "Boy, he's old." The man was younger than I am now. The prosecutor was an Italian-looking man with an Italian-sounding name. I believe it was Pusateri. I picture him as being dark, tall, and a bit slender. He dressed well in dark suits. I don't remember being particularly impressed with his presentation.

One of the prosecution's witnesses was Jean Young, a white woman who managed the apartment complex where the Panthers had their office and Pete had his residence. She claimed that Pete brought a weapon, which she could not identify, to her apartment and showed it to her husband, a black man named Harold Young. While researching this case years later, I learned that Jean Young had operated under numerous aliases, had a criminal record, and was a longtime paid FBI informant. None of this was revealed to the court during this trial. Below are Pete's comments on Jean Young's testimony and Harold Young's statement to him:

Jean Young was a dark-haired white woman. I always considered her my good friend. During her testimony, that woman was so nervous. She came on the stand with a pair of glasses in her hands.

The prosecutor spoke to her very gently, but she was so nervous she started to destroy the glasses. She twisted them until they broke. She was *almost* incoherent. She started to complain about things I did in an apartment. That I had made a bed out of a big spool of old electrical wire—a really nice looking thing—brought that thing into the apartment and left it there. She claimed I showed her husband [*Harold Young*] a shotgun and told him I had purchased it. But, her testimony was so jumbled that I didn't think anyone would give much credence to what she had to say.

Before the trial, Harold Young acknowledged that I had never told him anything like that. Shute may have a statement from him to that effect. I can remember trying to talk Harold Young into testifying and him not wanting to, being very, very reluctant. Now why he ultimately did not testify, I don't know. But it was at this time that he told me about how they—they being he and his wife, Jean Young—would let the FBI into my apartment to plant bugs and listening devices. [*The FBI did this illegally, without the necessary judicial warrants.*]

I can remember Tilly [*Pete's first wife*] flying all the way from California. She had moved to California where she got a good job with AT&T. She took off from her job at her own expense, flew to Kansas City to testify *strongly* on my behalf. Tilly tried everything she possibly could to convince the jurors (and she's a very elegant woman) and everyone else that what she was saying was the truth. [*Tilly testified that Pete brought the firearm in question to her apartment in Kansas, telling her it was for her protection. Pete left it there. Later, a Panther named Archie Weaver took the firearm away.*] I have a vague remembrance about wanting Archie Weaver to testify. I don't remember what put a block on that. [*Weaver did not testify at the trial.*]

Shute advised me not to testify. He may have been afraid that I might become a bit rhetorical and the prosecutor may have been able to manipulate me. Had the prosecutor pushed me, I would have adopted a revolutionary posture. Shute was probably aware of that and said it's best not to do that. For the Panthers, defending yourself and trying to prove your innocence was secondary. The party line was to use the courtroom as a forum to further the party philosophy and to edify the masses about the work the Black Panther Party was doing and what our goals and our aspirations were. Had

I testified, honestly, Paul, I'm telling you from my heart, I could not have sat there and not said something about the Black Panther Party and how I felt that the path we were following was really a path good for all Americans. I might have been a *hair* more diplomatic than the norm, but nonetheless I would have spoken up.

I was becoming apprehensive about the trial. Whenever Shute made motions, the judge denied them. So I started talking to all the brothers and sisters. They'd tell me, "Brother, we're with you and we're not going to let them do this. We know if you go to jail, they will kill you." Everybody agreed, "If it looks like you can't beat this thing, you've got to leave. Your best bet would be to get to Papa Rage." [*Eldridge Cleaver, known as Papa Rage, had been involved in a 1968 shoot-out with police and was charged with attempted murder. He fled the United States before his trial and found refuge in Algeria.*] The seed of our flight was planted then.

After conviction [*on count three of the indictment*], but before sentencing, Shute wanted me to do a probationary report. I didn't want to do it. "No, you should do it. You've got to go through the whole procedure." So we went down there and we filled out forms and filed everything. I remember a fat Mexican man was in charge. Of course, when I went to court his recommendation was that probation be denied. Then the judge sentenced me to four years in prison. But before he sentenced me, he asked me if I had anything to say. I did. I said, "Some time ago I made the decision to dedicate my life to the revolution. I am a revolutionary and nothing that happens here today can change that."

The judge then made an outburst that was so shocking I didn't even know what he was talking about. He raved, "The American flag was defaced and I'm going to put a letter into the appeal so that the circuit court is made aware of this situation." I had not seen him this venomous during the whole trial, and I didn't know what the hell he was talking about. He was ranting and raving. [*According to a brief article appearing in the* Kansas City Star, *the alleged desecration occurred in a courtroom that was reserved for O'Neal witnesses as they waited to testify.*[2] *Court attachés found that some unknown person or persons had placed stickers used to identify court exhibits over the flag's stars. Judge Stanley's enraged outburst and threat to negatively influence Pete's appeal with his gratuitous letter, without any evidence of Pete's involvement in the alleged desecration, evinced his bias and deficient judgment.*]

Austin Shute told me there were grounds to win an appeal. However, he said someone else, I've forgotten who, would represent me.[3] I should make it clear I was out on bail during the course of the entire trial. I went home every night, came back to court the next day. After the judge sentenced me to four years imprisonment, and after he made his venomous outburst, he then said (and this was very weird to me), "The defendant can continue with his bail during the appeal." Very unusual. He didn't ask me to put up another bond or increase it. Over the years I've wondered if he was manipulating me into leaving.

Escape

We had worked with a lot of left-wing whites in New York through a doctor we knew there. This friendly doctor would come to Kansas City and talk to us, trying to direct us on a strong communist path. When I made up my mind to leave, I told him, and he offered to get us plane tickets. He said, "All you got to do is get to New York and we'll get you out of the country."

Charlotte was a very young woman. She and I were married at this point. I told her, "You know, you got a lot of life in front of you. You really ought to think about this objectively." She said, "I'm with you. If you're going, I'm going." I said, "All right, but you're sure?" She said, "Yes."

We wanted friends in one of the other midwestern satellites to help us with passports. We gave them our photographs. Shortly before it was time for us to leave, passports were brought down with our pictures in them. They had gone into the passport office with our pictures (I guess all black folks look alike), signed up for the passports, and got them. Charlotte and I never touched an application form in any shape or form. Passports were put into our hands. My passport name was Norman Pickett, and Charlotte's was Dorothy Hunt. We and our friends raised about six or seven thousand dollars, a good piece of money in 1970.

The police at that time had us under strict surveillance. Policemen would park outside our house all day and all night. They would change shifts; there would be someone watching us at all times. The police had helicopters flying around, shining lights in our windows at night. One night we ordered pizza. A young white boy drove up in his little pizza-delivery wagon and walked up to our door. The police jumped out at him with guns drawn. The boy threw the pizzas up in the air and cried, "Please don't kill me! Please don't kill me!" I guess he thought he was being robbed.

One of our friends made arrangements for someone to drive up from Arkansas. We didn't want any cars that were known in Kansas City. This guy was supposed to park a few blocks from our house and wait for us. We were supposed to receive a coded telephone message that night around twelve o'clock letting us know this guy had arrived. We're waiting. I have on a very expensive cashmere coat, I've got a suit and tie on, my hair was marcelled back. Before my political days, I used to wear my hair like that. Charlotte wore a wig and an expensive fur coat. We looked like a couple of buppies (that's black yuppies), posing as newlyweds. Twelve o'clock is supposed to be signal time. It comes and goes. Two o'clock comes and goes. Three o'clock in the morning comes and goes. Charlotte and I decide he's not coming. "To hell with it, I'm going to court tomorrow. [*Pete was scheduled to appear in the Jackson County Circuit on November 9, 1970, to appeal the Linwood Church disruption conviction.*] Let the chips fall where they may." I took off this coat and the suit. Charlotte said, "This wig is itching." She took it off and we got in bed. Four o'clock in the morning we get the phone call and the coded message. This guy from Arkansas was around the corner. Time to go.

We crawled out the back door, into the next building's courtyard, out into the alley, dragging these little suitcases behind us. Charlotte gashed her knee; her knee's bleeding. The driver is sitting there with the trunk of the car open. He tells us to get in the trunk. So we get in. Charlotte starts shaking; she's claustrophobic. The driver closes the trunk and drives off. He drives for twenty-five minutes and stops the car on a side street. We get out of the trunk and into the car. We continue driving to St. Louis to catch a plane for New York. We hit a traffic jam. It looked like all of these white people were turning around and staring intently at us. I said, "Lord, they all know!" We get to the airport, start running to the gate to catch our plane before they close it. And I'm shouting, "Charlotte, come on! I mean, Dorothy, come on! Hurry up!" We get on the plane. Bam! We go to New York.

We get off at the airport in New York, get a cab, go to Long Island. Beautiful homes there. We walk up this manicured lawn and knock on the door. This man (an associate of our doctor friend) came to the door. I said, "I'm Pete O'Neal." I've never seen anything like it. His face went from pale to red and back to pale again. And he said, "Oh, my God!" You're not supposed to come here. Wait a minute, wait!" Then he puts us in his car and he drives us to an apartment. He then says, "I'm going to leave you here. People will start making arrangements." He asked for the names on our passports and said, "We'll get the tickets." Then we discussed where to go. We told him we were ultimately going to Algeria, but if he can get us to Sweden, we could hide there with a feeling of security. Sweden was being a bit sympathetic to what was happening in America. After he left, I saw a note in the apartment that someone had written to another member of their group. It said, "You've got to be careful with this guy, he's really a wild man in Kansas City. He's probably coming with guns. Be very careful." Charlotte and I had a big laugh about that.

I sat at the window and I looked out. I thought I could be gone up to two years. So what I need to do is imprint on my mind these last scenes of America. Across the street was a Jewish delicatessen. So I sat there all day watching people go in and come out. I could see a young black boy go in, give a note to the butcher, who would wrap stuff up in paper. Then he would go out. I saw an old woman go in with her little bags. They would chat and laugh. And I told myself, "Remember all of these things." These are some of the last memories I have of the United States of America.

A knock on the door. Didn't have—contrary to what they thought—I didn't have a weapon at all. I grabbed a fork. I thought, "Lord, I don't know who this is, but I'm not going without a fight." I opened the door. It was one of their friends. He saw the fork in my hand; he's scared to death now; he's trembling. He is so nervous he can barely talk. I told him, "I'm sorry, I didn't know who it was." He comes in, gives us the tickets and the shot health cards. He tells us our plane leaves in two or three hours and we should head for the airport now. I think he wants to get rid of us. He puts us in the car. It's night now. We're driving and I remember seeing the night lights of New York, some big tanks along the highways. On the radio we hear a little squeaky voice singing. It was twelve-year-old Michael Jackson singing "I'll Be There."

FIGURE 1. Pete O'Neal with Kansas City Black Panther Party comrades.

FIGURE 2. Pete O'Neal as a member of the Kansas City Black Panther Party.

FIGURE 3. Pete O'Neal
at age twenty-nine in
Kansas City.

FIGURE 4. Charlotte Hill
O'Neal, age eighteen,
during her Black Panther
Party days in Kansas
City.

FIGURE 5. A poster of Pete and Charlotte O'Neal that addresses "Revolutionary Love," 1970.

Right: FIGURE 6. Charlotte Hill O'Neal and son Malcolm, age two, in Dar es Salaam, around 1973.

Below: FIGURE 7. Pete and Charlotte O'Neal in front of Charlotte's artwork at the National Natural History Museum in Arusha, Tanzania.

FIGURE 8. Charlotte Hill O'Neal with her artwork at an art museum in Arusha, Tanzania.

FIGURE 9. Paul Magnarella with Charlotte and Pete O'Neal in front of the Heroes' Mural at the UAACC, 1997.

FIGURE 10. Ceremonial opening of the public water spigot, *left to right,* Pete O'Neal, Geronimo Ji Jaga Pratt, Joju Cleaver Ji Jaga Pratt, Imbaseni Village Chairman Emanuel Pallangyo.

FIGURE 11. Mwajabu Sadiki, director of Leaders of Tomorrow Children's Home, with some of its children.

FIGURE 12. Pete O'Neal, aka Babu, with some young members of the Leaders of Tomorrow Children's home in school uniforms before leaving for Imbaseni Primary School, around 2012.

Right: FIGURE 13. Faraja and Happiness, two members of the Leaders of Tomorrow Children's Home, holding secondary-school certificates of achievement.

Below: FIGURE 14. Pete O'Neal and Irene of the Leaders of Tomorrow Children's Home. Irene finished first in all her classes from primary to secondary school. The background mural at UAACC was created in part by Emory Douglas, former Black Panther Party minister of culture.

Above: FIGURE 15. Pete O'Neal with some participants in the UAACC children's program.

Left: FIGURE 16. Pete O'Neal and Charlotte Hill O'Neal, aka Mama C, 2017.

Right: FIGURE 17. Pete and Charlotte's children, Malcolm and Ann Wood O'Neal, 2018.

Below: FIGURE 18. Pete and Charlotte O'Neal, 2018.

6

Fleeing to Sweden and Algeria

Escape to Sweden

While on bail, prior to his appeals from the Jackson County Magistrate's
Court conviction for the Linwood Methodist Church disturbance and the
federal district court's gun-transportation conviction with its four-year
sentence, Pete and Charlotte escaped to New York and then to Sweden.
Pete recounted their getaway, which probably occurred in the early hours
of November 9, 1970.

> This doctor or lawyer drove us to JFK Airport and dropped us off.
> We had our tickets to Sweden on SAS Scandinavian Airline. Char-
> lotte and I got on the plane, and it hopped and jumped all the way
> to Sweden. On the way, we flew over some snow and ice-covered
> mountains that looked so desolate and depressing. When we landed
> in Sweden the airport looked depressing. There were ducks walking
> all around. Outdoors was freezing cold. Charlotte looked at all this,
> turned around, looked at me, and burst out crying.
>
> We got us a hotel there, and the next day we went around trying
> to make contact with some of the Vietnam-veteran organizations
> to see if they would help us. And most of them, quite frankly, were
> scared to death to become involved with us, and made no bones
> about it. A lot, in fact—African Americans who had deserted in the
> war—were terrified of being sent out of the country if they were
> caught associating with us. Incidentally, about two weeks later,
> friends in the States sent word that the authorities thought I had

headed for the Canadian or Mexican border and they were watching both.

Finally we made contact with a young woman who was part of the International Solidarity Committee that worked with the Panthers. Housing was impossible to get in Sweden. So she did the impossible. Through people she knew she got us a small apartment-like house on the outskirts that was very reminiscent of a Dr. Zhivago–Laura setting. We spent some romantic time there.

After staying about two-and-a-half months in this setting, we decided to take a state-subsidized trip to Tunisia and try to get into Algeria from there. We flew there, but found that the border with Algeria was closed. While in Tunisia, we met a young member of the Swedish Communist Party. Once back in Sweden we bared our souls to him, explaining to him our situation. He introduced us to a young group of Swedes who had formed a commune. We lived with them for another two, two-and-a-half months before we made another effort to get to Algeria.

This time we decided to go to Majorca, Spain, again on a Swedish state-subsidized trip. After we got off the plane, our tour leader met us and told us to follow. Charlotte and I said, "Yes, but first we're going to the restroom." Boom! We ran to the other part of the airport, got tickets on Air Algérie and flew straight on into Algeria. Incidentally, I should say we had got visas while we were in Sweden.

Meeting the Panthers in Algiers

We get off the plane in Algiers and go to the Hotel Royale. I am very apprehensive. I had told you about the difficulties we had with David Hilliard and national headquarters. Geronimo Pratt came to my house shortly before I left the States and told me that our problems with California were not at all unique. A lot of people were dissatisfied with national headquarters and were working to bring about a change. He indicated that Eldridge Cleaver and other Panthers, who had formed the International Section of the Black Panther Party in Algeria, were critical of national headquarters. That made me feel good, but I was still apprehensive. I didn't know for sure which side the brothers there supported. And if I made a mistake by contacting them, I very well could lose my life. So I told Charlotte, "I'm going to contact these brothers. You stay here. If you don't hear from me in say, eight to ten hours, get out of here. Get on a plane and try to get back to Sweden. If I can get out, I'll find you there. But leave this place."

I got their telephone number, called them. They were very suspicious of everybody. I found out later that was the norm. Anytime anyone would call, suspicions immediately would come to the fore. "Who are you?" "I'm Pete O'Neal." "Oh, yeah? Okay, why don't you come out here. Get a cab. Tell the driver you want to go to Neuf Deux de Tres in El Biar." I said, "Okay." I got a cab and I am scared to death. I get there and see this huge imposing villa with iron gates. Some brothers are standing up on the balcony, looking very stern. I'm thinking, "Oh, my goodness!" I call up to them, "I'm Pete O'Neal." They look down, but they don't say anything. They hit a buzzer—bzzz. Bump! The gates open, and I walk in.

One brother takes me into a huge room. Eldridge Cleaver is sitting there. He asks, "You Pete O'Neal?" I reply, "That's right, I'm Pete O'Neal." And he says, "Where in the hell have you been, man? Your mother's been writing. I got four or five letters from her. She told us to be on the lookout for you, that you were coming. We didn't know what had happened to you." Everybody embraced. It was so nice and so wonderful. Eldridge said, "I thought you were with your wife." Me: "My wife's at the hotel." Eldridge: "Larry Mack, take him over there and pick up his lady and you all come back."

Larry Mack had a deformed eye from a childhood accident. One of his eyes bulged out very dramatically. We went to get Charlotte. Knocked on the door. Charlotte opened the door and saw Larry Mack standing there. You could see the fear in her face. I guess she thought I was in the hands of an assassin! We returned to the Panther villa and were warmly, warmly, warmly received. So this is when I came back into the party. I later telephoned Kansas City and told brothers and sisters there that we were reinstated in the Black Panther Party. But it didn't make a hell of a lot of difference in Kansas City, because things there had withered away.

The Algerian Context

In 1834, Algeria became a French military colony, and the 1848 French Constitution declared Algeria an integral part of France. In 1954 the Algerian revolutionary movement, known as the FLN or *Front de Libération*

Nationale, broadcast calls to Algerian Muslims to join in a national fight
to create a sovereign, democratic, and socialist Algerian state inspired by
the principles of Islam. On July 3, 1962, after years of ruthless struggle,
French President Charles De Gaulle pronounced Algeria an independent
state. Ahmed Ben Bella, an Algerian socialist soldier and revolutionary,
became Algeria's first president (1963–65). In June 1965, Muhammad b.
Ibrāhīm Bū Kharūba, known by the *nom de guerre* Houari Boumédiène,
seized power in a bloodless coup. As chairman of the Revolutionary
Council of Algeria from 1965 to 1976 and thereafter as the second president of Algeria, Boumédiène pursued a policy of nonalignment, but supported freedom fighters and gave assistance to anti-colonial movements
across Africa and the Arab world, including the PLO (Palestinian Liberation Organization), ANC (African National Congress), SWAPO (South
West African People's Organization), and others.

The person, more than any other, who helped Cleaver get established
in Algeria was a white American named Elaine Klein. In 1960 at an international youth conference in Accra, Klein struck up a friendship with
Frantz Fanon, a roving ambassador for the Provisional Government of
the Algerian Republic. Later, in New York, she met Abdelkader Chanderli, the head of the unofficial Algerian mission at the United Nations.
Chanderli invited Klein to join his team, lobbying UN member states to
support Algerian independence. In 1962, with independence declared,
Klein went to Algeria to work in President Ahmed Ben Bella's press and
information office. She stayed on after the coup that brought Houari
Boumédiène to power in 1965. Late one night she received a call from
the representative of the Zimbabwe African People's Union, telling her
that the Black Panther Eldridge Cleaver was in Algiers and needed help.
She met with Eldridge and his wife, Kathleen, who was eight months
pregnant. Klein convinced Commandant Slimane Hoffman, who was
close to Boumédiène, to allow Cleaver and his fellow Black Panthers
to remain in the country. Klein arranged and accompanied Cleaver on
visits to the ambassadors of North Vietnam, China, and North Korea,
as well as representatives of the Palestinian liberation movement and
the National Liberation Front of South Vietnam (the Vietcong). Klein
also helped arrange for the International Section of the BPP to be recognized as a sponsored liberation movement, allowing it access to a range
of privileges and a monthly government stipend. The FLN assigned the
Panthers a villa formerly occupied by the Vietcong delegation in the El
Biar sector of the city. It also provided the Panthers with telephone and

telex connections and Algerian ID cards, permitting them to enter and leave Algeria without visas. The official opening of the headquarters of the International Section of the Black Panther Party took place on September 13, 1970.[1]

Kathleen Cleaver writes, "the daily call to prayer and veiled women attested to the resurgence of Algeria's Islamic heritage. . . . The complicated tribal and ethnic divisions among Arabs, Berbers, and Africans bewildered Panthers accustomed to simple stratification of color and class. . . . The daily juxtaposition of ancient and modern, North African and French, yielded unending confusion to the Black refugees."[2]

Klein writes (under her married name, "Mokhtefi"), "The Panthers may not have noticed, or perhaps didn't care, that Algeria itself was a conservative, closed society, that women were not really free, that a form of anti-black racism existed among the population, and that the Algerian establishment's generosity required certain codes of conduct and reciprocity on the part of their guests. The Panthers ignored whatever they didn't want to deal with."[3] Eldridge Cleaver took on a beautiful young Algerian mistress named Malika Ziri. Some of the Panther men openly dated attractive Algerian and European women.

Pete offers his perspective:

Elaine Klein was a very, very informative woman in matters political in Algeria. She knew all the liberation movements; she knew all of the revolutionary embassies. She would help us a great deal with translating. But much more than translating. Kathleen Cleaver spoke French well, so Kathleen could deal with that. But Elaine not only knew what the words meant, she knew what was meant behind the words. Elaine Klein was a confidant of Eldridge Cleaver. So when there was a problem, she would offer her advice to Eldridge or to us. However, some in the International Section felt that she was a little too close to Eldridge. We felt she was privy to a little too much of our business. So, she was resented by some.

Algeria was a haven for exiles and political refugees. And particularly, political refugees from the West or people in opposition to Western supported regimes. You had the ANC there, you had SWAPO, you had all the southern Africa organizations, you had the IRA [Irish Republican Army], you had the Baader-Meinhof gang [West Germany's Red Army faction], you had Black September [a Palestinian organization], you had all of these diverse organizations. The North

Vietnamese, Chinese, and North Koreans all had their embassies there. We interacted with these people on a daily basis.

The International Section had semi-ambassadorial status. We almost had diplomatic immunity. When unfortunate incidents occurred, when even serious transgressions of law occurred, the government worked with us to prevent those incidents from being exposed to the world. We were allowed to carry guns on our person. Everybody had guns either stuck in their pants or carried in their briefcases. We had heavy guns in our embassy. The government knew this, but it was not openly acknowledged.

We imported cars and all of our equipment. We'd have Volkswagen vans and private cars coming in. We never paid duty. We would go to the FLN [*Front de Libération Nationale*], something would be stamped and we would immediately go and collect it—the same way an embassy does with its diplomatic pouch. We had our own immigration forms. If people were coming to see or join us, we would fill out the forms and send them to the airport. When the people came in, completed and stamped forms would be there waiting. These people could come in without visas. Sometimes they came in without passports. They would be brought to our place. So that's very close to diplomatic status.

The Algerian government gave us a stipend and supplied us with villas and an apartment complex for twenty people. Eldridge Cleaver had, perhaps, two villas. Don Cox had a villa at Point Biscard on the Mediterranean. Charlotte and I, as our influence grew, got a villa in Kouba [*a suburb of Algiers*]. Very nice with very elaborate gardens and manicured grounds. I was aware that these were something of a symbiotic relationship. The government was using us, and we were using the government. The Algerian government was engaged in a propaganda war with America.

We had an ongoing relationship with the North Korean Embassy, the Chinese Embassy, and the North Vietnamese Embassy. Whenever they had functions, they would invite us. Whenever we approached these embassies for financial support for our speaking tours, they would help. But they wanted to be sure we were speaking to whites as well as blacks. It would have been so easy to say, "Oh yeah, we were on top of it." But, I think many of them, especially the North Vietnamese, sensed our inexperience. They would try to keep us as close to them as they could, believing we would benefit from being in their presence. The North Vietnamese supported us because of our strong antiwar policy. They gave us money and some guns, like AK-47s. When Kathleen Cleaver's speaking tour in the United States came up we approached the North Vietnamese and some monies were forthcoming. So, there was a fraternal relationship. I don't think it was developed as much as it could have been.

Quite frankly, we were politically naive to an extent. Once we were invited to the Chinese Embassy for a very elaborate and very protocol-conscious dinner. Beautiful long table, and the Chinese are so proper and elegant. We had this wonderful dinner and we're talking about revolution. As we get up to go, DC's [*Donald Cox*] gun falls through his pants leg—bam!—it hits the floor. The ambassador, who at the time was escorting us out, was so cool. He said, "Oh, pick it up." DC nervously picked it up and put it back in his pants and we apologized. The ambassador said, "Oh no, of course I understand. We're living dangerously here." He made a joke and laughed, and we went on our way.

We established some really good, meaningful relationships with other oppressed people of the world. But it could have been so much better if we had presented ourselves in a more serious and a more revolutionary manner. But in terms of creating some kind of bonds, I think we did so. We had good relations with ANC, with SWAPO, and with the Palestinian Liberation Front. Yasser Arafat came one time, and there was even a photo session. I had never done anything like this on an international level. We would hold functions, and we would invite all of the people and they would come. We would all mingle with the guests. Eldridge, who was our spokesperson, would give speeches. The guests would be very impressed when we told them about our struggle, the history of what we had undergone as a people. When we told them about slavery and the horrors of segregated life in the fifties and early sixties in America, it would almost bring tears to their eyes, as it would any compassionate human being. The people from African countries looked at us, correctly so, as their brothers. Of course there were a lot of blacks who had deserted the US military and came to Algeria to join us. One of our main activities was to help them and to work with them to influence others not to support the war.

We had a policy of nonfraternization with Western embassies. There was some animosity. America did not have an embassy; it had an Interests Section in the Swiss Embassy. I remember one time some brother went there and stole the passport stamping machine. [*Mokhtefi wrote that the thief was Eldridge Cleaver.*][4] They almost had a fit. They called the FLN. The FLN came and told us, "I don't blame you for taking it and I know what you want to use it for, but you've got to give it back." So, ultimately we ended up giving it back. The Americans, through the grapevine, made it known that they could not touch us in Algeria. But be aware, the moment we cross these borders, the chase will be on." [*Unknown to the Panthers at that time, the US Central Intelligence Agency was actively spying on them in Algeria. Reportedly, the CIA even managed to gain access to Eldridge Cleaver's living quarters.*][5]

Organization and Activities of the International Section

The organizational structure of the International Section in Algeria was very laissez faire. Eldridge Cleaver was considered its head. Then it went mostly on seniority. Don Cox was Eldridge's primary assistant. Then there were Sekou Odinga [*born Nathanial Burns*] and Larry Mack, with no specific titles. Most of the others were considered soldiers. When I started talking about the ways we could implement things, my influence grew. But, I met a lot of resistance. They would say, "Hey man, we're not in the military. There's no point in doing that." That was the odd attitude that existed there.

Most of our work was interacting with other people in our situation and trying to develop a networking system. The main function was trying to propagate the ideals of the Black Panther Party, what we were about, relating to other liberation movements, and trying to build up influence. But almost from the beginning the main players had their own personal agendas. Sekou Odinga was probably the most devoted individual to the concept of revolution that I've ever met. He saw himself as a soldier. His goal was to get back to the United States and participate in the revolution on the ground. In fact, he did do exactly that. As for Eldridge, the moment I arrived I was seeing the beginning of disillusionment building in him. His thinking was somewhere else.

We started working from the moment we walked in there. I mean, we did everything and never stopped until the day we left. I am an electronic technology buff, so the first thing I wanted to do was to organize the section's technology. I built a soundproof radio room with some really nice equipment contributed by the Red Army people, the Baader-Meinhof gang, and people like that out of Europe. As a matter of fact, Europeans would bring us some beautiful, brand-new, reel-to-reel tape recorders. I started a weekly program where I gave an overview of the international situation. I would interview people and send the tapes to Kansas City, where they would be played on radio stations. I also set up a telex machine. Boy, that was something back then! Now we had an additional radio room for the telex machines, shortwave radios, and other tape recorders. I designed a system whereby, whenever a phone was lifted anywhere in the Panthers' Embassy, tape recorders would start automatically. So we had an automatic taping system, and all we had to do periodically during the day was change the tapes.

We would welcome people in our huge sitting room where we had a full-wall world map. I put in a whole system of lights and a control panel on a chair so that, if we're talking about what's happening in a particular place, we could have lights light up on the wall map in that particular spot. If we're saying, "Now, in Oakland . . . ," bump, you hit the thing and the light would flash and blink over Oakland. I worked days on end hooking that up and enjoyed every minute of it.

One European who stands out was Lily Vanderberg. She was a white girl from the Netherlands or Switzerland, or somewhere thereabouts. From very wealthy people. She was one of the young white kids who wanted to be part of the revolution. So they come to Algiers. Lily would go to Europe to raise money from white organizations and bring it back to the party.

I don't want to try to demean our efforts there. I think, for the most part, we made a very serious effort, but I think this was terra incognita for most of us. This is something we had not dealt with before. And I doubt we had a level of political sophistication that was appropriate for our situation. For example, smoking marijuana in the sixties, my goodness my friend, if you found anybody involved in the struggle—and I'm talking about across the board, in America—that wasn't smoking marijuana, that would have been unusual. So when we went there, we went with these attitudes. Now a lot of people from other organizations wouldn't dream of involving themselves in anything like this. Word got around that we were smoking, and it lent a negative air to our work. And one of the biggest problems we had was Eldridge's Algerian mistress. Algerians had a very high level of political sophistication, but I think they had a very deep-seated racism towards blacks. They did not take kindly to Eldridge's having this Algerian mistress. So this added to this negative air that we had. Speaking of Eldridge Clever, when I say he had one of the most brilliant minds I've ever encountered, I mean that sincerely. He, like all of us, came from a street-cum-prison background, and we carried that baggage with us when we went to Algeria.

It would have served us better had we left that baggage in the United States. The womanizing, the marijuana, and things like that. In this Casablanca-like setting, stories and rumors got around. I even heard people refer to us as palace revolutionaries, because we were set up in the palaces and smoked dope. People would look at us and say, "You could be a bit more serious." Yet, in my heart of hearts I believe we did a lot of good revolutionary work. I do. It could have been done an awful lot better. But, after the hijacked planes started to come, things seriously started to fall apart.

Charlotte's Comments

In Algeria, there was a wonderful camaraderie. We lived communally and ate communally. After Malcolm was born, I worked mostly in the nursery. We had a day-care center for our little warriors, and I felt that that was a big contribution. We taught the children, even children four and five years old, our history. I didn't feel like I was less than anyone else because I worked in the day care.

There were women coming to Algeria from all over the world—European women, Americans, Caucasian women—coming for the simple purpose of meeting these brothers and latching on to them. Not for any revolutionary kind of work, but just for sex. Of course, sisters resented that. I remember when Pete and I came to Algeria from Sweden, the sisters were so relieved when they saw I was black.

The Split

While Huey Newton sat in prison in 1970, the Panthers' chief of staff, David Hilliard, attempted to rule the party from Oakland. He tolerated no disagreement with his decisions. Upon his release from prison in August 1970, Huey Newton assumed the new title of "supreme commander"

and began expelling people from the party either because they criticized him or because he mistrusted them. These included Geronimo
Pratt [*who changed his name to Ji Jaga*] and members of the New York
chapter, known as the "New York Twenty-One." These and other expul-
sions stunned many party members, who regarded Pratt, the leader of
the Panther revolutionary underground, a true hero. Newton reportedly mistrusted Eldridge Cleaver because of his charisma and popularity. Cleaver, who wanted the party to be the vanguard of a revolution in
his time, criticized Oakland's lack of support for revolutionary-minded
members. Tensions within the party were exacerbated by an FBI campaign of forged letters disguised as being from actual party members and
warning other members of conspiracies against them. Some of these letters warned Cleaver of plots by Newton to eliminate him. Others warned
Newton of similar Cleaver plots.

In an attempt to show the public that the party was not split, Newton
decided to have a public conversation with Cleaver via a televised international phone hookup on the *Jim Dunbar Show,* a program that covered
events in San Francisco. The conversation did not go as Newton had
hoped. In it, Cleaver criticized Newton for expelling Pratt and New York
members. He recommended that David Hilliard be replaced. He labeled
Oakland's stress on community-service programs as reformist, and
exhorted Panthers in the United States to engage in guerrilla warfare.
Cleaver also announced that he headed the real Black Panther Party from
Algiers. After the program ended, an irate Newton telephoned Cleaver
and accused him of killing a Panther in Algeria who allegedly had an affair with Kathleen Cleaver, beating his wife, and dealing in drugs. These
two men then expelled each other from the party. The New York faction
followed Cleaver while most of the other chapters stayed with Newton.
Pete offers his views of the Dunbar show and the party split.

Many people have said that Huey wanted to show solidarity in the
Dunbar Show. Really what Huey was doing was trying to box us into
a corner of declaring support for what he was doing. He needed that
support. Remember this was a time when he had just cast Geronimo
aside. Wouldn't let people testify on Geronimo's behalf—cast him
totally aside. [*Geronimo Pratt had been on trial for murder.*] We were
in opposition to this. To publicly, on this televised, radio talk show,
come out and support Huey Newton would have undermined all our
efforts to bring about change. Eldridge told him there are a lot of

things that we need to talk about because there are a lot of things that have to be straightened out in the party. Some people wrongly painted Eldridge's words as backstabbing. Quite the opposite. I think, had we taken a different position, had Eldridge tried to gloss over for the public's sake, the differences in the party, it would have undermined our efforts because there were people all across the country who were looking to us for leadership to bring about change in the party. So it had to be brought out into the open, and that's precisely what happened. People here agreed that David Hilliard must be removed. Huey Newton's megalomaniac tendencies had to be cut short immediately. We were all in the radio room as Eldridge was talking on the telephone. It's coming through the speakers and we're listening to the whole thing. And shortly after the program, Huey called Eldridge and said, "Yeah, you embarrassed me on that television show." And it developed into name-calling.

First of all, Huey had renamed himself the supreme commander. The central committee became a rubber stamp for any and every- thing he said. He would brook no dissension. They were beating people for disagreeing. Whereas before there had been criticism and self-criticism, and you were obliged, if you felt strongly about something, to take a stand and defend it. That was not tolerated under this new penthouse Huey Newton. His dictates were from the supreme commander and that was it. There was no criticism allowed whatsoever. There was a lot of animosity toward David Hilliard, who had abandoned the underground. Now, our position was there should be an underground to wage war, the revolution. A perfect example of that was Geronimo. Geronimo had an underground functioning. In one of the tapes Eldridge asked Huey, "Why are you all not helping Geronimo?" Huey responded, "Because he's a damn fool." Huey was pursuing his own agenda. And his agenda was not the Black Panther Party that we knew.

Huey Newton wanted an organization wherein he had total and absolute and undisputed control. And that was, I believe, what he did build in California with Elaine Brown. Someone once told me that people ought to look at the Black Panther Party as a nonstruc- tured gang with a leader. I really believe this is what Huey had after the split, after the Black Panther Party as we knew it fell apart. What he revived was a gang with a leader. You look at some of the things that happened. The beatings. How he would go into places and just beat people for no reason. Exercising, manifesting his authority. The poor girl everybody knows he killed, the seventeen-year-old girl that was a prostitute. He kills the girl, he goes to Cuba, all of these things. No, that wasn't the Black Panther Party I knew. That wasn't the Black Panther Party that inspired me. It was a gang with a leader.

When everybody speaks about the split, they talk about Newton and Cleaver. Well, it may be accurate to say Newton on one side because he was the supreme commander. Cleaver represented a large segment of the Black Panther Party—all of the New York Chapter, one of the most populous chapters and best chapters in the country. It withdrew absolutely. Huey abandoned the New York Twenty-One. He expelled them from the party and started undercutting their legal defense. Why? They were not viewing him as the supreme commander. Eldridge Cleaver represented all that I knew and all that I had been associated with in the Black Panther Party. It was because of him that I went back into the party.

Plane Hijackings to Algeria

During 1972 some American citizens who supported the International Section of the Black Panther Party hijacked two American airliners in the United States and had them flown to Algeria. Willie Roger Holder, a black Vietnam War veteran, and his white girlfriend, Catherine Marie Kerkow, hijacked Western Airlines Flight 701 on June 2, 1972, and arrived in Algiers with $500,000 in ransom money. Then, in July, five adults, with three children, hijacked Delta Air Lines Flight 841 in the United States and ordered it to be flown to Algiers with $1 million in ransom. The adults were members of the Black Liberation Army, a loosely organized underground movement comprised of Black Panthers and other revolutionaries. In both cases the Panthers in Algiers expected that the Algerian authorities would turn the ransom money over to them. Instead, the authorities returned the planes and most of the money to the United States, although they refused to extradite the hijackers, as the United States had requested.[6] Following are Pete's comments on the situation.

We really had nothing at all to do with those hijackings. But since it happened, the money was there, the money was supposed to be brought for us, we started pushing for it. A total of one-point-five million! The Algerian government said they would give it to us; they were lying. While they were saying they'll give it to us, we found out the money had already been sent back to the United States with the planes. But they kept telling us, "You're going to get your money. Don't worry. There are procedures we're going to have to work, you're going to get it." We also found out that the Algerian government and the American government, behind closed doors, were negotiating a billion-dollar natural gas deal. So it would be the epitome of foolishness to think that they would allow Black Panthers and one-point-five million dollars to jeopardize something of that magnitude.

According to a *New York Times* report dated August 11, 1972, Algerian authorities sealed off the headquarters of the International Black Panther Party, effectively putting those inside, including Eldridge Cleaver, Panther leader, under house arrest.[7] Authorities also cut off telephone and wire communications from the headquarters building, a villa on the outskirts of Algiers. These actions followed angry public demands by Cleaver for the ransom money taken in the hijacking of a Delta Air Lines plane from Florida to Algeria. Cleaver said that the money was needed for black revolution. Observers said that the Algerians had become increasingly embarrassed by the activities of Cleaver and the Panthers, whom they had welcomed three years ago as "fellow revolutionaries."

Pete comments:

We were arrested and put under house arrest, because of a letter Eldridge and I coauthored and sent to President Houari Boumédiène, telling him he would be blocking our revolution if he didn't give us the ransom money from recent plane hijackings. [*The Panthers also delivered the letter to the international press.*][8] The authorities came to our villas and took all guns they could find. They didn't find them all. But even after that we reached some sort of understanding and they started giving us the guns back.

Eldridge Withdraws and Pete Takes Over

There came a point where there was so much pressure on Eldridge Cleaver after our attempted coup [*against Newton*] failed that he really lost all interest and he just backed up, backed up. He recommended that I take over the International Section. I had been there now for over a year and a half. My influence was growing and I had earned a bit of respect. There was no opposition. Everybody agreed.[9] And I took over with the idea that I could get the section back on track, get it really organized the way we had the chapter in Kansas City at its height; I really thought I could do it. I brought up the idea to everybody that we can do this thing. We can make the International Section of the Black Panther Party outlive itself. But we've got to do something drastic. One of the things we could do was become involved in, believe it or not, agriculture. The government would have been glad to give us land. We could have started some sort of farming project. I'm not talking small, big farming project, perhaps a huge chicken farm. Something like that would benefit the country, would help us sustain ourselves and the work we wanted to do, and it would put us in harmony with the country that was basically agricultural. Now remember, everybody, in that section, including myself, came from an urban setting. Bear in mind while I was suggesting this, I knew nothing about agriculture at all. As a matter of fact, the idea got in my head because I had heard that people from Kansas City in Tanzania had started a chicken farm. And that planted a seed. So when I suggested the idea, first thing other members said was, "Do you know how to do this?" I said, "No I don't, but we can learn." Then they said, "You know, that's probably very technical, raising chickens and all. You have to have experts to know how to do these things; none of us know." So, no one supported the idea; it died as it was being suggested.

Understand, the people in the International Section were very individualistic, almost everyone had been a person of substance. So it was not going to be the way I did things in Kansas City, in terms of me, Pete O'Neal, telling everyone, "All right this is the way it's going to be and we'll do it this way and so on." As things began to crumble after the attempted coup, people started to talk about their individual plans. Sekou and Larry Mack were talking more and more about getting out of here and getting back, as they would phrase it, "on the ground." Eldridge played his cards close to his chest. He wouldn't say what he wanted to do, but I knew it was not continuing with what we had there. Eldridge just started pulling more and more away from the party.

Kathleen Cleaver wrote: "The colony of refugees in Algeria dwindled from nearly 30 people in 1971 to seven by the summer of 1972."[10] During his last years in Algeria, Eldridge Cleaver tried to establish the Revolutionary Peoples Communication Network for the revolutionary peoples of the world. In this effort, which ultimately failed, he tried to engage with Tony Soares, a postwar South Asian immigrant in London who found inspiration in contemporaneous African American struggles for rights and equality. Tony Soares was born Antonio Moushine Leo de Sousa in Portuguese Goa in the mid-1940s. He spent part of his teenage years in Mozambique, where he protested against Portuguese colonialism, before migrating to the United Kingdom in 1961 to escape persecution for his political activism.[11]

According to Kathleen Cleaver, Eldridge came to regard the back-to-Africa ideal as an emotional "skin game." He concluded that the kind of freedom American blacks needed did not exist in the socialist and Third World countries he had visited. After unsuccessfully seeking political asylum in France, Cleaver returned to the United States in 1975.[12] Nineteen-seventy-three marked the last year for Panthers in Algeria. Some members returned to the United States, others opted for African countries. Pete and Charlotte O'Neal and their son went to Tanzania.

Pete on Eldridge Cleaver

Eldridge Cleaver left Algeria in 1973 for France. He divorced himself from the party, but not from the struggle, or so he claimed. He started the Revolutionary People's Communication Network with some of our European allies. We had a video recorder we called "voodoo." It used huge tapes, about two inches wide. We started to propagandize with it, by sending video tapes back to the States. The recorder was a big huge machine. It took a strong man to hold it on his shoulder. When Eldridge left, he took *his* machine with him. He thought he was going to start something really good with it, but it died before he did anything. In France he came up with his codpiece pants idea. He wanted to make pants that "liberated the penis," he said. It got big play in the paper, but sounded like he had lost his mind. He tried to make that as a fashion statement. It flopped.

While in France, Eldridge became a born-again Christian. He said that one night he was standing on his balcony and there was a full moon. He's pondering the fates and the directions of life, and he looked into the moon and lo and behold and much to his amazement, there was the face of Che Guevara. He said that didn't touch him. He said he looked again and he saw the face of Mao Zedong, of Marx, of Castro, but it didn't touch him. He said he wiped his eyes, looked again, and saw the face of Jesus Christ. He said from that moment on that was him. So he went back to the States in 1975, and upon entering the States I read that he said, "The greatest threats to the security of America were communism and black militancy." And I said, "Oh, break my heart!"

He went to jail, but didn't spend much time in there at all. I'm talking four or five months. He had charges like attempted murder of police officers, etcetera. I have been led to believe that these charges were dropped because of the influence of right-wing forces which he had indicated he wanted to align himself with in America. I know while he was in jail he started the Eldridge Cleaver Crusade for Christ or for Jesus. Some right-wing philanthropist put up his bail money, put him in a hundred-thousand-dollar home, this was back in the mid-seventies now. [*Pete is referring to a multimillionaire and evangelical Christian, Arthur S. DeMoss, who founded the National Liberty Life Insurance Company and the Arthur S. DeMoss Foundation, which among other activities distributed a book titled* Power for Living *that promised a more personal relationship with Christ. DeMoss arranged Cleaver's $100,000 bail and covered many of his legal, personal, and family expenses. Reportedly, many of Cleaver's public statements conformed to DeMoss's beliefs.*][13]

Eldridge came out of prison and started hitting the speaking circuit, trying to promote his Eldridge Cleaver for Jesus, or whatever, program. And it was a humongous flop; no one responded to it. In the African American community it became a joke. That for me was particularly tragic because Eldridge Cleaver was such an icon. That tape I gave you, Paul, entitled "Dig," or something like that, was played in every chapter of the Black Panther Party every day all day long across America. It became our Bible, our daily inspiration. People would go around all day quoting Eldridge from that particular recording, the one he did when he spoke to the Peace and Freedom Party when he was running on their ticket for President of the United States. He was such an inspiration, and later people were so disappointed. Even I here. In spite of the difficulties, the problems we had with Eldridge. When I heard some of the moves he was making toward this ultra-conservative right wing, oh that just hurt me to my heart. It really did. In spite of that, there is one thing I cannot deny and I never will. While I disagreed with Eldridge as much as a human being can disagree with another in terms of his politics, I have to admit that I have a begrudging admiration for the fact that Eldridge Cleaver, Papa Rage, once again stood before the altar of conventional thought and declared himself in opposition. It took a hell of a lot of courage to stand up. I would like to think that it was a heartfelt conviction, that he really sincerely believed and was not doing this for some manipulative reasons.

Some Visitors to Algeria and the Black Panthers

While the Panthers were in Algeria, several notorious Americans landed in that country. In some cases, the authorities, not knowing how to handle them, turned them over to the Panthers. One arrival was Timothy Leary, a terminated lecturer in clinical psychology at Harvard University, who advocated the use of psychedelic drugs and became a prominent figure in 1960s counterculture. Leary became famous for catchy slogans, such as "Tune In, Turn On, Drop Out," and "Science is all metaphor." Because of the enthusiastic reception, especially by young people, of Leary's advocacy of LSD, then-President Richard Nixon described Leary as "the most dangerous man in America."[14]

In 1970 Leary was convicted of illegal substance possession and imprisoned in California. That same year he escaped from a minimum security prison with the help of the Weathermen (a violent offshoot of Students for a Democratic Society) and traveled to Algiers with his wife. Eldridge Cleaver thought he could convince Leary to denounce drugs and instead advocate a sober commitment to the revolution against capitalism and imperialism. Cleaver failed and concluded that Leary's mind had been blown by acid.[15] Leary continued to use LSD in Algeria, and his erratic behavior with followers and others embarrassed the Panthers, who felt responsible for his unrevolutionary decorum. Pete comments on this case:

Timothy Leary came to Algeria with his wife, Rosemary. The Algerians turned them over to us. We got him and Rosemary an apartment. From the moment he got there, Leary wanted to be the celebrity and mingle with all of the Western embassies. That was a very bad show. With all the revolutionary organizations in exile there—ANC, SWAPO, and others. That just gave a very bad picture of someone associated with us. This developed to the point that we had to put Timothy Leary under house arrest to prevent him from fraternizing with the Western governments. When we did that, white radicals in America went absolutely berserk. They were calling and asking, "Yes, we want to know what's happened to Timothy Leary. But why have you placed him under house arrest?" We tried to explain, "He's fine, but we just had to cool him down a bit. After that everything will be all right." I can't remember when he left, but shortly after we released him, he moved on to Europe. Eventually, he made his way back to the United States. I don't think much of anything happened to him. [*Leary traveled from Europe to Afghanistan, where he was arrested by an agent of the US Bureau of Narcotics and Dangerous Drugs. He was brought back to the United States and imprisoned. California Governor Jerry Brown released Leary from prison on April 21, 1976.*]

Doctor John Branion

On December 22, 1967, forty-one-year-old John Branion, a successful physician in Chicago, found his wife murdered in their home. Branion was convicted of her murder, and after exhausting his appeals, he fled to Algeria. Pete narrates:

Then there was Doc Branion. If ever there was an odyssey, Doc Branion's story most certainly is one. Doc Branion was a gynecologist out of Chicago, an African American. I remember reading about him in black magazines. He was considered one of the top ten gynecologists in the country. Well-to-do man, a wealthy man, and married to a socialite. I can't remember his wife's name, but I remember she was somehow related to Oscar Brown Jr.—a very well-known entertainer. That was his wife. Well, Doc Branion's wife was found shot to death. He and his son found her. The police alleged that he killed her and that there was an attempt to make it look like a burglary. He went to trial, was convicted. While out on appeal, he fled to Algeria. The Algerians turned him over to us. It was all over the papers about this wealthy gynecologist. Now he came with very little money. He had spent all of his money on legal battles.

You asked if Doc Branion was a Panther. Oh, my God no. Branion—the very elegant, sophisticated Doc Branion. My God, no. But he would spend a great deal of time at the Panther embassy. His presence was totally dependent on his financial situation. When Doc Branion had money, you wouldn't see him. He would be gone. When he was needy, he'd come to the embassy with a very sheepish smile, and he'd say, "I got a problem, brother." We'd always welcome him back. Be very critical of him, but bring him back on in.

When Doc Branion had no money he was right there with us. He examined Charlotte and told us that our baby was going to be small. Malcolm weighed five pounds, but everything was okay, and it turned out perfectly. Doc Branion was waiting for employment with the Algerian government. Algerians can be very bureaucratic. So they're going through their processes. Months are going by. Then some relatives or friends start to send money to Doc Branion. Now when he gets money, he changes. Doc Branion becomes the Doc Branion of old. He wants to go out and hang out at the cocktail parties, hold a drink in his hand and hold court. He's telling all of his business to all of the people in Algiers. Remember, Algiers was, I imagine, something like Casablanca in the film: city of intrigues. So Doc Branion's business is spreading all over town. He's telling our business as well. We started to rein him in. We told him, "You can't do this." He started to balk. We started to press down tighter on him. So after he'd been with us for some months he absconded one day and got out.

At that time, Charlotte's parents and my parents were coming to visit us. Charlotte and I went to the airport to meet them. We're standing there waiting for the plane to come in. Lo and behold we look over where people are waiting for departing planes, and who should we see with a cocktail glass in his hand, but Doc Branion. It shocked me. "Doc!" I called out. He looked at me and almost fainted he was so surprised. He came over and started talking, "Pete, I got to go and get my mind together. Please understand. Please forgive me, brother." I said, "Forgive you?" He flew out. Our parents flew in.

Interestingly, the day after Doc Branion left, the government sent a representative over. They had a house for him, a big, nice villa, cars, servants. They wanted him to take over a head position in the hospital, but he had left a day too soon. He went to the Sudan. The American government was hot on him. He was arrested and jailed there. Somehow, he escaped and made his way to Tanzania. In Tanzania he started to use an assumed name. But he had credentials on him, and when the Tanzanians saw his expertise they hired him at the main hospital in Dar es Salaam. He worked at the hospital and opened up an office. He was doing very well. Beach houses and everything, making a lot of money. But, Doc Branion fell into the same old trap: cocktail parties. He starts to talk, word gets around. The government finds out about his criminal case, and at the same time the American government finds his location and starts putting pressure on Tanzania. They kick him out.

Doc Branion makes his way to Uganda. He becomes a Ugandan citizen and Idi Amin's personal physician. So he's just having a ball. He's got a Ugandan passport now. He's traveling around. He visited us in Tanzania. The end of the seventies though, Idi Amin is over-thrown. Milton Obote, who had been in exile in Tanzania, goes back in power and takes over. One of his first acts was to revoke Doc Branion's citizenship, then arrest him and call in the US Marshals. They came, got him on a plane, and took him back to prison. I think he got twenty years to life. There was a big article about this in *Ebony*. In it the prison warden said, "Yes, I know of Branion's medical reputation, but he can't apply a Band-Aid here."

I've really given you the short version of something that would honestly make a damn, damn good film. [*Branion was arrested in 1983 and returned to the United States to serve his twenty-to-thirty-year prison term. Illinois Governor James R. Thompson commuted his sentence to time served on humanitarian grounds. Shortly thereafter on September 30, 1990, Branion died in hospital at age sixty-four.*]

About Mike

You have to bear in mind, everyone who came to Algeria was not po-litical. Some were criminals and had nowhere else to go. They would come to us. One example—and I'm not going to use this man's real name—was Mike. Mike was one of the biggest human beings I've ever seen. This man was about six foot three, weighed almost three hundred pounds and not an ounce of it fat. All of it just muscle, and he was a very intimidating person.

One day we were all sitting up in the embassy. We get a call from Mike. He says he wants to come over and talk to us. We tell him to come over. He arrives at the gate. We look down from the balcony and see this huge fellow. It was more than his size. There was something a bit disconcerting about him. Eldridge says, "Good Lord! Look at this brother!" Eldridge decides to bring him into the villa to talk. I told Eldridge that, while they're talking, I'll be sitting with an AK-47 in the adjoining restroom with the door cracked. Mike tells Eldridge (in his very intimidating voice), "Yes, I wanted to come and see if I could work with you brothers. I am well known in Oakland, very well known in Oakland." We're starting to think he's some hit man sent by Huey. Mike continues, "I got some legal cases there and I want to talk to you about them."

ELDRIDGE: "What are your cases?"
MIKE: "Well I don't want to tell everything now."
ELDRIDGE: "Well wait a minute, brother, I'll tell you what. You go and come back in a few days. We'll talk to some of our people in Oakland and then we'll talk here."
MIKE: "Okay, I'll come, but I want you to know one thing. I'm going to treat you with respect and seriously. I'd appreciate it if you would treat me in the same manner."

After he left, we sent a telex to Oakland, California, describing this man, and we got a hot telex back warning us: "Be extremely careful. This dude is a living legend in Oakland, and he is deadly!" So he comes back, and now we're all packing guns. So we sit there and we're talking, he's proposing things and asks, "Okay?" We respond, "Look here, this is what we'll do. We'll help you, but you've got to find your own place to stay. You can't stay here with us. We'll help you with whatever you need that doesn't jeopardize anything we're doing. But you have to understand, you can't be a part of what we're doing here." First of all we didn't trust him. It turns out that Mike was a notorious, big-time, I don't mean small-time, cocaine dealer. He fled from a big legal case in the States.

Mike got his own apartment. He would come by, and he and I

started talking. We struck up something of a friendship, as much of a friendship as you could with somebody like this. One day he told me, "Pete, I don't have any money now, but I'm going to have some before long. I got people who are going to send me money." So weeks go by. One day he comes to me and says, "Pete, my money came in. I want you to do something for me." I said, "Oh, what's that?" He said, "I want you to hold some money for me. But when I ask for my money back, I don't care what you do with it, but I want my money back." I say, "Okay." He pulled out thirty thousand dollars in hundred-dollar bills, put ten thousand on the table, and says, "Here, take this. Now when I ask for this money, I want it back." I say, "That's fine. You got it." Understand that we were always desperate for money for some project or the other.

I go to Eldridge and tell him that Mike gave me ten thousand dollars. He's surprised, and tells me that we need to use the money now. I explain that Mike said when he comes back for the money, he will want it. Eldridge tells me not to worry, he'll find the money then. So months go by. Mike returns. He says, "Well, Pete, I'm going to be leaving before long. I want my money." I said, "Oh, yeah. Sure, sure. Can you get it tomorrow?" He said, "Not a problem. But I want it tomorrow." I go to Eldridge and tell him to give me ten thousand dollars." Eldridge: "Give you what?!" I said, "Give me ten thousand dollars or let's go kill this man now. If you don't have ten thousand dollars let's go kill him now, because I am not going to die." Eldridge: "When does he want it?" Me: "Tomorrow." Eldridge: "You'll have it tomorrow." The next morning Eldridge Cleaver put ten thousand dollars in my hand, and I gave it back to Mike.

Now, during the time that Mike was in Algeria, he met Doc Branion, and Doc Branion latched onto him. They became something of friends. So when Doc Branion went to Tanzania, Mike went there as well. I told you Mike was a deadly, deadly dangerous person. I'm going to give you an example of what happened while he was in Tanzania. He's huge. Huge muscles. Huge! He walked into a German bar. This was a time when they had these German bars in Dar es Salaam, these big tough Germans in there. He and a little African American, called Cutslo, walked in there and the Germans looked and said, "What are they doing in here?" Mike didn't drink, but he's sitting next to the bar talking and some guy wanted to start some kind of trouble with Cutslo. Mike says, "I'm going to hurt people in here." And he put his back up against the wall and he said, "Damn it, I'll kill everybody." And the Germans charged him en mass. (This is the truth; they talk about this in Tanzania to this day.) Mike starts to knock out every one that comes up to him. Cutslo is cutting people, after he knocks them out. They lay waste to the bar. People are seriously cut, and seriously hurt. The Tanzanian authorities kicked them out of the country. Remember, African Americans had a certain kind of distinction, even when we messed up in those days. You'd go to jail forever now, but they kicked them out of the country.

Now let's jump again. Charlotte and I come to Tanzania. We leave Algeria. No money hardly at all. We're in Dar es Salaam now. I'm riding the bus every day to go shopping. One day there's a knock on the door. I go open the door and there's Mike. Malcolm, our baby boy, looks at him and starts crying. Mike was that intimidating. He invited me to his apartment at the Fordham Hotel in Dar es Salaam on the waterfront. I'd go down there and we'd talk. He'd tell me how he was going to Colombia to revive his businesses. I told him that I wasn't into that. He said, "I wouldn't want you to be and I wouldn't respect you if you did. But I'm not like I was in Algiers. I've got money now." He turned off the light in his hotel room. He says, "I don't want anybody shooting me through the window while I show you this." And he pulls out a box of money and lays it on the table. A lot of money! And he says, "This is not Christmas and I'm not Santa Claus, but I really respect the way you dealt with me in Algeria. I'm not going to go out of here and leave you like this." He took out five thousand dollars and put it in my hand. That just turned my life around! I didn't have a car. I went out and bought a really nice Volkswagen car. Charlotte and I began talking about moving up to Arusha. He said he was leaving, and he did. I never saw Mike again.

He went to Colombia. I would get postcards and letters from him that didn't make sense. I wondered if he was using drugs. He would write gibberish. At one time he even wrote, "I've taken care of you. And it's in safety deposit box number one." I said to myself, "Safety deposit box WHERE?" Then, years go by, I get a letter from Mexico. "I may be going back," he writes. He's talking about the States. Time goes by. Then I get a letter. "I'm in Leavenworth." So he's in Leavenworth Prison. He writes that he met people that I had had fights with years ago. "Even they respect you. All of your buddies are here talking about you." Years go by. Don't hear a thing from Mike. Then around 1990 I get a phone call from a guy I knew in Washington, DC. He tells me that he has a friend—sheikh whatever his name was then—for me to talk to. Mike then had an Islamic name. He had become a very important Islamic sheikh. Mike had traveled to Iran for Islamic education and teaching materials. Now he has a huge mosque in Washington, DC. And Mike is now talking to me like a preacher. He says, "In the name of Allah, the most beneficent," and he's going on. I say, "Well, Mike, how are you doing?" He said, "Oh, I'm quite all right. I'm going to send you some tapes of my teaching." And he sent me prerecorded tapes of his sermons. Today, Mike is a very well-respected man. That was about the darndest thing I've ever seen in my life. It was.

7

Leaving Algeria and Living in Tanzania

Leaving Algeria and Meeting Muammar Gaddafi

After the house arrest in Algiers, we decided to leave Algeria. We got on an Air Algérie plane. I had let people in Kansas City know that we were moving and that we were going through Tripoli, Libya. Charles Knox had very good ties with the Libyans. Charles had always been more of an internationalist than most of us. So we got there, and we were at the main hotel. After two days Charles came in and says, "Pete, I've made arrangements for you to meet some people in the government and perhaps to meet Gaddafi." He had sent Gaddafi a telex congratulating him on his coming into power and the wonderful work he was doing. This was a belated thing, but we had waxed eloquent and we had received a telex back welcoming us to Libya in revolutionary fraternity and things like that.

Knox picked us up and took us to a government building where we met some officials. One of them said, "Oh, we've heard about the difficulty that you've had in Algeria. Those people don't have a proper revolutionary perspective. We want you to know that, if ever there is a need, we will support you. You have brothers, you have comrades here." They took us to a room in a palace. We took our shoes off, walked in, and met Gaddafi. He wore a Bedouin headdress. He spoke with a very, very, *very* thick accent that I could barely understand. He said, "We want to thank you. How long are you going to be here?" I said, "Well, I'm moving because we're trying to get to

Tanzania." He said, "We want you to know that we support you. We have something for you that may be of help. I hope you are not offended by us." "Oh, I most certainly am not." I had visions of a large sum of money. He said, "And here's a token." He gave me an Islamic ring. This is what I'm showing you now. It's a silver ring. I said, "Oh, thank you. I am so honored. I will treasure this." After we left this very, very brief meeting, some of his people gave us an envelope. In that envelope was five thousand dollars. I don't know how much we had. The Algerians had given us a bit, but it didn't amount to a great deal.

We got on a plane to Egypt. On that very short plane ride I got very, very sick. I don't know what it was—pressure or tension or what. Remember, every time I would leave a safe place I would be totally apprehensive. I've got my baby, I've got Charlotte with me. We got to Egypt and stayed in a beautiful hotel and had a really wonderful time. I think we spent a week in Egypt, just trying to chill out and feeling relatively safe as long as no one knew who we were. We went to the Tanzanian embassy, telling them that we wanted visas. They said, "We've got to know that you have means to leave before we let you go in." Now, I had a money belt. So I remember pulling down my pants in the embassy, taking out the belt, and showing them the money. Finally they gave us the visas.

Arriving in Tanzania

We flew to Tanzania in September of 1972 on a Lufthansa airplane. We knew some African Americans from Kansas had settled there. They answered the call from the Tanzanian ambassador who had visited the University of Kansas and invited them to emigrate to Tanzania and contribute to nation building. Tanzania in 1972 had about five thousand African Americans. It had become something of a Mecca for African Americans because of Julius Nyerere's welcome and socialist policies.

You've heard the old saying about two men who looked out from prison bars, one saw the mud, the other saw the stars. When we landed at Dar-es-Salaam, the first things that caught my eye were rusted tin roofs and dirt roads. I said, "Oh, Lord. What have I allowed myself to get into!" And Charlotte's eyes were big and she said, "Oh, did you see what that woman had on. Did you see that cloth? Oh, did you see the way the earrings look?" I said, "What in the world is she talking about? We're dying here and she's talking about the women's clothes!" Charlotte was in seventh heaven. Oh, she was. But I was not at all impressed. I wasn't.

There was a brother here from Kansas City—Fred Johnson. We called him, he came and picked us up. We're in his car driving down roads with holes like I've never seen in any place in my life. He said, "Pete, let me tell you something. When you drive here, pretend that you're driving through a battle field. That's the best way to do it." He swerved and swerved. I said, "Oh, Lord! What is this?" And Charlotte's just beaming.

He took us to his house and then to the YMCA. We checked into the YMCA. Some of the brothers that were here had heard that these Black Panthers were coming. They came to talk to us. They were so happy talking. And we were telling them some of our experiences, some of our goals, our revolutionary goals. And this one guy, Kai Juko Leonard Dillon—he's still here and one of my best friends now—he says, "Brother, listen. Housing is very difficult to get here. I've got a brand new one-bedroom apartment that took three years to get. I'm single. Why don't you take it? I'll go stay with friends." I said, "Yeah, man, but I tell you, I've got a family. I'm not interested in sharing anything." He said, "It's yours." And he let us take it. So we moved into that thing.

Slowly, but surely, and I have told everybody that talks to me about this, there's something about Africa in general and Tanzania in particular that plants a hook in people's hearts. It does, Paul. And this is everybody who spends any time out here. The hook was slowly being planted. This is a different way of life. Remember, I had come from a very violent, very fast-moving, very dynamic kind of background. This was entirely laid back. Things moved at a slower pace. Entirely different lifestyle. I had moments where I'd try to be the old Pete O'Neal. I would be in town and get in arguments with people. Then I'd say, "Wait a minute, this is so out of place." It didn't fit in with what was happening in Tanzania. The hook was being planted. Seeds were being planted that would bear fruit later on down the road.

In 1998 I asked Charlotte why she thought Tanzania was a good place to resettle after leaving Algeria. She explained:

The main reason we chose Tanzania was Malcolm. I thought many Algerians were racist. We didn't want Malcolm growing up in an atmosphere like that. But, from the hindsight of age, I look at some of the people's attitudes and now I say, "That might not have been all racism. They might have thought that we were disrespectful to their religion, because of the way we dressed, miniskirts and shorts in a Muslim country!" You can imagine people didn't appreciate that. But being liberated, revolutionary women, that's the way we carried ourselves. So I look back on that now and say, all of that wasn't their fault. Some of it we brought upon ourselves.

My heart has always basically been in Africa, and we had a lot of Afro-American friends and acquaintances in Tanzania. A lot of people had been urging us to go to Tanzania. Socialist policy, the whole African culture thing. I don't have any regrets, and I don't think Pete does either.

Moving to Ngaramtoni

We stayed in Dar es Salaam, money's going. You know when you're trying to get established, money can go so quick. Even in a very cheap place like this. Not broke, but money's getting down low. Remember I told you about Mike coming to Tanzania and giving me five thousand dollars. This was the boost we needed. From the Yugoslavian embassy I bought a nearly brand-new car—a 1969 Volkswagen station wagon Variant. Here that's brand new, man. Know how much I bought it for? Ten thousand shillings! The exchange rate then was about eighteen to a dollar. I bought this and Charlotte and I, oh, we were just so happy! Now we could move, we're mobile. Had the damnedest time learning to drive on the other side of the road—kept drifting over to the one I was accustomed to. I told Charlotte that I wanted to drive up to Ngaramtoni to visit an African American named Michael Monk. He was living in Ngaramtoni on the Manyara Coffee Estate that was run by an Indian.

I drove up by myself; Charlotte stayed behind with Malcolm. This place looked different. The air felt different. In Dar I had been sick for almost nine months. I was in and out running to the doctors to the hospital—headaches, nausea, weakness. I didn't know what it was. Just sick all the time. Dar was unbelievably hot, humid, muggy, and dirty. After I came up here to Ngaramtoni, my ailments started going away. I couldn't believe it. I went back and told Charlotte, "You got to see this place."

Charlotte and I drove up here and we saw it. A friend of ours, a Maasai fellow, who's a friend of Bill Whitfield, named Husein Lisa, told us that there were some white boys renting a really beautiful house on a hill from some Asians. We went out there and saw these young white guys, who'd been in Tanzania all their lives. Their parents had been old colonial people. Europeans. They had their little girlfriends in and out of the house. It was the most beautiful thing I had ever seen. They said, "We're getting out of here. We can't afford this anymore." I said, "Let me take it." So they sublet it to me. This was 1973.

We went back to Dar to pack up. But Charlotte didn't want to move. Every move we've ever made, Charlotte has resisted. It's some kind of security thing. It's breaking up the security. "We better not do that. Don't need to do that." "But, come on, Charlotte, let's do it." We packed everything up on the Volkswagen. It's loaded down to the ground. We drive up here and arrive at night. The white boys had gone. We broke in the door and moved in. It was a beautiful place, the house on the hill with four acres of farmland. Six months later we experienced an international tragedy.

The Big Bust

Before I talk about the big bust, I'd like to give you a brief history of Ngaramtoni. Remember I told you I was sick living in Dar es Salaam. It was hot and muggy, dusty, and dirty. I came up to Ngaramtoni to visit an African American named Michael Monk. I fell in love with the place. He lived in a house that African Americans occupied from 1969 to 1996. It would change hands, from one group of African Americans to another. This became known as our tribal house. Later, my brother Gary lived in that house for about fifteen years. He raised his family there. The house I sublet was on the same estate in Ngaramtoni as the one Monk lived in.

Shortly after we moved there, my mother came to visit. At that time she was working as a key-punch operator for the Treasury Department. Ironically, Treasury is the parent organization of the Alcohol, Tobacco, and Firearms Department that arrested me in 1969. Because of my difficulties with the federal government, some higher-ups made every effort they could to attack her, simply because she was my mother. They tried to get her fired. All of her bosses, all of her coworkers rallied around her and protected her. Her boss told her that they were putting pressure on him to get rid of her because of me. But he simply refused to fire her. He said, "I just won't do it. I cannot. This woman has been a good and faithful employee, and I just won't do it."

Our house in Ngaramtoni was up on a hill. Every year there would be a flood that would cut off the road to my house. The flood could last for three days. My mother said, "Listen, I'm going to send you some walkie-talkies so you can be in contact with Michael Monk (whose house wasn't affected by the flood) if you get stuck up here." She did send them to me. The walkie-talkies will play an important part in this story.

The Tanzanian ambassador had visited the University of Kansas and invited African Americans to go to Tanzania and contribute to nation building—*ujamaa* [*"socialism," a political concept used by President Julius Nyerere as the basis for a national development project*]. This inspired a group of African Americans to contribute to Tanzanian nation building. So they went around the United States, soliciting and gathering all sorts of equipment, from tractors to generators, to water pumps, to harrows, to plows, etcetera, sufficient to fill four large shipping-cargo containers. Back then it was shocking to see a consignment that large coming into Dar es Salaam for African Americans.

Tanzanian customs officials examined the cargo and found some things that were not on the manifest: two old shotguns, a couple of old rifles, and a pistol. "My God," the Tanzanians thought, "this could be a CIA plot, trying to undermine and destroy our socialist policy." They suspected the African Americans to be a fifth column, waiting for a signal to overthrow their government.

Security officials began detaining African Americans at the pleasure of the president. They were held in detention, incommunicado. They are just held there until the president decides he will or will not release them. They started arresting people from Kansas in Dar es Salaam. And then it started spreading. They began holding women in detention—some of the African American women with babies. The police searched homes. Now remember, we're talking about young people, products of the sixties. If you go into their houses looking for things, nine times out of ten you're going to find something that is not 100 percent kosher. And this was the case. Although the little things that were found—maybe it was marijuana, maybe it was something else—people weren't charged with them, but simply because they had such things, they were put into detention as well.

The government was aware of my particular political situation. Security people made a surprise raid on my house in Ngaramtoni. They searched the house and found the walkie-talkie my mother had sent. The police looked at it and said, "My God, this is highly illegal in Tanzania. You're not allowed to possess things like this without a special license. Listen, we want to work with you. First register this and then start the procedure to get a license." Now they had already arrested Bill Whitfield [a former Panther from Kansas City] in Arusha. The police had gone to his house and found ten guns and box after box of ammunition. Now they're convinced there's a plot. So Bill was in jail, in detention. His wife, Jimmie, was there by herself. The police warned me, "We know your friend is in jail. We want to try everything we can not to arrest you because of your circumstances. Try to get a license for this." I said, "Okay."

In the meantime Charlotte and I would go out to Jimmie's house almost daily. We couldn't just leave her out there while Bill was in jail. Every day the security forces would be there. They asked us, "What are you doing here now? We've already talked to you." We explained that we couldn't leave Jimmie alone. We had to check on her. They cautioned, "You're interfering with our investigation. You better be careful."

The next thing that happened is difficult to believe. First let me explain that I'm fascinated with things technological. I've always been that way, I can't help it. I was in town the next day. I walked into an Indian's second-hand shop and saw a radio call transmitter receiver, big huge thing, about four times the size of this TV here. It had all sorts of dials, microphones, and antennas, and stuff that just makes my heart skip a beat. So I said, "Oh man, that looks so nice! Listen, I have a reel-to-reel tape recorder. I'll trade you." The shop owner said, "Bring it in." So, I brought it in the next day and took the transmitter receiver home.

A day or two later, I'm sitting at home playing with this thing. I got wires going out the windows, flying antennas, I'm just trying to see what I can pick up. I got the microphone, "Testing one, two, three." Turning dials and flipping switches. I hear the door open behind me. Turn around and look. Here are the security forces standing. They look from me to the radio call, back to me, back to the radio call. They said, "Oh, no, this is going a little bit too far." Surprisingly, they didn't arrest me then. But I knew arrest had to be imminent. They said, "We're going to have to report this and we'll let you know what our superiors say."

The next day I told Charlotte, "I'm going to Dar es Salaam to try to see President Nyerere before they arrest me. Perhaps I can block it." I got as far as the Air Tanzania office in Arusha. The security people came up to me and said, "Have you bought your ticket?" I answered, "Yeah, I got it in my hand." They said, "Well, I don't know how easy it's going to be to get your money back but, my friend, we're placing you under arrest." So they put me under arrest and took me to the CID Building, Criminal Investigation Department Building.[1] They also arrested Michael Monk because he had the other walkie-talkie. They took us both in. They wanted us to sleep on the floor in an office until they could decide what to do with us. Michael Monk and I said, "No, we're going on a hunger strike." We refused to eat. After some days, we were transferred to the jail.

I've been in jails in many places around the world. I think I can honestly say that I would rather do a year—a year might be a stretch—I'll say six months, I'd rather do six months anywhere that I've been in jail, particularly anywhere in the West, than do another thirty days in the place that I was in, in conditions that existed in Tanzania in 1974. The jail was filthy. It was nasty. And we were given preferential treatment as political detainees! They put us in a dark, dingy cell that had a hole in the floor for a toilet. They would let us out in the daytime to sit in the yard. But at night we had to go back into this smelly, dirty place. We were on a hunger strike, but even had we not been, we couldn't have eaten the food. The food was nasty. So I'm wasting away. Bill Whitfield's in the jail too, but he's on a different side. When we go to the yard I could talk to him. He was working in the kitchen. He said, "I can slip you some food." I said, "Man, I don't want the food. We're on a hunger strike. I wouldn't eat it anyway." I'm starting to get thinner and thinner. The guards came and asked me, "Listen, would you eat if we had your wife cook food and bring it in to you." I said, "Nope. I'm not eating anything."

Charlotte was pregnant with our daughter, Stormy. Malcolm was a small child. The security forces brought Jimmie, Bill Whitfield's wife, from her house to our house in Ngaramtoni. They placed her and my family under house arrest there.

So I'm continuing with the hunger strike. They would take me daily to the warden's office and he would try to convince me to eat. I would refuse. One day he walked out of the room. On his desk I saw in Swahili a telegram saying, "Bring O'Neal and Monk to Dar es Salaam." It was signed by Rashidi Kawawa, the prime minister, who was the driving force behind this big bust in the first place. Finally the time came. They said, "We're transferring you to Dar es Salaam." They loaded us up into a Land Rover.

I can remember we're in that Land Rover, we're handcuffed, and we're so thin and weak from not eating. Before we take off on this journey to Dar es Salaam, they drive to a petro in Arusha. It was dark. To this day, I don't know Tanzania at night. So I'm sitting there, watching the blinking lights and I think, "I wonder if I'll ever see Charlotte again."

We took off on the long journey to Dar es Salaam. We're on the way and the car breaks down. Now, Michael Monk was a damn good mechanic. He built a Land Rover from the chassis up. He had come to Tanzania as an engineer to help build General Tire. I think he helped build the boilers. The car's not running, and the driver and guards are sitting there without the slightest idea of what to do. It was obviously a problem with the fuel line. Michael Monk said, "This is obviously not a big problem. I can fix this thing." The guards talk among themselves, then one says, "Okay, fix it." Monk said, "First, you got to take the handcuffs off. There's no way in the world I can do anything with handcuffs on." The other guard warns, "Don't take them off! Don't take them off! They all know karate!" There were these popular black exploitation films that showed all of these African Americans as martial arts masters. And I suppose these guards being influenced by these films thought we were deadly. So we sat there all night in the Land Rover. We had to wait until they could make contact for a mechanic to come out and repair. Finally we take off and get to Dar es Salaam.

We go to Keko Prison. Now Keko is a big prison. We go into Keko and see that all the African Americans from Kansas are there. "Hey how are you doing? How's everything? What's happening man? Are we ever going to get out?" "I don't know." I'm called to the office. There was this security guy, a very sharply dressed guy with a suit and a tie. He was just so slick. He started out like this, "Peter, Peter, Peter. What is wrong with you? Why are you being so difficult by not eating?" I said, "Being difficult? I'm being difficult because you had me in jail for absolutely no reason, when I have done nothing. I don't know if I'm going to live to see tomorrow. So I'm fighting back in the only way I know how." He said, "Listen to me. My brother, we know your history and we're with you. I have it on the highest authority that you're going to be out of here before you know it." I said, "Really?" He said, "I'm telling you to cooperate with us." I said, "Okay." Then he said, "Guard, bring the potatoes and milk." They brought the potatoes and milk and I'm eating. I go back to Monk. Monk says, "You're eating!" I told him, "Yeah, they told me we're out of here." So we both start eating.

The next day, the day after, two days, three days we're still there. I said, "They tricked us, Monk. They sent somebody in here to trick us. We're going back on a hunger strike." So now I'm not eating anymore and I make the declaration we're not going to eat food, regardless. And that night, it was on a Thursday—why I should remember that, I don't know—the guards came in and said, "O'Neal! Monk! Get your stuff together. You're getting out of here." And so we're slapping fives, telling all the brothers goodbye. We take our little bundles and we walk out. We're talking about how we are going to get home. Maybe we'll spend the night in Dar es Salaam and catch a bus tomorrow. We walked out to the foyer and see four or five security guys standing there with guns pointed at us. They shout, "Get up against the wall! Get up against the damn wall!" We get up against the wall, and Monk tells me, "Pete, they're going to kill us!" Monk is scared to death. I'm scared to death. Then they blindfold us and take us out to a car. They put our heads down so we wouldn't bump them as we got in. We're sitting there, someone on either side of us. We're all cramped together in this car. Bam! They close the doors and they take off driving. So we're driving and driving. It seemed like we're driving forever. But at one point I would hear the car go over something that seemed like railroad tracks. Boom, boom, boom, boom. And as soon as that happened I heard a man and a woman talking softly. They are talking about whatever men and women talk about in the evening. We went on. And after about ten minutes I felt the same thing: boom, boom, boom, boom. And I heard the same man and woman talking! Obviously, I thought, "We're going in circles."

So finally the car stops. Monk is pressing up against me, "They're going to kill us now! They're going to kill us now!" I said, "Yeah, they probably are." They order us out of the car and into a building. The door closes behind us. Next thing I know, I don't hear Michael Monk with me anymore. I'm pushed into another room and a door closes behind me. I'm standing there trying to make my peace now, preparing for whatever is coming. A guy reaches up and takes the blindfold off my eyes. And lo and behold I find myself in a beautifully laid out bedroom with a bed, with a canopy, beautiful stuffed chair in one corner, writing table with pens and papers. Then this guy says, "Well, Mr. O'Neal this will be your home for the time being. If there is anything that you need, would you please let me know." I said, "I most certainly shall." And so he left and locked the door. This was a security safe-house. They had taken Michael Monk to another room and locked him in there.

The next day the guy came back, pointed to the paper, gave me pens and said, "Now, Mr. O'Neal, what we want you to do is to write down your entire history, as far back as you can remember, if you can from the day you were born to the present. And leave out no details." I never liked writing by long hand. It's always rather laborious for me. But I sat there and labored away.

One day security people came to my room in a rage. They thrust a telegram into my hand and demanded, "What is the meaning of this? Our president is very upset." And I said, "Why? How the hell do you think I feel!?" The telegram was from the Black Lawyers Association of America's chairman, Dr. Charles Knox. It said, "Your Excellency, we are concerned about the incarceration of our brother Pete O'Neal. We are asking you please clarify why you have arrested him. And under no circumstances should he be extradited to the United States." So there were inquiries coming from the States and particularly the Kansas City area.

So I go back to scratching and scribbling my story. I'm going on and on and on. After a few days the security guy came back, took the papers, and said, "You left out a great deal." I said, "I know. It's difficult for me." He said, "Well, we have a committee and they want you to tell them your story." They took me into a big conference hall with a big, long table. There are security people sitting all up and down this table. One of them was the president's representative. They're sitting there stern, almost glaring at me. "Sit down there, please Mr. O'Neal. We now want you to tell us your life history." Paul, I can tell a story. If I can't do many things else, I can do that. So I started out. And I'm getting into the story. Fifteen minutes later, half an hour later, you can see their ties are pulled away, they've opened their shirts and I got the story going. "What happens next, Pete?" And I'm telling them tales about Kansas City and I'm telling them how Charlotte and I ran through the hospital and the police are chasing us. "Did they catch you?" "No, they didn't." So they were very much into it. They listened to my story and they listened to the stories of the other people they had arrested as well. They finally said, "You know we're beginning to get the impression that a mistake has been made here. But things move very slowly in Tanzania. We really don't think you have much to worry about. We're just asking you to hold on."

I won't give you the long version of what happened next. Ultimately they took us out of that building. We had to go back to prison before we could go back to Arusha. The next day a Land Rover took us back to Arusha and put us back in the jail here. Then the next day they took us to court. They had to find a charge to justify all of this. So they charged each of us with possession of a walkie-talkie without a license and fined us five hundred shillings. I was only in jail for thirty-two days. Most other people, like Whitfield, served four to five months. I remember being in the safe house in Dar es Salaam on my thirty-fourth birthday, which was July 27, 1974.

Charlotte had gotten huge during her house arrest, gained a lot of weight and for some reason cut all her hair off. She came to pick me up. Now Charlotte can't drive worth a lick in the world. She's probably the worst driver ever. She's driving my car, running all up the sides of the roads trying to get to the courthouse. She got there and saw me, this little thin emaciated looking guy. She grabbed me in a bear hug and lifted me off the ground. Almost broke my back. Bill Whitfield's wife was there too, so we had a celebration. We went back to the house and I ate so much greasy food that I had dreamt about, it made me sick.

Ultimately all of the African Americans were released. It was a horrendous experience for young people who thought they were coming to Tanzania to participate in something grand and unique. President Julius Nyerere made what, I guess, constitutes an apology.

He said, "I fear our security forces overreacted." And that was the end of it. No one was sentenced to any time in jail; everyone was released. But that ended a particular chapter in the interaction between African Americans and Tanzania. There was a mass exodus out of here.

There's an aspect of this that has never been talked about, Paul. Families were destroyed as a result of this overreaction. Michael Monk's wife left a couple of weeks before he got out. Their marriage was destroyed. They had a small baby. She took her baby and their marriage was over. There are people who cannot take that kind of pressure. That kind of drama. Marriages, relationships were destroyed. "I fear our security forces overreacted!"

Return to Life in Ngaramtoni

Now when we moved into this house on the hill, I didn't know how you planted corn. I honestly didn't. I didn't know if you took the seeds and threw them across the ground, or if you dug a hole in there and stomped on the seed. There was a WaChagga man who laughed when I told him, "Don't you take the corn and just throw it across the ground?" He said, "Oh, son. Listen. I'm a farmer. I'm going to bring my tractor up and show you how to do this." So for the first time, we learned to farm. We learned to bring in huge crops (well, for four acres). I've had up to thirty one-hundred-kilo bags of corn in the storehouse. We harvested a mountain of beans. I'll show you the pictures. I didn't know how to mix cement. I tried to do it without sand. An Asian man told me I needed sand and had to mix it in certain proportions. Raising a chicken—in spite of my ideas that I tried to press on people in Algeria—I hadn't the slightest idea about that. I thought Safeway provided chickens, thought they made them in the back room somehow. With help from others, we went into the chicken business. People helping us along the way.

This is part of the transformation that was taking place. How to learn to interact with people. How to learn to accept people not expecting anything from them. Not being fearful of what they wanted or what they might do to me. Accepting people for people. And that is one of the best experiences I've ever had. My experiences in Tanzania with Tanzanian people, ironically, Tanzanians of all colors. Really. There are so many whites that have been here for generations. All of these people helped me. All of them said, "No, don't do it that way, do it this way." When the motor on my Volkswagen Variant burned up and I was without a car, the same WaChagga man said, "Well, listen, why don't I loan you the money to buy a car." He did. He gave me fifteen thousand shillings, a huge sum of money. I went and bought a nice Land Rover from some Europeans who were leaving. People were constantly helping. People were constantly pushing us. I would backslide. The negative baggage that you heard me refer to before was very much a part of me. Every now and then I'd have it and I'd get into some kind of hassle. But the lessons that I was learning in Tanzania served me well and eventually I was able to put a great deal of this behind me.

So Charlotte and I started there in the house on the hill. We became farmers. We made and sold cakes. We made birthday cakes. I've even made breakfast cereal. Would you believe I made things like Cheerios, where you stamp out each individual one! I'd then put them in plastic bags and sell them. We made and sold doughnuts. Back then, there wasn't much on the market, very few imported goods. It was a growing, a learning experience, and it was a heck of a lot of fun. The hook that I was telling you about, it had me now. The man who came to Tanzania and said, "Oh, my God, we're dead now." I could not, and to this day cannot envision breaking ties with Tanzania completely.

Everything that we embarked on was new to us, very different from the experiences we had had in Kansas City. We became something of a symbol for African Americans because we applied the same tenacity to our lives here that we did in Kansas City with the Black Panther Party. People would come from Dar es Salaam to visit us and they'd say, "Boy, we really admire the way you all are doing." We were doing, we weren't just talking. We'd get an idea and move immediately to implementation. And if we didn't have the money or the means, we'd move simply on the strength of our will. We made sacrifices that you wouldn't believe.

Talk about making sausages, Charlotte and I would stay up all night making them. There would be meat all over the table. Once you make the sausage now, you got to go ahead and pack them. We got a little hand stuffer. We would get natural skins from the slaughter houses. We're up to three and four o'clock in the morning, turning these things and stuffing sausages. Doing this without a break.

We have worked harder, I think, than most people have worked in their lives. I think you might even see a little bit of that now. We can't sit back and sit on our laurels and talk about things, we still have to do it. So, learning lessons in Tanzania.

And one of those lessons was our adventures with Dick Stanley and the Arusha Appropriate Technology Project, AATP. Dick and I built windmills, wind generators, methane generators, and wind-powered water pumps. The logo on the side of my farm was "Pete's Experimental Farm: New Methods and Technology to Aid Development" (or something to that effect). Dick and I did so many things. We built hang gliders and jumped off hills with them. He broke his shoulder and his collar bone, and I broke my wrist—a crazy white boy and a crazy Black Panther from Kansas City. But we had a lot of fun times together. Dick Stanley is now in Zimbabwe, still doing appropriate technology work. We like to get together and reminisce about the good old bad days that we shared together.

All of this is part and parcel of our experiences here. Experiences that are laced very heavily with a very, very sound work ethic. This is what has allowed us, with some difficulty, to establish the lifestyle that we have in Tanzania.

Meeting Jim Ross

One of my most profound learning experiences began with a man that I despised when I first saw him. He was an Oklahoma cracker, named Jim Ross. You talk about the old Pete O'Neal. I honestly had thoughts of wanting to physically hurt this man. We're selling chickens and eggs and here comes Jim Ross, a short rotund kind of guy, very active man, probably in his forties. He came to the house. He wanted to buy chicken and eggs. He was a talker and a know-it-all, and damn it he wasn't afraid to say so. He said, "I work for General Tire; what are you doing here?" He had this Oklahoma accent that was making me mad from the beginning. I asked him how many chickens and eggs he wanted. He said what he wanted and we got his order there. Then he asks, "How do you like this place, Tanzania? I think this is the silliest damn place I've ever been." I thought, "Oh, shit! Here he goes." Now, I try to do my little business with the chickens and eggs and let it go at that. He continued, "This is the silliest place I've ever been. They don't even have frozen orange juice here." I went berserk then. I said, "Oh man, I don't know what you're talking about. You're coming in here. . . ." And he and I began to argue. And we argued. And we moved from the sitting room to the dining room. And we argued. And then we went out on the porch and we continued to argue. And he's talking about how bad Tanzania is and I'm telling him, "No you're looking at it wrong because you have such provincial views. You don't have any kind of international understanding." And we argued. He must have felt he didn't finish his part because he came back the next week—to buy more eggs and more chickens so that we could continue to argue. And if that wasn't good enough, he said, "Do you fish?" I said, "No, I don't fish, but I can learn." He said, "Why don't you come fishing and we can finish." I said, "Let's do it." And so we would go fishing at Lake Dilut, and it became an every-week thing now. We would sit out there and we would fish and we would argue back and forth. Jim Ross made rich people money working for General Tire. He had a very good position. One of the things that made me mad about him, he would have hams flown in from Tennessee to eat. He lived like a rich man.

Now, of course, Jim Ross had a lot of prejudices, a lot of biases, a lot of narrow provincial thinking, but he was a damn good human being. He really was. He and I became fast friends as a result of arguing. I know I changed his way of thinking. I know I made him temper some of his more outlandish ways of thinking. And he had the same effect on me. One day we were talking about politics. And I must admit I do have a very narrow political view, often times, that does not allow anything that doesn't fit into my political scenario. He told me, "You know, Pete, you're a very smart man. But you know what you do. You look at one side. It's like looking at Mount Meru. You look at one side and you know it well, but you won't even acknowledge that there's another side there." That really made me think.

Jim Ross and I became fast friends. At this time I'm going to his house almost every day for lunch. We don't even argue any more. We talk. We discuss. We reason. One day Charlotte said, "You know, I want to become a vegetarian. This is important to me." We had no passport and no extra money. You couldn't buy anything here and we couldn't go abroad to buy things. Jim heard Charlotte. He got in his car, a brand new Range Rover, drove to Nairobi, and bought

Charlotte one of the best juicers you could ever see. He came back and said, "Here, I don't know why you want to eat rabbit food, but here take this." Jim Ross was that kind of person.

Jim Ross got us a huge contract to supply all the chickens at General Tire. Now, I knew nothing about business or business planning. Jim would come over and ask, "Pete, how's business going for you?" I say, "I think it's pretty good; we got chickens here." And he say, "Wait, let's look at it. Let's do some projections. Let's look at how long it takes to raise chickens. Let's look at how many chickens you have on hand. Let's look at how many orders you have, and let's project all of this for the next six months." I said, "Next six months!" He said, "Yes, six months and even a year." And we would look at it and he'd say, "Pete, look at the figures. You're already in trouble." And he was right in terms of being able to supply. He said, "There is no way you'll be able to supply chickens nine months from now. About seven months from now, you're going to run out. You'll have small chickens on hand, but you won't have enough big ones to meet your supply needs." So, another learning experience.

Jim Ross had a really weird effect on my life. Jim Ross left here, I believe, in 1976. Before going, he told me, "Well, I'm getting ready to go back to the States, Pete. I'm going to move to California and open an air conditioning business. This is something I've wanted to do for a long time. You'll be my assistant. Yeah, we'll do it, doggone it." But, of course, I couldn't join him. Jim Ross went back to the United States—cried when it was time for him to leave. Remember, the hook gets in people's hearts, all kinds of people—cried when he had to leave here. He went back, opened his air conditioning business. Then he started going around to all these civil rights organizations—NAACP, CORE, all of them—this old Oklahoma cracker. They don't know who he is. He'd tell them, "I want you all to do something for Pete O'Neal." They'd say, "What are you talking about?" He'd write, "Today, Pete, I went to this [*civil rights*] organization. They didn't act like they wanted to talk to me, but I'm going back again tomorrow." So it went on like that. His wife called me in 1990 to say that Jim Ross had died of bone cancer.

I hope you see the purpose of my telling you this. This place works in ways that affect people. It affected me. Jim Ross was one of the better experiences that I've had here. So I just wanted to share that with you.

8

Settling in Imbaseni Village

Moving to Imbaseni Village

After renting a house and land in Ngaramtoni for five years, Charlotte and Pete decided to establish themselves in their own place in Embaseni village, near the city of Arusha. They have lived there ever since, starting off as pioneers on a vacant piece of rocky land and eventually turning it into a multibuilding compound consisting of their home, guesthouse, dormitories for visiting students, dining facility, classrooms, workshops, and a home for over twenty underprivileged Tanzanian children. Pete describes the process:

> So our life continued and we stayed in this house on the top of the hill in Ngaramtoni until 1979. The house at the bottom of the hill, Michael Monk's old house, had changed hands. One African American couple that came in was Randy Flippin and his wife, Sheila, both of them from Washington, DC. Both of them were good friends of ours. Sheila was a particularly good friend of Charlotte's. She was vegetarian; she didn't believe in eating meat or any kind of animal products. She even went to the extreme of not taking medicine for ailments. In 1979 Sheila contracted typhoid. The community, Charlotte, and I tried to put pressure on her to take medicine. She wouldn't. She wanted to prove to the African American community that she could deal with it her way. She died out here of typhoid. The African American community had the first loss of one of its members.

We continued renting this house, and the ownership of the estate changed hands. Now some Europeans owned the place. We thought that was a bit of a contradiction. Here we are, Africans of the Diaspora returning to the mother land and renting land from Europeans. Something just wasn't kosher there. We had a beautiful setting. A beautiful farm. But Charlotte and I said, "You know, maybe we need to plant some real roots here. Maybe we need to start building."

I had a Maasai friend named Zephenia Lija. He owned about twenty acres of land in a village called Imbaseni. I used to make ketchup and sausages. He was the store's manager at the Danish Volunteer Center at that time. So he would buy ketchup and sausages from us. I told him that Charlotte and I wanted to get out of here. He said, "Pete, I'll tell you what, I'll try to find you some land in the area where I live." I said, "Okay." A few weeks, a few months went by. Every time I would see him, he'd say, "I haven't heard anything yet, but I've got a lead and I'm working on it." So then I started pushing a little harder, going to him every week. He said, "Pete, I haven't found anything and quite frankly, I don't know if I'm going to be able to. I tried the best I could." I said, "Man, I can't go on like this. This feels too unreal. We've got to develop a stronger sense of permanence with our situation. And the only way to do this is to build something." He said, "Look, man, what if I gave you a little bit of my land." I said, "Good." He said, "I'll sell it to you very cheap." I said, "Fine." He said, "If I do that, when do you want to start?" I said, "Tomorrow." Now I love Zephenia with all my heart and soul. I love him, he's my brother, he's my friend. He'll laugh and he'll joke, if he hears me saying this, if he ever reads this, he's going to talk about me, but he sold me the worst, rockiest piece of the land! But I was grateful.

It was four Tanzanian acres. Boy, when people sell you land here, they will stretch it beyond belief. If this is three acres, it's good. But I'll always refer to it as four because that's what's on the paper. Zephenia sold me this land for the sum of four thousand shillings. The exchange rate then was about eighteen to a dollar. At the time I had ten shillings in my pocket. Had my old Land Rover, and we'd just go from day to day, selling chickens and sausage. I said, "I'm going to have to owe you four thousand." He said, "No problem." Charlotte and I came out the next day with Randy Flippin, our friend. We started putting out sisal string and measuring off the house. We said, "Boy, we're ready to go!"

I am not a spiritual person, and I am not a religious person, but I'm telling you what happened is so damned spooky, I don't understand it to this day. I had no money. And the next day when I wanted to start building, a sum of money came my way. Not a grand sum. But enough to enable me to buy seventy-five bags of cement, which was a hell of a lot, to buy sand, and to get the foundation in the ground. I couldn't believe it. The money came from some interactions I had with some Asians or something like that—nothing illegal. Something like that would come up at every step of the way. I'd have nothing and I'd say, "Well, I don't have any more cement, so let's just go out there today and put water on the bricks." While I'm out here something would happen that would enable us to go to the next step.

I went to my friends at the Appropriate Technology Project, and they gave me a cinva ram machine, which is a machine that was developed in Venezuela to make stabilized soil bricks. You can make very strong bricks by using dirt. Put a little stabilizing agent in there, perhaps a little lime, and a good strong brick, almost as strong as cement comes out. This is what we built the first portion of this house with. We worked harder than I have ever worked in my entire life. We would get up at three or four o'clock in the morning, every morning at Ngaramtoni, and we'd try to pump ourselves up. We had a record player. There was a song by Al Jarreau; it was, "Follow the Fellow Who Follows the Dream." We would play this at four o'clock in the morning. Charlotte and I would start dancing in the bedroom. And we'd be just dancing trying to get ourselves pumped up for the day's work. Now, remember, Ngaramtoni is thirty miles from our new home site in Imbaseni Village. I would have to take Malcolm to school. I would have to ferry supplies. And in between I would be working. I lost weight. I went down to 135 pounds. We would work at night, and when we could no longer see we would take the old Land Rover and turn the lights on the plot so we could keep on working. We would get back home sometimes at eleven, twelve o'clock at night and collapse in the bed, waiting to get up in the next few hours.

It took us two and a half months to complete this house to the point that we were able to move in. But, conditions were very Spartan there. We had put the iron-sheet roof on, no ceiling, no floor, just a rough concrete slab. Rough, dusty concrete slab. No windows.

We put plastic up to the windows and plastic up to the doors. In 1979 we moved in, with the very wise idea that it would be cheaper if we didn't have to keep ferrying from one place to another.

Meeting Mzee Mketi

During all of this time we had never contacted the village elders here. Now this village is a tribal homeland. I have no title deed to anything here. I have a piece of paper from Zephenia Lija that he sold me this land. All of the elders in this village know that this is my land. If they were to die today, their sons know that this is my land. Technically, in Tanzania, to this day there is no private ownership of land, unless the law has been changed and I don't know about it, and I doubt that very seriously. The government—this is a socialist government—owns all land and your title deed entitles you to use the land. You can get a ninety-nine-year lease. There is no private ownership. So we were here, hadn't contacted anybody, and put up the house.

So one day I'm here working, and this old man, named Mzee Mketi [*Elder Mketi*] came up to me, speaking Swahili he said, "*Hodi, hodi?*" [*May I come in? May I come in?*] I said, "*Karibu*" [*Welcome*]. He came in and, continuing in Swahili, he said, "Aha. You just noticed before I came in I said, '*Hodi.*'" I said [*in Swahili*], "Yes, and I said, '*karibu*'" [*welcome*]. He said, "Aha, so you know how to do that. I was thinking you were the kind of person that just comes into someone's house without saying, *hodi, hodi*. That seems to be what you've done when you came into our village." I said, "Oh! I'm so sorry." He said, "Where are you from?" And I told him, "I'm from America." He said, "Oh. Are you those people I read about that used to be slaves?" I said, "Yes, I am." He said, "I want you to tell me about that some time." I said, "I most certainly will." He said, "But I'm going to tell you something now. How long have you been in Tanzania?" I said, "I've been here for seven years now." He said, "Let me tell you one thing. The way you started off is not good. What you should have done, you should have given the elders their respect. You should have bought a keg of beer, you should have bought some goat meat, you should have invited everybody, and you should have told everybody, 'I am requesting permission.' This is the way we do things in

Tanzania. We have a great deal of respect for tradition, and this is an important part of our tradition. Do you understand that?" I said, "Yes sir, I do. I am so sorry. I just honestly didn't know. I bought the land from Zephenia." He said, "Let me tell you. That buying means nothing. If we didn't want you in our village, you'd be gone before the sun set." I said, "Yes, sir, I do understand." He said, "Now I don't have any bad feeling about you. I can see that you are a nice young man. But you need to be very careful not to do that." I said, "Well, sir, let me tell you one thing. I'm going to ask you a favor now. I'm a long way from home, a long way from home. There are a lot of things I simply don't know. If I was around my father, maybe I could ask him for support and advice. My father is thousands and thousands of miles away. May I consider you my father here in Tanzania? And when I need advice, will you help me?" He said, "Give me your hand." He took my hand and shook it. Then he said, "Sasa u mtoto wangu" [Now you are my son] and embraced me. Very touching. Mzee Mketi was my friend from then on.

I had an opportunity to really make up for that oversight about a year later. I bought a two-acre plot of farmland right down the road from here. I bought it from a Tanzanian man for my young brother, Charley. I invited all the elders. I had beer and roasted meat. I addressed the elders in Swahili, "Sirs, I am asking permission to buy this shamba [farm]." Mzee Mketi looked at me and let out a laugh. He slapped his leg and said, "Now you know!" I said, "Yes, sir, I do."

So I bought that land for Charley. I'm going to come back to that in a moment. First, I want to tell you about an incident that just touched me to my heart.

Getting Water

Bear in mind when we moved here, there was no electricity. Electricity didn't come until 1983. Moved here in '79, no electricity until '83. No water. I had a Land Rover and I had three oil drums—of course, they were cleaned out, and we hauled water in them. Three forty-four-gallon drums, and I would have to make two trips a day. Miles to haul water. I put water in a tank I built up high. I had an underground tank that I would pour the water into, then pump it up to a thing that would gravity feed the house. We reused water. Water that we washed dishes with, we would use to flush toilets. Charlotte and I would bathe together to cut down on the usage of water. We had to do it this way.

Finally, in 1981 the water line is coming in to a seminary about a mile from us. Now we've got to lay a mile of water pipe. Several families went in together and we put up the money to buy pipe and the labor to put it all in. We had to do this ourselves. That meant we had to dig a trench one mile long, we had to buy one-and-one-half-inch plastic piping, and we had to bury it in the trench. Some places we could only go down two or three inches because we'd hit solid rock. Where we couldn't dig, some of the pipe would be partially exposed. But we finished the project and we got water.

I have always been kind of the keeper of the water. Everybody relies on me and a young man who worked with me, to deal with the maintenance of this water line. One day this young man comes to me and says, "There's a man, named Enoch, halfway on your water line. He's cut your water line in half. He's put his tap into it and water's going to his house." Now there wasn't enough water in this one-and-one-half-inch water line for the people who had paid all of this money, and this man just cut it. I went up to his farm, looked at the pipe, and disconnected his water line. I poured cement all around where he had made the joint.

So he brought charges against me. Said that I had cut his pipeline. In a village setting, you deal with things locally first to see if they can be resolved at the village level. If it cannot, then it goes to the state courts. The people from the village said, "Mr. Enoch has filed charges against you. He said you destroyed his water line, and we're going to have a hearing about this next Saturday morning." Man, I was nervous! This was a Tanzanian man and a man who knows the workings of village life. And here I'm a new person in this village. This is my first experience with anything like this. They told me, "The meeting will be held up under the big tree there, Saturday morning at nine o'clock." Thursday and Friday I could see Enoch's Land Rover moving up and down through the village. He's going to all the elders, lobbying. I said, "Boy, they might ask me to leave here. I really don't know what to do." I went to see Zephenia, but he wasn't here. He has another wife and another home, so he was away.

Saturday comes and we go to the meeting place. I see Zephenia is there for the gathering. We're sitting there under the tree and people

are speaking in Kimeru [*a Bantu language of the Niger-Congo family*].
A lot of it I can't understand, so Zephenia is translating. Enoch said,
"This fellow here is the one that cut my pipeline and not only do I
want him kicked out of the village. I want him to pay for the damage
he caused to my line. This man is a perfect example of people coming
in from outside and thinking they own Tanzania's water." I heard
that and I thought, "Oh boy, this is the end of it now." Then Mzee
Mketi, my Tanzanian father, stands up and addresses the other elders: "First of all, we want to talk about this water line. *Bwana* Peter
[*Mr. Peter*] and his friends and his neighbors put out a lot of money
and a lot of effort to bring this water line down. Now the first thing
they did when they brought that water line down was not connect
it immediately to their houses (and this is the truth); the first thing
they did was put up a public tap so that our wives and our daughters
don't have to walk for miles to get water. They did this before they
even had water go into their own houses." He continued, "Yes, he's
not a Tanzanian, but he helped Tanzanians." (You could hear everybody murmuring then.) And so the discussions went on and on. He
said, "As I said before *Bwana* Peter is not a Tanzanian, but he seems
to be a good person, he and his family. He seems to be somebody
who is concerned about the welfare of our village, and *Bwana* Enoch,
it is our opinion that you are the one who has committed the wrong.
You came in and you cut someone's line, without asking permission
from the village elders or from the people who put in the line. You
very selfishly ran that pipe to your house, taking water that they
didn't have enough of for themselves in the first place, and now you
want to bring charges? No, no, no!" I'm beaming by this time. Mzee
Mketi continued, "You *Bwana* Enoch are the one. If anybody has to
leave this village, it should be you. Not only that, if ever you touch
that line again, we are going to take this case to town and there will
be legal action taken against you. For this hearing today we are finding in favor of *Bwana* Peter. We are instructing you not to touch that
line and we're ordering you (listen to this, Paul) to pay *Bwana* Peter
one male cow." I said, "Oh my goodness, look at this!" I just leaned
back and beamed. Enoch was fuming. He was furious.

That was the first time that I really had a first-hand experience
with the real basic fairness that transcends race, that transcends
nationality and deals with the very basic stuff. Is this a good person?
Is that a bad person? Is what he's doing good for everybody? Is what

he's doing selfish? I think that's an inherent part of African culture. Perhaps, more specifically, Tanzanian culture. It's very impressive and very important. Mr. Enoch never paid me the cow, but he never touched my water line again. I see him periodically, perhaps once every few years. Each time he says, "Now I still got my land. I'll want to have a talk with you, so we can try and work out something about water." I'd say, "Oh, please come. We'll have a talk." Nothing ever comes of it.

Roy Wilkins was head of the NAACP back in the sixties. We used to call him "an Uncle Tom"! I remember once he said, "All of you people are talking about how much you love Africa and want to return to Africa. Let me tell you one thing. You won't find one African country that will give you one piece of land." You know for years before I moved here, and particularly when I was angry after the big bust, I said, "I wonder if that man was right." So you can see how important this was to me when Zephenia put paid to that lie and gave me this land; when Mzee Mketi and the elders in this village put paid to that lie and welcomed us as family members, if you will, in this village. This was very, very important to us.

Meeting Christopher

In 1980 we were working in our bedroom in the back of the house. We were putting in a stepped-up platform. We had a rough-looking wooden fence around the place. I hear knocking on the fence. I go out there and see this little kid. Tanzanians can look so young sometimes. He looked like he was about fifteen years old. He said, "My name is Christopher, and I want a job." I said, "Okay, what can you do?" He said, "Well, I don't know, but I can work very hard." I said, "Okay, come in." We're building something here. You come in and start hauling." I remember Christopher had a yellow sweater on. The first thing he did was lay down that yellow sweater. Then he started hauling dirt and throwing dirt through the window to fill up the platform that we're building. He was a very hard worker, but particularly unskilled. I can remember one day we had these galvanized iron sheets and I had the tin snips used to cut them. I gave the snips to Christopher and told him to cut an iron sheet in half. I drew a line across the middle of the iron sheet and said, "Just take this and cut it." He picked the snips up in his hand, holds them awkwardly and he's trying to cut. But he's not cutting straight; the cut is jagged. I said, "What's wrong with you?" I snatched the snips out of his hand. (I can get a little like that at times.) "Here man, take your time; try again." But he couldn't do it. I said, "Good Lord!" I'd give him some hammering to do, and he'd try to hammer but miss the nails. I told Charlotte, "There's something wrong with that boy. I've never seen anybody in my life that can't hammer a nail."

Well, interestingly enough, Christopher has been with me now since 1980 so that makes it eighteen years. Christopher has become a master craftsman. He can do carpentry, masonry, plumbing, electricity, he can do automobile mechanics. A great deal of this I taught him the basics of, a lot of it he's gone on beyond that. Certainly, I couldn't begin to hold his coattail in terms of masonry. This man has built houses for other people. And Christopher's loyalty to me transcends employee-employer relationship; he's more like a devoted son. He really is. Just recently Christopher fulfilled one of his life's dreams. He bought, by Tanzanian standards, a brand-new fifteen-seat *Matatu,* one of those minibuses that they use to ferry passengers all over town and from one little township to another. His runs from town all the way to Usa River, past Madyachi, and on to Kika. He is so proud. He bought this about three months ago, and his whole persona has changed since then. The first thing Christopher asked me when he bought it was, "Do you want to use it first? If you have problems with your car now I can help you out." So this is my Tanzanian son, Christopher Unko, who is a WaMeru; he comes from this village.

Back in 1983, Christopher had been with me a couple of years, there was a WaMeru ceremony, and Charlotte said, "Oh, I want to go see this." We had our video camera. I was busy, I said, "Okay, take the camera, maybe you can get some footage." So she went there and very respectfully asked the elders if she could film, and they said, "Yes, please, go ahead. No problem, you're part of our village." The WaMeru are very funny about cameras. They do not like people taking their pictures at all. But they agreed.

So Charlotte's filming part of the ceremony that had something to do with young people making the transition to manhood. Some of the young men looked at her and they started to scowl. They didn't like this woman from outside doing this film. They started complaining and raising a little bit of hell. Christopher's father said,

"Stop. Stop the ceremony." Everyone stopped. You know when one of the elders speaks here in a village setting, that carries a great deal of authority. He said, "What is this complaining I'm hearing?" The young men said, "Well, we don't think it's right that this foreigner is coming in here and filming our ceremony." He said, "But we gave her permission to do so." They said, "Yes sir, but we still. . . ." He said, "I don't give a damn what you think. We are your elders, we made a decision; we gave this woman permission." He held up his stick—Charlotte tells this story so well—held up his stick and he said, "If anybody else has any more complaints about this, I will break my stick of authority." All of the elders in this tribe carry their *fimbo*, their stick. It's their walking stick, the stick they would kill a snake with, their symbol of authority. And so for an elder of the WaMeru tribe to say, "I will break my stick of authority." My goodness, everybody said, "Now don't you do it!" Now when people want to calm down and please an elder, they stroke his beard. The young people said, "Oh, please, please, don't be angry. Please forgive us, forgive us." The elder said, "To make sure that this doesn't happen again, we're going to move this ceremony to the *WaNegro* (that's what they called us now), to the WaNegro's house. We're going to have the ceremony there, and they are going to be WaMeru." So they came here.

I was here working and I heard all this marching and singing, marching and singing. Charlotte's coming in, excited. She's telling me the story. She said, "The elder said we're going to be WaMeru." So they came in and Christopher's daddy there and the young men who had complained the most were dancing and jumping the highest and embracing me and embracing Charlotte. Oh, it was a very, very festive time! That was how we became honorary members of the WaMeru tribe. That is an honor that may not have been bestowed on anyone else. It's one that we accepted with a great deal of honor.

In 1990, Christopher came to me and said, "Mzee, at the bottom of the hill the village has taken over a huge farm. They're going to cut it up into plots and give them to people in this area. But you have to put in a request. I've already got mine in. Why don't you put one in?" I said, "Christopher, that's silly. There's no way in the world, they'd give me something like that." He said, "But you could at least try." I said, "But Christopher, it doesn't make sense. I'm not a Tanzanian citizen." He said, "But you should try because people have a lot of respect for you. I'll write it for you." I can't write Kiswahili well. I said, "Okay." Christopher writes slow and laboriously, but he writes well. He reads it to me, trying to make me understand. He explained, "Now, it requires a five-hundred-shillings deposit that you don't get back." I said, "Okay." So I give the money to him and forget about this thing. Christopher came back some months later and said, "Mzee, guess what? They divided up the plots and I've got one and you've got one too! And we both got good plots right on the road." I said, "My goodness!" That's how we got the land for the United African American Community Center.

O'Neal Initiates Community Programs

Long before we had any Heal the Community Program or United African American Community Village Center we did some form of community work. Charlotte worked with women and young people in the village, teaching them papier-mâché and art, with the idea that this would be some way for women to be able to develop skills that would supplement their income. We had had young people come in here and work with us. Christopher would put them on a job similar to on-the-job training and teach them masonry. We'd teach them the rudiments of carpentry. A lot of village masons, not so young any more, started here with Christopher teaching them how to throw and smooth plaster, how to lay brick. We did this with the idea of contributing to the community. I'd like to think this played a part in their reasoning for giving us a building plot down on the main road.

I think it was in 1991 that I met Omar Jamal, a businessman and an entrepreneur, from Washington, DC. He came out here to export coffee to the United States. At the same time he wanted to make a contribution to Tanzania, as most African Americans do to the motherland. Well, Charlotte and I began to tell him about our ideas to start an organization that would open up avenues for all African Americans to make a contribution to Tanzania's development. I explained, "We've got this land down by the main road, but that's all we got. We don't have any money to build on it." He said, "Okay, here, let me give you some money." He started giving me money to start putting up a community center. He gave me five thousand dollars and then he'd leave. He'd come back five or six months later and give me another five thousand, and we'd do more building. So it went on like this. Now, Omar Jamal had bought a beautiful van in Dar es Salaam. He left that van here. He said, "Here, you just use it." When we completed the building, he became the president of the United African American Community Village Center and I became the managing director. For all intents and purposes Omar was not interested in the day-to-day activities, so that was left to Charlotte and me.

Our idea was to make a contribution to Tanzanian development, and at the same time we began to see the opportunity to share with African Americans the beauty of Tanzanian traditions. If you go to the poorest, most isolated family in the most remote village in Tanzania, you would find a family structure that was vibrant, that was dynamic, that was thriving. In this village you see families that by American standards own very little. Yet they have a family structure that is thriving. They cooperate with each other on a scale that's almost unheard of in the West. The family's child is entrusted with almost their entire wealth, the cows, the goats. So we thought this could serve as an inspiring example to young African Americans.

When Africa ultimately rises out of its present chaos, the strength and the dynamism of family structure is going to play a very, very important part in that resurrection. We believe that to build a strong nation you must first build strong communities. To build strong communities, you have to have strong vibrant families. We look at what's happening in America with African American family life, and if the statistics that we hear can be believed, the family structure is dying. We felt we could make a contribution to African American life from afar by creating programs that could contribute to the rebirth and the rebuilding of the family structure. Our Heal the Community program came about with the idea that we could bring young African Americans, ultimately young people of all races, out here and expose them to African family traditions. And if it impresses them as it has impressed us, maybe, they'll be able to take this back, share it with their compatriots, and it could serve as a model for the big task they have of rebuilding their families, their communities, their nation. This was the basic idea of Heal the Community.

We've had some notable successes with that. Some have been less successful than others, but I think the basic idea is very sound. Even though, sadly, I must admit while we're pursuing this program, we have learned that this African family structure may be dying a bit, itself. A great many people that we've talked to said that urban influences and outside influences are beginning to erode it. But while it's here, we think it can serve as an inspiration. Initially, we were able to ask KLM Airlines to donate a ticket to kick-start the first program. In 1994 we brought a young woman here from Kansas City's De LaSalle [*an alternative charter high school*]. She made a huge turnaround. Her mother was on crack. Her brother was a gangster. She had no sense of a family structure or self-worth. After six weeks here, she returned with a sense of identity; she finished her education and married a Nigerian doctor. But the program is not a panacea for everyone. We plan to expand this program, but of course, the problem is finding the funding.

Pete's Marriage and Siblings

When we talk about family life, I think it might be well to talk about my particular family here. I had been married before. A failed marriage and so I came into this marriage with Charlotte determined to make it work. I was inspired further by the fact that we had a revolutionary love for each other. That was a binding factor for both of us. I've said many, many times how hard Charlotte and I worked together. You know I do a lot of cooking. But most things with the household we do in a more conventional manner, more in harmony with African life. Charlotte deals with the kitchen for the most part and the running of the household. I do the things that require going to town. There was a long period of time when Charlotte would not go into town at all. As she became more involved in civic and community activities, she goes a great deal now. She was a housewife and she was a damned good one. She raised our children, she *taught* our children through home studies. She got them through their grade school and their high school, which is a hell of a task. Anybody that tells you that teaching your own children is not hell, trust me, it is. She did all of this, and she did it well. But, Charlotte has taken a lot of flack from many women because of her conventional way of dealing with the family structure. Charlotte's position always has been, "Well, this is my family, and I do this because I want to."

I've had the same experience with some men. They'd criticize me for doing women's kitchen work. I'll go in the kitchen in a minute if I feel a need to help out with the cooking. If Charlotte's cooking something, I'll ask, "Do you want me to cook this?" I think nothing of it. Men will also come to me and complain about their wives. I don't have those complaints. In fact, I don't have anything negative to say about Charlotte. Nothing. Nothing whatsoever.

Charlotte has also taught me how to deal with people in a different manner. That is very true. Paul, let me tell you, I am the most distrustful person, probably, that you'll ever meet in your life. I've always been that way; it's always been a defense mechanism for me. The less I trust, the less harm that can come my way. And Charlotte has often told me, "Yeah, that might make it a little bit safer, but safe for what?" She opens herself up to people, so that has enabled me to do so to an extent. Charlotte is a very kind person. I am a great deal more cynical than she is. But, I'm working on it, and perhaps growing out of it to some degree. But I have a very different background from Charlotte's. Charlotte's was always open and loving, mine was always cautious, defensive, and manipulative.

Charlotte is an extremely artistic and extremely cultural person. Back in the States as Panthers we did not completely ignore culture. But we relegated it to an almost insignificant position. Our thinking was that it played no great part in the grand scheme of things and that there were forces that were much more powerful and important. We stressed the whole concept of class and the political interaction of people. You know how you make statements to people and later you say, "My God how could I ever have said anything that dumb." I can remember speaking somewhere and saying that I felt that culture in its totality was completely insignificant in the development of mankind. That's one of the stupidest things I've ever said in my life. Charlotte has always been very artistic and always culturally inclined. I've watched that grow with her. She likes to claim that I'm cultured too. And perhaps I am in a quiet kind of way. I'm certainly much more tolerant of things than I was then. I am not an artist. She says I am in my own way. But I'm not. I don't have the passion that she has regarding art unless it lies in the circuit boards of computers or things like that.

Both of my brothers, Charlie and Gary, came out here in 1978. Gary had been here in 1976 to visit and later came back. Charlie had never been here, heard about it, and wanted to come. So in 1978 the three O'Neal brothers were here together. Gary and I,

characteristically, did not get along together for very long. He stayed
with us for a while, then after a month or two, he moved out and
started staying with friends in town.

Charlie was different. Charlie stayed with us, and when we moved
out here to Embaseni, Charlie started having difficulties with the
police, getting into one scrap after another. Finally, I got him a farm.
I said, "Charlie, I bought this two-acre farm. It's for you. I'll build
you a house." I built him a little house on it. Charlie had a young
girlfriend in this village named Makti that he wanted to marry. He
said, "Man, I want to marry." I thought, "That's good. Maybe this will
calm Charlie down a bit." So Charlie got married. They had a son and
they moved into the house I built for them. Now it's getting on to
1980–81. Charlie's just living from hand to mouth. He saw that Gary
had developed his peanut-butter machine, and I was still making
sausages and food products. Charlie tried to make some Skinny Man
Candy, he called it. It never did take off. But he would always keep
something going, just enough to survive. Not well. But just enough
to survive.

It's so interesting that there's such a vast space of time between
our ages, I'm thirteen years older than he is, yet we could be so close.
I can remember when Charlie would come here every morning. He
had a smoker's cough, so I could hear him walking up the road when
he's coming here, wanting to get a ride into town. We'd go into town
together. Charlie would talk to me about anything and nothing. But
he'd talk all the way to town. I used to just love to hear him talk. He'd
tell me stories. He'd tell me about a movie he saw years ago. He told
me about a movie called *The Getaway* with Steve McQueen. He told
it so well, it made me feel like I'd seen the thing. We had a lot of fun
riding together. I began to take Charlie's presence and the comfort of
it for granted. One day while I was in a little sitting area with flowers
in the backyard, Charlie came. He said, "I want to talk to you." I said,
"Okay." He said, "Pete, I'm not a farmer." I said, "Okay. I got that." I
could see that he was having difficulty with this. He said, "Pete, I've
got to go back to the States." I said, "Oh, really." He said, "You know,
man, I want some burst of color in my life. All I see in Tanzania are
shades of grey." I said, "Oh, I hear you Charlie. I really do." That was
so very touching and it was so very well put. Remember this is Charlie Brian from the Black Panther Party, fifteen years old, sitting on
the roof behind the chimney with a rifle when we were getting ready

to defend against a police assault. In a way he was really kind of saying, "Give me your blessings on this." And I most certainly did. I said, "Sure, man. I certainly do understand." So he took his young wife, who didn't speak a word of English, and their child and went back to the States. That was in 1982. They've been there ever since. Wife never got back here to this day. They keep planning it, but just never can get it going. Charlie now has a business that deals with artifacts from Africa and other places. I have on occasion sent him things. We worked out deals where I've sent him some carvings, batiks, and things of that nature. He sells them. I think he's doing good. Not getting rich, but he's supporting his family.

[*In 1998, I asked Charlotte to describe her life in Tanzania. She responded by discussing her family, marriage, art, and spirituality.*]

Our son Malcolm was born in Algeria; our daughter Stormy [*Ann Wood*][1] was born in Tanzania. They grew up playing with local, bush children, herding cattle, speaking Kiswahili. But the other children considered ours to be the "rich kids on the block." It was such a contradiction to our whole goal. Sometimes that would bother us. The fact that our children were a part of this community, but still somewhat separate.

I homeschooled both of them. We wrote to our people and friends in Kansas City, and they rallied together, sending us teacher's editions, student editions, schoolwork manuals, etcetera. We supplemented them with our knowledge of African and African American history and our revolutionary history. I think I did a good job. Sometimes I would be real nervous, because I'm a high-school graduate. But I'm very well read. I'd spend hours studying and preparing lessons. Sometimes there were problems with scheduling. It's hard dealing with a household plus classes every day. When Stormy went into the school system, she did okay. Her problem was discipline, because she basically wasn't used to strict times, scheduling, and people telling her what to do. All in all it went well. I would recommend homeschooling, because it brings your children closer to you. But it is hard work, very hard.

In 1990 the children and I went back to the States. It was the first time back for me, and the first time ever for the children. Stormy was fifteen; Malcolm was eighteen. It was very traumatic for me, because it was the first time, other than when Pete was jailed in Tanzania for about a month, that we were apart. I was like a baby in the woods, crying every day. The children had no problem. People would say, "You mean these kids have never been here? They act like they've been here all their life."

A lot of times I feel more comfortable expressing myself in my poetry and my art than in more conventional ways. I've developed the courage over the years to acknowledge myself as an artist. I started exhibiting in '86, but I'd been doing art since I was a little kid. For me to say, "I'm an artist" is a very big step, because I'm really putting myself out there. Pete has been instrumental over the years to give me courage, to express myself as an artist and also as a poet. I can't emphasize enough how he has been such a continuing positive influence. In '93, I was thinking about how Pete's life on the streets was before we met and how he made such a complete turnaround with the Black Panther Party. I was thinking about the parallels between his life and Malcolm X's life. I wrote a poem, "The Malcolm X Factor in My Man," that expresses my thoughts on that. I write poetry all the time. A lot of it is very personal, and I wouldn't be able to share. But here's one that's called, "A Five Letter Word for Pete." You know how couples can sometimes argue over little silly things and find it hard to say I'm sorry. Over the years when we've had disagreements we've remembered something that my Mom told me. She said, "Don't ever go to sleep angry." That's one of the reasons that our marriage and our partnership have been so successful.

This is a painting that I did called "Pete's Kind of Day." It has this poem with it. Then, did you see this thing here? It's called "Pulse of the Sixties." It's the only large abstract I've ever done. It expresses my feelings about the atmosphere during the height of the Black Panther Party, and here's a poem that goes with it. I have always felt great reverence for our African history and our ancestors. This is a poem I wrote a few years ago called "Those Who've Gone before Us." It's dedicated to our ancestors. Then, I don't know if you knew Pete was a poet. I've taken the liberty of sharing this, "Kilimanjaro Morning," with you by Pete.[2]

I received these facial scarification marks last year. I did these to honor both my mother, who had passed away in January last year, and to honor my ancestors—those that I know and those I don't know because of the history of slavery and the way the records were wiped out. When we first came to Tanzania in 1972 I saw that many native women in our apartment complex had scarification marks on their cheeks. I didn't know their tribe. But I thought that was the most beautiful thing. And I said, "Man, I'd like to do that." Then I started reading about scarification, and I learned that's part of the history of our West African ancestors. It's part of tribal markings; it's a part of various initiation ceremonies. For twenty-some years I said, "I'd like to get my marks." But I never had a reason to do it, and I didn't want it to lower this ritual to just cosmetic desire. So when we got word that my Mom was expected not to live, I went to see her and I told her, "Mama it came to me in a dream. I'm thinking about going through the scarification rites to honor you and my ancestors." In the last five years the ancestors have really started talking to me. At first I refused to listen. Then I started relaxing and opening myself up to it and gaining the courage to express some of the messages the ancestors give me. So after Mama passed I even told Daddy while I was in Kansas City, "I think I'm going to have this done to honor her." He, of course, wanted to come and attend the ritual. I talked with the spiritual leader of the Maasai community. At first I thought he should be the one to perform the ritual. But then I had a vision of a woman doing it. So I told him, "I'd rather have woman energy in this." So one of his wives consented to do this rite. Funny, I had never witnessed this ritual before, but it had come to me in a dream, full of leaves and chanting, people calling out our ancestors' names.

At my scarification ceremony I invited everyone present to participate by calling on the names of their ancestors. When this happened, a powerful wind came into the room. It blew the papers off the table. Roosters started crowing; the whole atmosphere was just electric. I had goose pimples, I was crying. I know that my mother's spirit and the spirits of a lot of the people's ancestors were right in that room. It was so powerful that, when the time came for the lady to actually do the marks, I felt nothing. The ritual unfolded just like the ancestors in my dream told me it would. There must be a thread of knowledge running through the universe, and if you're open to it, you can tap into it.

Pete on His Exile from the United States

I'd like to state that over the many years that I have been in exile, and let's be clear, I very definitely consider this exile, I have had more people than I can probably count approach me—some people who may have good connections, some who don't, some who just think it's a pleasing thing to say, "You know, I can do something for you. I know Senator So-and-So. My Aunt knows the president." This has gone on and on and on. Rarely have I given any indication to anyone directly that I wanted them to do something for me. Probably one of the first approaches that was made to me, surprisingly, was by an official of the American Embassy in 1983. I don't know whether this guy was the vice counsel or what, but he came to Arusha and was seeing Americans to help them solve problems. I had been engaged in a long battle with the embassy, trying to legally get a passport. I was being refused because they said I had obtained a passport fraudulently when I left the States. Charlotte couldn't have one. I couldn't have one. I made an appointment to see him. We meet in a building that they used here in Arusha for their official business. I told him, "I'm still adamant. I think I have a right to have a passport. I don't think you have the right to deny me." So I'm going on and on. This guy said, "Wait a minute, Pete. Just a minute. You know you're going about this thing the wrong way." I said, "What do you mean?" He said, "Do you know. In the grand scheme of things, your case is not that big a deal. This thing could be straightened out tomorrow and be put behind you. According to your record you're forty-three years old. It would be so nice to get this thing settled now before you're fifty-three." I'm almost fifty-eight now [*in 1998*]. I said, "No, I'm not going to prison for something I believed in." He said, "Who's talking about prison. You know people in the States. You have the ability to write. You can talk to people. All you've got to do is make a sincere effort to express that you feel that all you were involved in back then was wrong. You've seen the light now, you've come to your senses. You'd be surprised how quickly problems disappear." I swear to you that was what he said. I laughed and said, "I want my passport." I believe the next year they gave us passports for Charlotte, me, and our children.

Then in 1986 or '87 there was a group of American missionaries of the Southern Baptist Church. They helped me by buying my products, so we became rather friendly. I had a big twenty-six-seater bus. So I was hired to pick the group of twenty-six up every morning and transport them to various sites. I had all these southern accents ringing around my bus. Two of these people were lawyers, not ministers. In the course of their time here, they told me, "You know, we're lawyers. We could look into your case." I said, "Oh, that would be fine. Particularly, if something could be done that I wouldn't have to make compromises and would not have to go to prison." They said, "Okay, we're going to give this a try." They went back to the States. I got a letter from them indicating that they were going to deal with things. Then, I had an interview with a newspaper, probably one in Kansas City. I expressed my views. One of the lawyers saw the article and sent me a rather scathing letter indicating that I was creating a backlash, making it difficult for them, and they didn't know what they could do now. Somehow, according to them I had screwed things up. Of course, anything that prevents me from stating what I sincerely believe, I have absolutely no interest in. So I never heard anymore from them, nor did I ever try to contact them again. Bear in mind, I did not ask, even these people, to get involved.

In 1987 or '88, I lost my passport, and I went to the American Embassy for the first time ever. A friend of mine, Joe Straus, who helped me with the Panther tapes, told me, "Pete, I got it all set up. The marines are not going to grab you and hold you hostage." Believe it or not, these kinds of things allegedly have happened in Tanzania before. I went into the embassy, saw the vice counselor, her name was Sally Light, a very personable woman. She and I kind of hit it off. She said, "Okay, no problem. Here's your new passport." Then she pulled out a folder and in this folder, much to my amazement, was every clipping I have ever seen in my life about me. She said, "Look, we've got a whole file on you. Now just tell me, what is it going to take to get you to go back to the States? Another year, another two years? It would be a tremendous feather in my cap if I could say, 'I got Pete O'Neal back in the States.'" We had a laugh about that. I left and, of course, made no kind of agreement with her whatsoever. In the nineties, there was another resurgence of interest in my case. This kind of thing is cyclic. Newspapers, even nationwide, will start to write about exiles. And so when this stuff is in the news media, the Good Samaritans come up. There was a guy named Alvin Sikes. I remember this guy contacted Melvin McCray and told him he was going to call me because he had to talk to me. He never contacted me; I never talked to him. To this day [1998], I have had no direct correspondence with him whatsoever. The next thing I know, somebody sends me a tape and here's Alvin Sikes saying, "My lawyers have filed a motion representing Pete O'Neal and we're going to guarantee that he'll be able to come home without doing any time." This was in 1993. Never heard another thing from him whatsoever.

I have a great deal of respect for Kansas City Mayor Emanuel Cleaver, and I do not want anything that I'm saying to indicate that there is a lessening of respect and admiration for him and the very good work that he has done. He has indicated to me over the years that he was working on something that involved the president, that involved Janet Reno [*then US attorney general*]. This is my understanding. It's all been rather vague. I have no details as to what he has or has not done. When he came here he told me, "Don't you worry, Pete, I'm working on things." I told him then, "Emanuel, you'll never know how much I appreciate this. But you must be very clear, I am not willing in any form to compromise my principles in order to get something that I personally might want." He said to me, "Pete, I wouldn't have the respect that I have for you if you felt otherwise." I took him to the airport. He left. Again, I have no direct information or very clear information as to what he actually has or has not done. So the point I've tried to make is that I cannot recall ever having asked anyone to do anything on my behalf. Some people have indicated that they would do some things, and I have agreed to go along with them as long as they did not compromise my principles.

And then, in 1997, Paul Magnarella was a guest in my house, a professor of anthropology and a lawyer as well. His visit in my home coincided with the release of Geronimo Pratt. Geronimo is a very good friend of mine. I have suffered the tragedy of his unjust incarceration over the years that I have been out of America. He was in jail for over twenty years, up into 1997. I had communicated with him, received messages from him. Then when I heard that Geronimo was being freed, it was as if I was in total isolation. I can remember we were in the kitchen. I said, "Wait a minute, Paul, wait a minute. Let me ask you something. Do you think you could do anything on my case?" I came to you. That was not easy for me to do. But I was so filled with something, with this feeling of just being alone. It's like all of the people that I knew out here, and I've known a lot of them, had all gone back to the States. They had all embraced themselves in the American flag. I joke with you not. Some of them told me, "Yes, when I got back, I sang the 'Star Spangled Banner.'" Well, I would die and go to hell five times, before I would do anything like that if I had to compromise my principles. But at that particular moment, I was ready to initiate something to see what could be done.

You and I had talked a great deal. We talked about your work at the UN criminal tribunals, your work at The Hague. I'm a layman in terms of law, but I knew that you knew how to research law. Now that was clear to me. I have always felt in my heart of hearts that my conviction was absolutely unjust. I knew this whole thing came about as a result of the government's attempt to silence, not just me, but the Black Panther Party. Was Pete O'Neal that important? Was it me or was it the Black Panther Party that J. Edgar Hoover characterized as being the most serious threat to the internal security of the United States? But, I got caught up in the mix. At this time I said, "Well, let's give it a shot." I approached you and you said, "I'll look into it; I'll see what I can do." After we did that, I won't tell you that I was bubbling with optimism and hopeful. It was only later when you told me the details of your petition that I could allow myself to develop a little bit of hope. I thought, "Hey maybe something will come of this. Maybe, who knows, maybe I'll be able to see children that I have not seen in more than a quarter of a century. Maybe I'll have an opportunity to say good-bye to my father, to look him in his face and, perhaps, embrace him and tell him, "Hey man, I love you." And say goodbye to him in that manner. I talked to Charlotte, and Charlotte would get excited, "Oh, this might be it!" I'd say, "No, no, no." Defense mechanism again, the old Pete of days of yore comes to the fore again, protective. "No, no, no. This probably won't happen." I expected nothing, but for the first time I allowed myself to hope for everything.

Now, I want to talk about what that hope involves. When you gave me the overview of your petition to the court in e-mail communications, I said, "Oh man!" and I began to hope again. But when you came here and I read the petition, I really got fired up then. It made so much sense to me. It was so very, very clear. The very point that the convictions that I had in California as a very young man were regarded by California as mere misdemeanors that California wiped away after I served my time. That meant that the federal court in Kansas could not use them to prosecute me as a felon who violated the Gun Control Act. I realized for the first time that the State of California was, in effect, saying, "Go young man and err no more." It really amounted to that. "Here's your next chance." It seems that the government, motivated by J. Edgar Hoover, turned all of that around. The whole thing about the testimony of Jean Young was farcical. It makes you say, this wasn't American jurisprudence at its best. Having read the petition, I'm now in a state of reserved optimism.

In our conversations here, I've tried to share with you what I feel in my heart. We've talked about a lot of people. I probably have not avoided the temptation of making myself appear saintlike and everybody else screwed up. That was not my intention. So I'd like to clarify that a little bit now. If I have not adequately expressed it, Paul, I made more mistakes than you can ever count over the many years. I was not and am not an expert in this field of community work, but I found something that had so much meaning for me that I grabbed hold of it and refused to let go. I think in doing so, it saved my life. I think it pulled me away from an abyss that I was on the verge of tumbling into. So that is what I've tried to explain. With me there is a bottom line that is the end all be all. I believe the ideals of what we struggled for back in those days in Kansas City were absolutely correct. I believe that with all my heart and soul. Perhaps we erred in our methodology, perhaps there were times when we turned one direction, we should have gone in another, perhaps I was imprudent in the manner in which I expressed those ideals. But the ideals were correct. They dealt with the dignity and the humanity of human beings on this planet earth. Now, I'm getting emotional about this. I will never ever as long as there is breath in my body, I will never back off of that. And I ask you as my friend not to put me in that position. I consider you a friend. More than a lawyer. You are somebody I met and like.

I mean that from my heart. I don't want to yield. I want people to say, "You know what, old Pete, he never backed." And I won't. Regardless of what that entails. If it means that I will never touch those shores and those communities that I knew so long ago then, hey, so be it. I really honestly feel that way. I'm not saying that I'm being arrogant and I want people to apologize to me. I don't expect that. But I will never ever, ever say that what we struggled for was wrong and that we were wrong in doing so. So that's that.

You know, one of the things that I wanted to make perfectly clear. Now I have hope. I'm optimistic. I have a very meaningful life here. It can be frustrating as hell, like today, trying to repair these damn cords and blenders and things like that, but I have a meaningful life that has significance. I'm doing community work that makes me feel good. But exile cuts to the quick, my friend. Because it separates me from the things I knew. And sometimes it can work in subtle ways. I can have e-mail communications on a daily basis with my family. But my father's dying and I can't touch him. I can't look at him. Every time I get an e-mail I'm always worried, "Oh, oh. This is it. It's probably coming now." When I don't hear from them I think, "The reason is they're trying to spare me." I have a daughter that's thirty years old and the last time I saw her she was only two. She feels like I wasn't there. I most certainly was not there for her. I can't do it with e-mail. I want to touch her and tell her, "I love you." Those are some of the aspects of this exile that I am a bit hopeful will end. I'm not saying, "Help me, help me, I broke my wing." Not that.

You and I have spent many an hour here, Paul, going over these things and, quite frankly, I told Charlotte tonight I'm getting tired of hearing my own voice. I've been going on and on forever. I pity you or the poor individuals that have to transcribe my ramblings.

Okay, I'm through. All right, that's it. [*My interviews with Pete ended on a warm night in June 1998 at Pete's home in Imbaseni Village, Tanzania. These interviews took place before we received the results of my first petition on Pete's behalf to the US District Court of Kansas.*]

PART II

9

From The Hague to Arusha to Kansas Federal Court

In 1995 I went to The Hague, the Netherlands, to work with the UN Criminal Tribunal for the Former Yugoslavia at the invitation of then–Tribunal President Antonio Cassese. I was given the title "Expert on Mission" and assigned the task of developing procedures whereby victims of the atrocities (especially rape victims) in the former Yugoslavia could testify in court without risking retaliation against them personally or against their families still living in that war-torn country. The judges were concerned for the victims' and their families' welfare, but also with the legal rights of the accused to be able to confront witnesses testifying against them.

That experience intensified my interest in international human rights and humanitarian law. In 1994, a genocide had occurred in Rwanda, and the UN Security Council created a special criminal tribunal to prosecute those responsible. That tribunal was located in Arusha, Tanzania, so consequently, two years later I would travel to Arusha to offer my legal services to and study the UN Criminal Tribunal for Rwanda. Before I left, I contacted Dr. Jim Dougherty, the American liaison to the Kansas City–Arusha Sister City program. Jim connected me with Charlotte O'Neal in Tanzania, who was instrumental in establishing the program in Arusha. Charlotte contacted me via e-mail, graciously offering to have her husband, Pete, pick me up at the Mt. Kilimanjaro airport when I arrived and inviting me to stay at the O'Neal homestead. Enthusiastically, I accepted both the offer of transportation and the invitation.

Because the O'Neals reside in Imbaseni Village, about eighteen miles outside of Arusha, I divided my time between a hotel in Arusha during the week, when the tribunal was in session, and the O'Neal homestead on weekends. The O'Neals' warm welcome and assistance made my stay most pleasant, and as time went by, we became friends. While I was there the O'Neals joyously received news of Black Panther Geronimo Ji Jaga Pratt's release from prison after serving twenty-seven years for his alleged murder of a schoolteacher in California. His attorneys, Stuart Hanlon and William Paparian, had finally convinced a judge that Pratt's prosecutors had wrongfully failed to inform the judge and jury that their main witness was a government-paid informant. Geronimo's liberation from prison caused Pete to experience a flicker of hope that his own conviction might be overturned and his years of exile ended. So, he asked me to look into his case. I agreed to do so on a *pro bono* basis and became his attorney of record.

Once back in the States, I contacted Austin Shute, Pete's counselor in his 1970 conviction case. Even though Shute had not been Pete's attorney of record since that case, he initially sounded indignant that I was taking on Pete's legal cause and claimed he didn't remember what Michael Lerner, Pete's post-conviction attorney, planned to base Pete's appeal on. Lerner had subsequently been disbarred for unrelated reasons and had dropped out of sight. Eventually, Shute became more cordial, even friendly, and agreed to assist me by reading my petitions and delivering them to the US District Court of Kansas. Because neither Austin Shute nor I were members of the Federal Bar in Kansas, we needed a Bar member to sponsor us to practice before the federal district court in which Pete had been convicted. At Shute's request, attorney Kurt D. Marquart kindly agreed to be our sponsor. Upon his application, the district court admitted us to practice *pro hoc vice* (for this occasion).

I secured copies of the trial documents and reviewed them. It became apparent that the trial's presiding judge, Arthur J. Stanley, had issued a series of erroneous rulings on both California and federal law. I decided to learn more about Judge Stanley.

Judge A. J. Stanley

On October 30, 1969, about two weeks after Pete had gone to Washington, DC, in an attempt to allege to a Senate Investigating Committee that the Kansas City, Missouri, chief of police, Clarence Kelley, had sold guns to the right-wing Minutemen organization, ATF agents arrested Pete and charged him with violations of the US Gun Control Act of 1968.

ATF agents arrested Pete in Kansas City, Missouri, but drove him out of state to Kansas where he would be indicted and prosecuted. Pete's defense attorney, Austin Shute, had earlier represented and won the case of a Panther in the Kansas City, Missouri, federal court who had been indicted on nearly identical charges. That case had disturbed US Representative Ichord (Republican, Missouri), who ordered that the name of the presiding judge and case documents be sent to the House Judiciary Committee. It appears that the ATF agents intentionally avoided the Missouri federal court and forum-shopped for a pro-prosecution judge in Kansas. They found Judge Arthur J. Stanley.

Arthur Jehu Stanley Jr. (1901–2001) was born in Kansas.[1] After serving in the US military, he earned his LLB from the Kansas City Law School and then joined his father's law practice in 1928. In 1934, running as a Republican, he was elected Wyandotte County prosecutor and served in that capacity for six years. He ran successfully for the Kansas State Senate as a Republican in 1940, but was soon recalled to active military duty to serve in World War II. He received the Bronze Star and later retired as a lieutenant colonel in the reserve. After the war, he returned to law practice and politics, running unsuccessfully as the Republican candidate for the Kansas State Senate in 1948. In 1958, Republican President Dwight Eisenhower appointed him judge in the US District Court of Kansas. Judge Stanley's most famous cases were the 1964 trial of alleged atomic spy George John Gessner and the 1970 trial of Black Panther and Sons of Malcolm leader Pete O'Neal.[2] Unfortunately, Judge Stanley failed to distinguish himself in either of these cases.

The Gessner Case

At the time of his March 22, 1961, arrest on the charge of desertion, George John Gessner[3] was a twenty-four-year-old private first-class nuclear weapons maintenance specialist and a member of the Ordnance Special Weapons Unit at Fort Bliss, Texas. He had become deeply religious and developed a strong aversion to war and weapons of mass destruction. His military service and personal conduct rapidly deteriorated. On one occasion he reportedly told his barrack mates he planned to plant a nuclear weapon in the United Nations building during Soviet

Premier Nikita Khrushchev's visit and then threaten to ignite it unless the assembled world leaders agreed to an international peace treaty. On December 2, 1960, he complained to the chaplain of his aversion to working with weapons of mass destruction and expressed his desire for a transfer to a medical unit. Four days later, Gessner's commanding officer lodged court-martial charges against him for forging sick slips. That evening Gessner called his mother and told her he couldn't take it any more: "I will not help them kill. I got to get away."

On December 6, 1960, Gessner went AWOL from his Fort Bliss unit and remained absent without leave until his arrest by military authorities in Panama on March 22, 1961. He was subsequently tried by court-martial for desertion, found guilty, and sentenced to one year's confinement at the Disciplinary Barracks, Fort Leavenworth, Kansas. While in confinement, Gessner was interrogated intensely by a team of commissioned and noncommissioned officers constituting a Counter Intelligence Corps (CIC). The questioning by the CIC and the gentle proddings of the base chaplain, in whom Gessner had confided, finally resulted in Gessner confessing to violations of the Atomic Energy Act.

Upon his release from confinement in March 1962, civil authorities arrested Gessner and charged him with violations of 42 U.S.C. § 2274 (communicating restrictive data related to nuclear weapons with agents of Soviet Russia with the intent of injuring the United Sates). He was tried before a jury in the US District Court of Kansas, Judge Arthur J. Stanley presiding.

The prosecution's main evidence against Gessner was his confession to the CIC while in custody at Fort Leavenworth. Gessner's defense counsel contended that Gessner was not mentally competent to stand trial, and that his confession was inadmissible as a matter of law because the undisputed evidence showed Gessner's mental condition at the time was such that it rendered him incapable of making a voluntary confession. Judge Stanley addressed the defense's first contention by ordering Gessner to be sent to the medical center for federal prisoners in Springfield, Kansas, for psychiatric examination. Four psychiatric reports followed in succession. Judge Stanley determined that the first psychiatric report showed that Gessner was mentally incompetent and could not assist in his own defense. The second report concluded that Gessner was mentally competent. On the basis of the third report, Judge Stanley found "the defendant now so incompetent that he cannot at this time assist in his own defense."[4] A fourth report was filed on January 23, 1964, and on

April 11 Judge Stanley determined that Gessner was then competent and set trial for May 25, 1964. Judge Stanley also denied the defense's motion to exclude Gessner's confession as a matter of law. That is, he did not believe there was a legally sufficient basis for him to bar the prosecution's key evidence.

According to Gessner's confession, he met with Russian Soviet authorities in Mexico. (However, because Gessner's mental competence and state of mind were in question throughout this period, his purported description of his activities in Mexico City and, in particular, his contacts with the Russians, which were not independently verified, should not be treated as facts.) Gessner "confessed" that he left Fort Bliss after calling his mother, hitchhiked across the border to Juarez, Mexico, and caught a bus to Mexico City. He took with him a small canvas bag containing five unclassified training manuals, a few clothes, and personal items. He said he arrived on December 9 in Mexico City and went the following morning to the Russian Embassy, using the unclassified training manuals and his training diploma as certificates of introduction. The first meeting with the Russians was spent mainly filling out application forms for a visa and political asylum. For several days thereafter, Gessner purportedly met with Russian representatives at various spots throughout the city and divulged restricted data. The Russians, however, denied his applications for a visa and political asylum and offered him no help. (Given these denials, it appears that the Russians did not regard Gessner as a valuable source of information.) Gessner then purportedly visited the Czech, Polish, and Cuban representatives in Mexico City, attempting to secure a visa or other assistance, but was unsuccessful. Thereafter, he journeyed through Central America, spending several weeks with some missionaries in Costa Rica and eventually reaching Panama, where he was arrested as a deserter by the US military. While in custody for seven days in Panama, Gessner refused to eat, move, or speak. The military police then carried him bodily to a plane, flew him to Texas, and installed him in the Fort Hood stockade. From April 3 until June 7 the CIC interrogated him extensively and intensively. During this period, Gessner broke down, attempted suicide, and confessed to violations of the Atomic Energy Act.

The military's interrogation of Gessner had been recorded and transcribed. It totaled thousands of pages, but prosecutors refused to release much of it at trial, claiming it contained secret data. Judge Stanley, siding with the prosecution, ruled that much of Gessner's interrogation need not be released to the court, thereby depriving Gessner's lawyers of the ability to examine it.

The jury heard that part of the confession that the government chose to make available to the court and found Gessner guilty. Upon the jury's recommendation, Judge Stanley sentenced Gessner to life imprisonment. Gessner's attorney filed an appeal with the US Tenth Circuit Court of Appeals. The appellate court accepted the case. A panel of three judges reviewed the trial and issued their ruling on December 2, 1965. They reversed the judgment of Stanley's court and remanded the case for a new trial, holding, among other things, that Gessner's confession was coerced as a matter of law. The judges emphasized that

> Gessner first admitted his compromise [when] he was in the company of the CIC team members from 8:30 a.m. until 9:00 p.m. Gessner was without counsel during the entire interrogation, was never advised of his civilian rights nor taken before a judicial officer until a year after his confession. . . . Applying the ultimate test we conclude that the undisputed evidence negatives the existence of a question of fact concerning the voluntariness of Gessner's confession and compels a finding of legal coercion violating the Fifth Amendment. Appellant [*that is, Gessner*] was mentally ill, alone and without counsel, uninformed of his rights as they pertain to this prosecution, subjected to an extended and prolonged interrogation by six interrogators who used a technique of "half-truths" hinting lenience. A confession obtained by unconstitutional means for intelligence purposes cannot subsequently be used with immunity in a civilian criminal prosecution.

The Appellate Court judges stressed that a court should not suspend the constitutional protections of a US citizen to satisfy the needs of government. This principle was well-stated in an 1886 US Supreme Court case, which the judges quoted: "No doctrine, involving more pernicious consequences, was ever invented by the wit of man than that any of its (constitutional) provisions can be suspended during any . . . exigencies of government."[5] Without the coerced confession of a mentally ill man, the government realized it could not successfully win a conviction in a new trial. Hence, Gessner was released.

One might wonder how Judge Stanley reacted to three circuit court judges telling him that, but for their intervention, he would have denied a US citizen his Fifth Amendment constitutional rights by allowing the government to present to the jury the confession of a mentally ill person who had been coerced into confessing by the US military, with the consequence being life imprisonment.

A brief biographical piece about federal judges of the District Court of Kansas offers a glimpse of Judge Stanley's reaction: "Judge Stanley was not pleased and told the press: "I sure hated to do this [*release Gessner*]. But the Atomic Energy Commission classified so much in this case that we just didn't have any evidence. Without that confession, we couldn't do it, and the confession is a secret."[6]

If this quote is accurate, Judge Stanley failed to hear what the circuit court judges had told him. He also sounded like a disappointed prosecutor, rather than an evenhanded judge who had learned a lesson about the US Constitution. After his release from prison, Gessner was asked why he had signed the confession. He replied: "Because of continued interrogation month after month and promise of total immunity. Of course, it was not true."[7]

10
First Petition

After reading the 1970 trial[1] transcript, it became clear to me that, had Judge Arthur J. Stanley followed the law, Pete would not have been eligible for prosecution on the firearm-transportation charge under the Gun Control Act of 1968. Judge Stanley misrepresented the relationship between California law and federal law. He approved unconstitutional FBI wiretaps, and at the end of all testimony, when it became doubtful that the prosecution could prove its case against Pete, Judge Stanley came to its aid by preparing jury instructions favorable to the government. Judge Stanley consistently overruled defense attorney Shute's objections.

Submitting the trial's many defects to a court for review twenty-eight years after the fact presented a challenge. The time limits on ordinary appeals had run out long ago. The popular writ of *habeas corpus,* used to bring a prisoner before a court to challenge the lawfulness of his detention, did not apply, because Pete was not in custody. Fortunately, there was the common law writ of *coram nobis* that had originated in the English legal system during the sixteenth century and was subsequently adopted by the US federal courts. A convicted person not in custody can use this writ without time limitation to petition his or her original court to address fundamental errors that affected the validity of the judgment against him.

Pete's fugitive status presented another obstacle. He had jumped bail in 1970, escaped to Europe, and ignored court orders to present himself to serve his sentence. In such cases, federal judges may invoke the "fugitive disentitlement doctrine" to punish fugitive petitioners by denying them any further court consideration. The doctrine is wholly judge-made and discretionary. A petitioning fugitive may overcome the disentitlement doctrine only by convincing the presiding judge that he or she left the court's jurisdiction for reasons beyond his or her control. With these challenges facing me, I prepared the first petition.

What follows is my description of the issues I addressed in my petition of coram nobis. In my description, I am critical of Judge Stanley by name. In the actual petition, however, I made no reference to the judge by name, nor did I attach any personal criticisms to him. I did not use the terms "incompetence" or "bias." Doing so in a legal petition is regarded as inappropriate and unwise. Here, however, I speak frankly.

The First Petition

Petition Coram Nobis

The petition began by arguing, with the support of numerous federal court opinions, that the writ of coram nobis was appropriate in Pete's case. The petition was coming twenty-eight years after Pete's conviction; the time for most judicial remedies was long gone. The US Tenth Circuit Court had stated that the writ of coram nobis is available "to correct errors that result in a complete miscarriage of justice."[2] Accordingly, I argued that Judge Stanley's erroneous ruling on the legal issue of Pete's felon status had resulted in a complete miscarriage of justice, because an essential element of the crime for which he was convicted was lacking. The federal judge in the case of *Pyles v. Boles*[3] wrote that the writ of coram nobis "can be employed to review, modify, or vacate an erroneous judgment in the same court in which it was rendered." And the judges in *United States v. Wainwright*[4] held that the imposition of an illegal sentence constitutes plain error which may be corrected *at any time.*

Overcoming Pete's Fugitive Status

Next, I had to convince the court that, because Pete had fled the court's jurisdiction for reasons beyond his control, it should not deny his petition. As the former deputy chairman of the Black Panther Party in Kansas City and later leader of the Sons of Malcolm, Pete had enemies both within and outside of law enforcement agencies. Pete joined the Black Panther Party in Kansas City, Missouri, on or about February 1, 1969. His practice of following police patrol cars for the stated purpose of witnessing and preventing police brutality against black citizens soon caused him to become a thorn in the side of local police. Even earlier, Pete had earned the animosity of local police by accusing Judy Brockhoff, wife of patrolman Larry Brockhoff, of having made derogatory comments with racial overtones against him at a public meeting of the United Campaign on November 15, 1968. O'Neal's charges against Mrs. Brockhoff were dismissed in Municipal Court on November 23, 1968.[5] Subsequently, both Pete and his first wife had been receiving threatening phone calls.

Pete O'Neal further infuriated local police and federal officials by making a vociferous appearance on October 12, 1969, in Washington, DC, at a Senate hearing during the testimony of Kansas City Police Chief Clarence Kelley. Eighteen days later, on October 30, 1969, O'Neal was arrested in Kansas City, Missouri, by agents from the Bureau of Alcohol, Tobacco, and Firearms for allegedly having transported a shotgun across the state line from Kansas City, Kansas, to Kansas City, Missouri, nine months earlier, on February 5, 1969. Local police had seized the shotgun from Archie Weaver, not Pete O'Neal. To shed light on my review of his story so many decades before, Pete emailed me the following statement on December 21, 1997.

> I most certainly thought that the police were plotting to assassinate me!!! I was convinced that if I went to prison I would never come out alive!! Many times policemen would smirk when I was going to trial and whisper that I was going to be on their turf in prison. To really appreciate how vehement they were toward me you must remember that I had a policeman's wife in court for verbal assault. Also remember that I accused their Chief of illegal acts in front of the US Senate! They wanted me dead and I was well aware of that fact!! Paul, believe me when I tell you that beyond the shadow of a doubt I would have died in prison!!!

I also included in the petition the affidavit of Thomas Sanders, who served as a detective in the Intelligence Unit of the Kansas City Police Department when Pete was active in the BPP. Sanders stated:

> If Pete had been caught alone by white officers I believe that he would have been in danger. There is no doubt in my mind about this. The message on the force was that he was armed and dangerous.

Sometimes I would hear officers talk about what they would do if they caught him. However they wouldn't talk much around me. There were rumors that some police officers at the time belonged to the Ku Klux Klan and the Minutemen.[6]

On September 8, 1968, FBI Director J. Edgar Hoover let it be known in the pages of the *New York Times* that he considered the Panthers "the greatest threat to the internal security of the country." Much of the operational history of the FBI campaigns against politically active African American individuals and organizations is detailed in the voluminous reports of the US Senate Select Committee to Study Government Operations with Respect to Intelligence Activities.[7] A number of other books and government reports document the FBI's illegal activities against the Panthers.[8] Especially revealing has been the book *FBI Secrets: An Agent's Exposé* by a former FBI agent, M. Wesley Swearingen.

The background history given below of the relationship between the FBI and the Black Panther Party (BPP) is taken verbatim from the facts produced at trial in the case of *Hampton v. Hanrahan*.[9]

In August 1967 the FBI initiated a national covert counterintelligence program called "COINTELPRO" which was designed to neutralize a variety of political organizations including those which the Bureau characterized as "Black Nationalist Hate Groups." Directives from Washington ordered the Chicago office of the FBI to implement the program in the Chicago area. While the Black Panther Party was not an original target of this program, it was included within the ambit of COINTELPRO's scrutiny by September 1968. The organizations originally the subject of COINTELPRO included the Southern Christian Leadership Conference (SCLC), the Student Nonviolent Coordinating Committee (SNCC), and the Nation of Islam. The trial court's Summary stated that the "purpose of the counterintelligence program, as it was implemented in Chicago as to the Panthers, was to prevent violence." The plaintiffs, however, presented considerable evidence to compel a different conclusion. . . . Perhaps the most damning evidence indicating the COINTELPRO was intended to do much more than simply "prevent violence" comes from the files of the FBI itself. An FBI memorandum from February 1968 described the goals of COINTELPRO as:

1. Prevent a coalition of militant black nationalist groups. . . .
2. Prevent the rise of a messiah who could unify and electrify the militant nationalist movement. . . . Martin Luther King, Stokely Carmichael and Elijah Muhammad all aspire to this position. . . .
3. Prevent violence on the part of black nationalist groups. . . .
4. Prevent militant black nationalist groups and leaders from gaining respectability by discrediting them. . . .
5. . . . prevent the long-range growth of militant black nationalist organizations, especially among youth.

These goals were incorporated into the various directives which Marlin Johnson, the special agent-in-charge of the Chicago FBI office, received instructing him to establish the program in Chicago. . . . The national COINTELPRO program adopted a variety of tactics which seemingly were aimed not at preventing violence, but at neutralizing the BPP as a political entity. These tactics included efforts to discredit the BPP among "liberal" whites, the promotion of violent conflicts between the BPP and other groups. For example, in Southern California the FBI mounted a covert operation to escalate a "gang war" between the BPP and an organization called the "United Slaves." [*This gang war resulted in the killing of four Panthers by members of the United Slaves, numerous beatings and shootings, the encouragement of dissension within the BPP, and the disruption of the BPP's Breakfast Program for Children.*] Memoranda from Washington directing the local employment of such tactics were transmitted to Johnson, Robert Piper (after March 1969 the chief of the Racial Matters Squad of the Chicago FBI which was responsible for FBI programs regarding the BPP), and Roy M. Mitchell (special agent assigned to the Racial Matters Squad in Chicago).

The *Hampton* case stemmed from an incident that occurred on December 4, 1969 (only thirty-five days after Pete O'Neal's October 30 arrest in Kansas City, Missouri), when fourteen Chicago policemen, working in close cooperation with the FBI, stormed a residential apartment at 4:30 a.m. with their guns blazing on the pretext of serving a search warrant. They fired at least ninety shots, killing two Black Panthers (leader Fred Hampton and Mark Clark) and wounding four others.[10] Only one shot came from a Black Panther weapon.

Subsequently, the surviving Black Panthers and the mothers of the two deceased brought a civil rights action for monetary damages against the FBI agents, the state's attorney and assistant state's attorneys, and the Chicago police officers allegedly involved. After the district court directed verdicts in favor of the defendants, the plaintiffs (Panthers) appealed to the US Court of Appeals, Seventh Circuit.

The appellate court held that the plaintiffs had established a *prima facie* case for several different violations, including conspiracy, use of excessive force, assault, battery, and wrongful death. The court specifically stated:

> We believe that plaintiffs have presented a prima facie case, not of a single conspiracy, but of two conspiracies designed to violate their rights in distinct ways. These conspiracies share many of the same participants who form the common nucleus of separate conspiracies, . . . but they are not identical conspiracies. The first conspiracy, as we view the evidence, involves the state and federal defendants who participated in the pre-raid preparations and planning, and the raid itself. The second conspiracy, involving many of these same defendants, was the alleged cover-up of evidence regarding the instigation, preparation and execution of the raid, and the post-raid legal harassment of the plaintiffs. These two conspiracies required entirely different kinds of activities, both legal and illegal, to achieve their ends. But more importantly, these two conspiracies had distinct objectives. The first conspiracy was designed to subvert and eliminate the Black Panther Party and its members, thereby suppressing both a potential source of unrest, turmoil, and even violence in the black community, and a vital, radical-black political organization. The second conspiracy harassed the survivors of the raid. Moreover, the post-raid conspiracy was intended to frustrate any redress the plaintiffs might seek and, more importantly, to conceal the true character of the pre-raid and raid activities of the defendants involved in the first conspiracy.[11]

The court further stated that the plaintiff's case rested on evidence of excessive force, assault, battery, and wrongful death, which a jury could conclude constituted reckless disregard of the plaintiffs' civil rights. With respect to some of the COINTELPRO tactics that the FBI in Chicago used against the Black Panther Party (BPP), the *Hampton* judges said:

> The evidence presented by plaintiffs indicates that when the local chapter of the BPP opened in Chicago in November 1968, the

Chicago FBI was quick to implement the tactics mandated by Washington. One of the key figures in the Chicago FBI's program to disrupt the Panthers was William O'Neal [*no relation to Pete O'Neal*]. [William] O'Neal was a paid FBI informant whom [Roy M.] Mitchell [*special agent assigned to the Racial Matters Squad in Chicago*] originally had contacted while [William] O'Neal was incarcerated in the Cook County Jail. Mitchell recontacted [William] O'Neal and instructed him to join the BPP. [William] O'Neal walked into the BPP office at 2350 West Madison Street the day it opened in November 1968 and joined, soon becoming the local chief of security for the Panthers.

The local FBI was able to effectuate many of its plans to disrupt the BPP through [William] O'Neal. [William] O'Neal informed Mitchell about a proposed merger between the BPP and a local black gang, the Blackstone Rangers. The Chicago office, with Johnson's approval, then sent an anonymous letter to Jeff Fort, the leader of the Rangers, telling Fort that the Panthers had a "hit out" on him. The purpose of the letter was to prevent a merger and to induce the Rangers to initiate reprisals against the BPP. [William] O'Neal also falsely accused a member of the Vice Lords, another black Chicago gang, of being a police informant, thereby squelching another possible merger. [William] O'Neal, according to plaintiffs' evidence, encouraged the Panthers to initiate and participate in various criminal activities, to obtain more weapons, and to increase their use of violent tactics.

[William] O'Neal also facilitated the FBI's efforts to discredit the BPP leadership and to frustrate their attempts to garner support among white groups. [William] O'Neal provided Mitchell with information that enabled local police to serve an arrest warrant on Fred Hampton, the leader of the BPP in Chicago, just prior to his appearance on a local television interview show. [William] O'Neal also encouraged the distribution of racist BPP cartoons, thereby fostering a rift between the BPP and the Students for a Democratic Society (SDS). For his efforts, [William] O'Neal received several pay raises from Mitchell with Johnson's approval. [*From January 1969 to June 1970,* [William] *O'Neal's monthly pay for his services as an FBI informant ranged from $100 to $500.*] After March 1969

[Robert] Piper [*supervisor of the FBI's Chicago Racial Matters*

Squad] also lent his approval to [William] O'Neal's efforts as a part of the FBI's counterintelligence program.

The FBI had other means of monitoring the BPP in Chicago. [Marlin] Johnson [*special agent-in-charge of the FBI's Chicago office*] and [Robert] Piper requested and received authorization for a warrantless wiretap on BPP headquarters.[12]

The *Hampton* judges also noted that FBI files that were eventually turned over to the plaintiffs, after unwarranted delays, included "counterintelligence documents which called for the destruction of the [BPP] Breakfast Program and for the use of local police to harass the BPP for possession of guns."[13]

The appellate court remanded the case to the district court with the recommendation that "sanctions should be imposed . . . against the federal defendants and counsel representing them at the first trial for repeatedly disobeying court orders to produce documentary material."[14] In November 1982, District Court Judge John F. Grady approved, and the plaintiffs accepted, the defendants' (City of Chicago, Cook County, and US government's) offer of a $1.85 million settlement of the case.[15]

The Chicago police raid on the Black Panther apartment took place only thirty-five days after Pete O'Neal's arrest in Kansas City. Pete and many other African Americans believed the purpose of the FBI and police in the Chicago raid was to assassinate BPP leader Fred Hampton and other Panthers. Pete feared that he, as head of the Kansas City BPP, was also on the FBI's list of Black Panthers to be eliminated.

One of the main reasons why a group of African Americans created the Black Panther Party in 1966 was to stop what they regarded as police brutality against, and murder of, fellow African Americans. Point 7 of the BPP Platform and Program, entitled "What We Want; What We Believe," addressed this issue: "We want an immediate end to POLICE BRUTALITY and MURDER of Black people. We believe we can end police brutality in our Black community by organizing Black self-defense groups that are dedicated to defending our Black community from racist police oppression and brutality. The Second Amendment to the Constitution of the United States gives a man a right to bear arms. We therefore believe that all Black people should arm themselves for self-defense."[16] In July 1968, the BPP requested UN observer teams for cities throughout the United States because the Panthers claimed to fear that "the racist power structure in this imperialist country is preparing to unleash a war of genocide against her black colonial subjects."[17]

The FBI COINTELPRO tactics described by the US Circuit Court in the *Hampton* case, which involved violent provocation, incitement, misrepresentation, and murder; the FBI's use of informant-provocateurs, such as William O'Neal in Chicago; and the police raid on the Chicago Black Panther apartment on December 4, 1969, resulting in the deaths of two Panthers and the wounding of four others only reinforced the Panthers' belief that law enforcement agencies were out to kill them.

The January 10, 1970, issue of the *Black Panther* newspaper contained an article about alleged police brutality against blacks in Kansas City. That issue also included the following statement: "The people now realize that this nation's plan to carry out acts of mass genocide has an ultimate goal of not only wiping out the Black Panther Party, and other revolutionaries, but all poor and oppressed people who stand up and try to take their freedom."

In my petition for Pete O'Neal, I urged the court to exercise its discretion in a positive, humane manner and to consider the petition on its merits, rather than dismiss it. As the Supreme Court of the United States had stated in *Molinaro v. New Jersey* in 1970, "Dismissal of fugitive appeals is always discretionary, in the sense that fugitivity does not strip the case of its character as an adjudicable case or controversy." And US Supreme Court Justice Stewart noted in his dissenting opinion in *Estelle v. Dorrough*, "If an escaped felon has been convicted in violation of law, the loss of his right to appeal results in his serving a sentence that under law was erroneously imposed."[18]

I pointed out that Supreme Court Justice Frank Murphy's opinion in *Eisler v. United States*[19] was applicable to Pete's case. During the height of the Red Scare in the United States, Eisler—a communist and alien—was convicted for contempt of Congress by the US District Court for the District of Columbia. After a US Court of Appeals confirmed his conviction, Eisler invoked the jurisdiction of the Supreme Court by a petition for *certiorari* (request for judicial review). While the court was considering his case, Eisler fled the country, thereby becoming a fugitive from justice. The court, with four dissenting votes, decided to remove Eisler's case from its docket pending his return. The following excerpt from Justice Murphy's eloquent dissent applies well to O'Neal's Petition: "Law is at its loftiest when it examines claimed injustice even at the instance of one to whom the public is bitterly hostile. We should be loath to shirk our obligations, whatever the creed of the particular petitioner. Our country takes pride in requiring of its institutions the examination and correction of alleged injustice whenever it occurs. We should not permit an affront of this sort [*Eisler's escape*] to distract us from the performance of our constitutional duties."

O'Neal had a well-founded fear that, as long as he remained in the United States, whether out on bail or in prison, his life was in danger. His subsequent legal position was hampered by his remote location in rural Tanzania and his inability to travel outside of certain African countries. His court-appointed attorney, Michael Lerner, had been disbarred. Through the years various US citizens, including lawyers, had announced that they were taking up O'Neal's case. Unfortunately, none of them actually did so.

Given the passage of time, ordinary appeals were not available to O'Neal. Hence, he was relying on *coram nobis,* which is available without time limitation. In *United States v. Cariola,*[20] the court held that, because the writ of error *coram nobis* was available at common law without limitation of time, there was no merit to the government's position that plaintiff Cariola was barred from relief because he had delayed twenty-four years in seeking it, because if the petitioner had been denied a fundamental constitutional right, passage of time would not preclude him from relief. Given Pete's dangerous situation in the United States, I asked the court to exercise its discretion in a merciful and positive manner and to consider O'Neal's petition.

Wrongful Interpretation and Misapplication of Law

When Judge Arthur Stanley decided that Pete O'Neal was eligible for conviction under 18 U.S.C. § 922(g)(1) of the Gun Control Act, he erred in two ways. First, he misrepresented California law; and, second, he contradicted the intent of Congress when it drafted section 922(g)(1) of the Gun Control Act. In doing so, Judge Stanley violated O'Neal's right to substantive due process under the Fifth Amendment to the US Constitution. In essence, O'Neal did not qualify for indictment under the Gun Control Act, and but for Judge Stanley's misrepresentation of it, Pete would not even have been tried.

On September 3, 1970, O'Neal was convicted on count 3 of a three-count indictment that stated he "knowingly and unlawfully transport[ed] a firearm, . . . in interstate commerce from Kansas City, Kansas to Kansas

City, Missouri, having been previously convicted of a crime punishable by imprisonment for a term exceeding one year, in violation of 18 U.S.C. 922(g)(1)."

18 U.S.C. § 922(g)(1) provides that:

It shall be unlawful for any person—
(1) who is under indictment for, or who has been convicted in any court of, a crime punishable by imprisonment for a term exceeding one year;
. . . to ship or transport any firearm or ammunition in interstate or foreign commerce.

18 U.S.C. Subsection 921(a)(20) provides that:

The term "crime punishable by imprisonment for a term exceeding one year" [as used in § 922(g)(1)] shall not include . . . (B) *any State offense . . . classified by the laws of the State as a misdemeanor and punishable by a term of imprisonment of two years or less* [emphasis added because this wording is critical to Pete's erroneous conviction].

The following excerpt from Judge Stanley's May 8, 1970, *Memorandum and Order* convicting O'Neal conveys the pertinent facts and Judge Stanley's erroneous method for determining that O'Neal met the conditions of 18 U.S.C. § 922 (g)(1) as modified by § 921(a)(20):

The defendant admits that he has been twice convicted of crimes committed in the State of California, specifically, receiving stolen property and escape, but challenges the legality of the use of those convictions to support the charges upon the basis of the exclusion contained in § 921(a)(20). That subsection provides that:
The term "crime punishable by imprisonment for a term exceeding one year" [as used in § 922] shall not include . . . (B) any State offense . . . classified by the laws of the State as a misdemeanor and punishable by a term of imprisonment of two years or less.
Pete O'Neal contends that both of his prior convictions fall within the purview of this exclusion. It will therefore be necessary to consider the defendant's prior convictions and the classifications given them by California law. . . .
The defendant was convicted on November 7, 1960 [*while a youth*] of receiving stolen property in violation of California Penal Code Section 496, and sentenced to imprisonment in a county jail for

nine months. Shortly after his commitment to a county jail farm, he escaped. He was subsequently recaptured, returned to California, and convicted of escape in violation of California Penal Code Section 4532(a). A state prison sentence was imposed, but *O'Neal was referred to, and accepted by, the California Youth Authority* [*emphasis added*].

Under Section 17 of the California Penal Code, a felony is a crime which is punishable with death or by imprisonment in the state prison. Both the crimes of escape and receiving stolen property are punishable by imprisonment in the state prison, although each may be alternatively punished by confinement in a county jail, and the maximum punishment for both offenses is greater than two years. The controversy arises in our case because Section 17 provides that when a crime is punishable by imprisonment in a county jail, it shall be deemed a misdemeanor for all purposes after a judgment providing other than imprisonment in the state prison. There is an additional feature of Section 17, applicable to our case, which in essence provides that when a defendant is accepted by the California Youth Authority after conviction of a crime alternatively punishable by a state prison sentence or by a fine or confinement in a county jail, the offense shall be deemed a misdemeanor. The defendant contends that since under California law both of his convictions, because of the punishments actually imposed, were misdemeanors, they fall within the exclusion contained in 18 U.S.C. § 921(a)(20). . . .

A review of California law on the subject of classification of crimes indicates that Section 17 is prospective and not retroactive in operation [*emphasis added*], so that an alternatively punishable crime should be regarded as a misdemeanor only for purposes subsequent to a judgment imposing a fine or a county jail sentence. *People v. Weaver* (1943);[21] *Ex Parte Miller* (1933).[22] In *People v. Johnson* (1958),[23] the court said:

Where an offense is punishable either as a felony by imprisonment in the state prison or as a misdemeanor by fine or by imprisonment in a jail, the offense is a felony up to the time the *sentence* is imposed.

[*Curiously or suspiciously, Judge Stanley chose to ignore the sentence immediately preceding the one he quotes here. The ignored sentence is most pertinent, because it alone addresses the California Youth*

*Authority. By intentionally omitting it, Judge Stanley made O'Neal
the victim of an unjustified prosecution.*]

Judge Stanley continued: "It therefore appears to this court that the
State of California has recognized limitations on the mitigating effect
of Section 17. Although it seems to be beyond dispute that Mr. O'Neal's
convictions are now classified by the State of California as misdemeanors
because of the punishments that were actually imposed, the *crimes* of
which he was convicted are *punishable* by imprisonment for more than
two years." Therefore, Judge Stanley held that Pete O'Neal's prior youthful convictions in California were sufficient to make him eligible for prosecution under 18 U.S.C. § 922 (g)(1) despite the qualifications contained
in 18 U.S.C. § 921(a)(20), which excluded conviction for misdemeanors
punishable by a term of imprisonment of two years or less.

Unfortunately, for this crucial analysis, Judge Stanley misrepresented
California law by relying on outdated and irrelevant California cases.
Section 17 of the California Penal Code was significantly amended in
1959—one year after the *Johnson* case, upon which Judge Stanley relied.
The *Weaver* (1943) and *Miller* (1933) cases, to which Judge Stanley referred, are even older and, more importantly, neither dealt directly with
the California Youth Authority.

The 1959 amendment of the California Penal Code made the intent of
the California legislature clear in the treatment of youthful offenders. In
People v. Navarro (1972),[24] the Supreme Court of California stated:

> In 1959 [Section 17 of the Cal. Penal Code] was amended to provide:
> "Where a court commits a defendant to the [California] Youth Au-
> thority upon conviction of a crime punishable, in the discretion of
> the court, by imprisonment in the state prison or fine or imprison-
> ment in a county jail, the crime shall be deemed a misdemeanor."
> This section has since been recast into lettered subdivisions but
> still provides, in present subdivision (b)(2), that *such an offense is a
> misdemeanor for all purposes* when the court commits the convicted
> person to the [California Youth] authority [*emphasis added*].
> . . .
> In *People v. Hannon* (1971),[25] this court had for consideration the
> effect of the 1959 amendment to section 17 of the Penal Code upon
> a 1968 commitment to the [California Youth] authority based upon
> an optional sentence offense. The contention there raised was that

the 1959 amendment made such offenses misdemeanors only conditionally, so that if the person committed was thereafter returned to court by the authority pursuant to section 1737.1, he could then be sentenced as a felon. We rejected that contention, holding that under the statute the offense was a misdemeanor thereafter "for all purposes."

The *Navarro* court also explained that the intent of the California legislature was to rehabilitate convicted youths and give them a new start in life, not "to hold out an apple and then withdraw it (in the discretion of the judge) for some future act. . . ."

At the times of O'Neal's California convictions, the pertinent provisions of the California Welfare and Institutions Code, chapter 1, section 1700, were as follows: "The purpose of this chapter is to protect society more effectively by substituting for retributive punishment methods of training and treatment directed toward the correction and rehabilitation of young persons found guilty of public offenses. To this end, it is the intent of the legislature that the chapter be liberally interpreted in conformity with its declared purpose."

California Welfare and Institutions Code, section 1772: "Every person honorably discharged from control by the [California Youth] Authority who has not, during the period of control by the Authority, been placed by the Authority in a state prison *shall thereafter be released from all penalties and disabilities resulting from the offense or crime for which he was committed . . .*" [*emphasis added*].

Why did Judge Stanley choose out-of-date cases and language that omitted the intent of the California legislature, knowing as he did that Pete had been turned over to the California Youth Authority? Judge Stanley not only misapplied California and federal law, but also he contradicted congressional intent, which was to give effect to state reforms with respect to youthful offenders. What constitutes a conviction for purposes of 18 U.S.C. § 922(g) "shall be determined in accordance with the law of the jurisdiction in which the proceedings were held" (*United States v. Thompson*).[26] When determining whether a defendant's prior youthful conviction in California qualified him for prosecution under 18 U.S.C. 922(g)(1), the US Appeals Court for the Ninth Circuit stated: "We defer to the California Supreme Court's interpretation of its own law because 'the intent of Congress [*in creating the exception to section 922(g)*]

(1) in section 921(a)(20)] was to give effect to state reforms with respect to the status of ex-convicts' *United States v. Cassidy,*"[27] *United States v. Varela.*[28]

According to federal legislation, in cases involving state law, section 921(g)(1) of the Federal Gun Control Law and the misdemeanor exception to it (sec. 921(a)(20)) must be applied in accordance with section 927, which provides that Congress did not intend to "occupy the field" when states had laws on the same subject matter, and that it would not trump state law except in the case of an irreconcilable conflict.

Therefore, because:

1. Section 921(a)(20) excluded offenses classified by states as a misdemeanor and punishable by two years or less of imprisonment;

2. Section 17 of California's penal code had reduced O'Neal's youthful convictions to misdemeanors punishable by less than two years of imprisonment "for all purposes," and thereby released him from "all penalties and disabilities resulting from the offense or crime for which he was committed";

3. the Supreme Court of California issued clear statements in *Navarro, Hannon,* and *In re Herrera* that Section 17 operates both retroactively and prospectively ("for all purposes"), and not only prospectively as Judge Stanley wrongfully held;

4. the California legislature intended to use the California Youth Authority to give convicted youths a new start in life;

5. Section 927 of the Gun Control Act stated that "no provision of this chapter shall be construed as indicating an intent on the part of the Congress to occupy the field in which such provision operates to the exclusion of the law of any state on the same subject matter"; and

6. "the intent of Congress [*in creating the exception to section 922(g) (1) in section 921(a)(20)*] was to give effect to state reforms with respect to the status of ex-convicts," *United States v. Cassidy* (6th Cir. 1990),

it is clear that Judge Stanley's conclusion that Section 17 applied only prospectively, and that O'Neal was eligible for prosecution under 18 U.S.C. § 922(g)(1), wrongly represented California law, federal law, and US congressional intent. Consequently, Judge Stanley's failure to apply the law fairly violated O'Neal's Fifth Amendment right to due process.

Judge Errs in His Ruling on Government Electronic Surveillance

As part of its campaign against the BPP, federal investigators conducted electronic surveillance of Kansas City Black Panther telephone conversations without first obtaining the necessary judicial warrant. In the September 1, 1970, morning session of Pete O'Neal's trial, Judge Stanley told the government and defense attorneys: "I have examined *in camera* [in chambers] the logs of the telephone, intercepted telephone conversations, and I find that all of the interceptions were after the effective date of the Crime Control Act and all were after the date of January 16, 1969, the date the offense is alleged to have been committed and that none of them have any significance with respect to the offenses charged in the three counts in this case and that all were authorized by the President acting through the Attorney General."[29] Having found the electronic surveillance constitutional, Judge Stanley then ordered the surveillance records sealed and returned to the attorney general. This meant that the defendant would never see the records of the wiretaps of his own phones. Both parts of this ruling—that the surveillance was constitutional and that the surveillance records need not be seen by O'Neal— were contrary to well-settled law. Shortly after the *O'Neal* case, Judge Keith, US district judge for the Eastern District of Michigan, pointed out how erroneous Judge Stanley had been.

In *United States v. Sinclair* (1971),[30] Judge Keith held that electronic surveillance authorized by the US attorney general in a "national security" case violated the defendant's Fourth Amendment rights. In that case, Judge Keith stated:

> In presenting its oral argument the Government relies heavily upon *United States v. Felix Lindsey O'Neal*,[31] a case in which the District Judge [Stanley] made an in-court ruling that surveillance pursuant to the authorization of the Attorney General was lawful. . . . In the instant case the Government apparently ignores the overwhelming precedents[32] . . . and argues that the President, acting through the Attorney General, has the inherent Constitutional power: (1) to authorize without judicial warrant electronic surveillance in "national security" cases; and (2) to determine unilaterally whether a given situation is a matter within the scope of national security. This Court is unable to accept this proposition. We are a country of laws and not of men.

[T]he Government submits that the President should also have the constitutional power to gather information concerning domestic organizations which seek to attack and subvert the Government by unlawful means. . . . In the opinion of this Court, the position of the Attorney General is untenable.

This Court adopts the holding of Judge Warren J. Ferguson in *United States v. Smith*, (1971),[33] which was that: " . . . in wholly domestic situations there is no national security exception from the warrant requirement of the Fourth Amendment. Since there is no reason why the government could not have complied with this requirement by obtaining the impartial judgment of a court before conducting the electronic surveillance in question here, it was obtained in violation of the Fourth Amendment."

The US Supreme Court also addressed the constitutionality issue in *United States vs. U.S. District Court for the Eastern District of Michigan*, (1972).[34] In that case, the United States charged three defendants with conspiring to destroy, and one of them with destroying, government property. In response to the defendants' pretrial motion for disclosure of electronic surveillance information, the government filed an affidavit in which the attorney general stated he had approved the wiretaps for the purpose of gathering intelligence information he deemed necessary to protect the nation from attempts of domestic organizations to attack and subvert the existing structure of the government.

On the basis of the affidavit and surveillance logs, which had been filed in a sealed exhibit, the government claimed that the surveillance, though warrantless, was lawful as a reasonable exercise of presidential power to protect national security. The district court held that the surveillance violated the Fourth Amendment and issued an order to disclose the overheard conversations, which the court of appeals upheld. The Supreme Court affirmed the lower courts' rulings. It held, among other things, that (1) the Fourth Amendment's guarantee from unreasonable search means that the government must obtain prior judicial approval for this type of domestic security surveillance; (2) the freedoms of the Fourth Amendment cannot be guaranteed if the Executive Branch has sole discretion to conduct domestic security surveillances, without the detached judgment of a neutral magistrate; and (3) obtaining a warrant would not frustrate the legitimate purposes of domestic security searches.

Because *United States v. Felix Lindsey O'Neal* involved a wholly domestic situation, electronic surveillance of defendant O'Neal authorized by the attorney general, but conducted without a constitutionally required judicial warrant, violated O'Neal's Fourth Amendment rights. Consequently, District Court Judge Stanley's erroneous ruling in *O'Neal* that the surveillance conducted on O'Neal without a warrant was lawful endorsed that violation.

Not only did Judge Stanley err when he approved unwarranted surveillance, but he also erred when he refused to allow O'Neal to view the surveillance records. Alone, in his private chamber, Judge Stanley determined that the electronic surveillance records did not affect the case. His decision not to reveal those records to the defense was contrary to the US Supreme Court's decision in *Alderman v. United States* (1969).[35] In *Alderman* the court concluded that "surveillance records as to which any petitioner has standing to object should be turned over to him without being screened in camera by the trial judge. . . . [W]innowing material from those items which might have made a substantial contribution to the case against a petitioner is a task which should not be entrusted wholly to the court in the first instance."

The *Alderman* case and many of the federal cases that Judge Keith cited above preceded Pete O'Neal's trial. A federal judge's failure to either know the pertinent rulings in those cases or properly apply them can be attributed to either incompetence or bias.

Judge Stanley Gives More Help to the Prosecution

Count 3 of the indictment, for which Pete O'Neal was convicted, stated that O'Neal "did knowingly and unlawfully transport a firearm . . . in interstate commerce from Kansas City, Kansas to Kansas City, Missouri."[36] In his opening statement to the jury, the US attorney correctly stated that "it will be incumbent upon the government to show the transportation of a gun purchased by Mr. O'Neal, *transported by him*, into the State of Missouri."[37]

At trial, however, the government could produce no evidence proving that O'Neal had transported the firearm across the state line. As an aid to the prosecution's case, Judge Stanley decided to add a strong "aiding and abetting" element to his instructions to the jury, which he gave at the end of the trial. O'Neal's attorney, Austin Shute, objected, but Judge Stanley overruled the objection. However, even the so-called aiding and abetting evidence was weak and circumstantial, not rising to the level of "beyond a reasonable doubt." The prosecution failed to establish whom Pete allegedly aided and abetted. The prosecution based its evidence largely on the confused testimony of Ms. Jean M. Young, Pete's landlady, who at first denied, but later partially admitted, that she was a paid government informant. Nevertheless, the jury convicted Pete on this count. In this respect, O'Neal's trial is reminiscent of the 1972 illegal conviction of Black Panther Geronimo Pratt on the basis of evidence provided by a paid government informant.[38]

Pete O'Neal's Good Character Supported the Petition

In addition to documenting many of the trial's defects, I wanted to present Pete's good character as one more reason for a fair judge to consider his petition on its merits. The following paragraphs come from the petition:

As a youth, Pete O'Neal grew up in a United States that was not fair to its black citizens. Housing, schools, and jobs were either legally or illegally segregated or closed completely to Blacks. O'Neal was 28 years old when the great civil rights leader Martin Luther King was assassinated by a White racist in 1968. One year later, O'Neal joined the BPP and became the object of the government's unconstitutional electronic surveillance and a target of the FBI, ATF agents, and local police. On October 30, 1969 ATF agents arrested O'Neal for allegedly having transported a shotgun across a state line some nine months earlier.

After being convicted in a trial that involved violations of his due process rights, fearing for his life, Pete O'Neal and his wife, Charlotte, fled the U.S. They moved to Tanzania—one of the poorest countries in the world—in 1972. They have worked extremely hard, struggling to survive by engaging in farming and small business enterprises, such as making and marketing mustard, barbecue sauce, relish, and sausage; promoting low cost home construction and wind generated energy. In addition, they created a United African American Community Center to promote local arts and crafts, improved nutrition and health for Tanzanian villagers, and educational opportunities for Tanzanian and American youths of all races. They have worked with a Vermont-based organization that organizes overseas experiences for American college students. Over the years, they have hosted dozens of American students (mostly white) at their homestead and have introduced them to Tanzanian village life. The O'Neals have also spearheaded the Kansas City–Arusha Sister City Project and student exchanges between the two cities.

Because of their community work, the O'Neals have won the respect of the Tanzanians and have promoted positive linkages between Tanzania and the United States. They have also raised and home-educated their son and daughter in Tanzania. The fact that their children (now young adults) presently live in the U.S. evidences that the O'Neals instilled in them a positive affinity for the U.S.

Over a quarter of a century has passed since Pete O'Neal left the U.S. in 1970. Now at age 58, he is an older, wiser, temperate person. He has expressed regret for parts of his past. For example, he wishes he could redo his Navy service. He had joined as a troubled teenager. Even though he experienced racism in the Navy, he now concludes that he had failed to take advantage of what could have been an enriching experience. He also expressed regret for some of the tactics that he and his fellow Black Panther Party members had employed back in the sixties. He firmly believes that they had some very worthy goals, such as creating breakfast programs and a health clinic to promote better nutrition and health for inner-city youths and families, but their tactics were sometimes too confrontational. Today Pete O'Neal advocates dialogue, conciliation and integration. He admires how Tanzanian villagers resolve their conflicts peacefully by bringing them before their respected village elders, who mediate them within the context of community and familial values.

Pete O'Neal also strongly opposes violence and the use of guns. The following quote from a 1993 article in the *Kansas City Star* is relevant here:

The years in exile have changed O'Neal. Gone is the ideological rhetoric, the thoughts of revolution and his penchant for danger. What remains is a father deeply committed to his wife, family and village. If he ever returns to the United States, he'd like to work with youth. "One of the greatest problems facing black America seems to me to be the drug problem," he said recently. . . . Once

O'Neal advocated revolution. Now he advocates inclusion. [According to O'Neal], America isn't Utopia, but it's still the best nation in the world.[39]

With respect to the use of violence, former Kansas City Police Chief Clarence Kelley is quoted in the February 20, 1993 issue of the *Kansas City Star*: "O'Neal kept a lid on any violence. . . . They [the Kansas City Panthers] were young. They were exuberant about the possibility of doing some great things. Instead of doing it the way it should have been done, they went about it all wrong. But I don't recall anything too forceful. They made an awful lot of noise. But this was the age of booming out. They used a lot of language, boasts, and a lot of promises, but there weren't any real bad situations."

In Tanzania, Pete O'Neal is a loving father and husband, a clean-living, hard-working and respected village elder, who gives priority to family and community. Given his present character and the passage of more than a quarter of a century, a reasonable person cannot see how the imprisonment of Pete O'Neal would serve American society or the State.

Prayer to Vacate Conviction

Given that Pete O'Neal was convicted and sentenced illegally in violation of Fourth Amendment rights and his Fifth Amendment right to due process, and given the other extra-legal circumstances surrounding and impinging on his trial, we ask this honorable court to issue a writ of coram nobis and vacate Petitioner's conviction. We beseech the court in its compassion and wisdom to answer Petitioner's prayer.

We are convinced that a careful consideration of this Petition would lead to a fair resolution that would allow Pete O'Neal to live with his family in the United States as the model citizen that he has already proven to be in Tanzania. Given the facts delineated in this Petition, Americans of goodwill would conclude that more than sufficient justification exists for closing this chapter of Kansas City's history in a conciliatory manner. Such a decision will increase the community's faith in and respect for American justice.

As Supreme Court Justice Frank Murphy has stated, our country takes pride in requiring our institutions to examine and correct alleged injustice whenever it occurs.

Respectfully submitted by attorneys for Petitioner,
Paul J. Magnarella, Austin F. Shute, Kurt D. Marquart

11

Submission, Responses, and Final Orders

Attorney Austin Shute delivered our petition for writ of coram nobis to the US District Court of Kansas in Kansas City. Judge Arthur Stanley had retired, and his longtime colleague Judge Earl E. O'Connor had taken over Pete's case. He accepted our petition, directed the US attorney to file a response by June 19, 1998, and allowed us to file a reply thereafter. On June 19, I received the government's response, written by an assistant US attorney. What follows are his main contentions and my responses to them.

Fugitive Disentitlement Doctrine

The US attorney recommended that the court invoke the fugitive disentitlement doctrine because, he argued, O'Neal could have litigated all of his claims on appeal to the Tenth Circuit Court twenty-eight years before his attorney filed the petition for writ of coram nobis. Instead, O'Neal had fled the country. Even if he fled then for security reasons, the US attorney saw no evidence of continuing threats against him. Therefore, the government insisted that O'Neal return to the United States to serve his sentence.

In my response, I explained that the US attorney's recommendation was designed to avoid the serious constitutional questions raised in O'Neal's petition and to defeat his plea for justice. The US attorney should know full well that as soon as Pete O'Neal reentered the United States he would be taken into custody by US Marshals and sent to prison to serve the sentence for a crime for which he was erroneously tried and convicted. Once in custody, his coram nobis petition would become void, as a condition of the petition is that the petitioner not be in custody. O'Neal would then lose his one chance for justice. Rather than defeat O'Neal's petition on this technicality and thereby avoid the grave constitutional and fundamental fairness issues in this case, I asked this court to consider the petition on its merits.

Coram Nobis

The US attorney also claimed, with an embarrassingly weak show of legal authority, that the writ of coram nobis "was all but extinct." He quoted from a US Supreme Court case, *Carlisle v. United States*:[1] "[It] is difficult to conceive of a situation in a federal criminal case today where [a writ of coram nobis] would be necessary or appropriate." The US attorney referred to this quote as "controlling authority."

In response, I noted that what the US attorney quoted was not a ruling of the Supreme Court at all, but what is referred to as dictum: a judge's individual opinion that goes beyond the facts before the court and therefore is not binding in subsequent cases as legal precedent. In the *Carlisle* case the petitioner had not asked for a writ of coram nobis, nor had the lower court issued such a writ. Consequently, the writ was not an issue argued in *Carlisle*. Dictum is not "controlling authority."

Profession of Innocence

The US attorney again misrepresented case law and Pete's position by stating: "For some *inexplicable reason* [*emphasis added*], the defendant offers no sworn affidavits or even a profession of actual innocence to support his contentions." Then the US attorney maintained that in *United States v. Bustillos*[2] the court held that coram nobis relief was inappropriate for the defendant because he did not assert his innocence of the charge against him. In response, I showed that the government's characterization of *Bustillos* seriously misrepresented the case, incorrectly analogized it to O'Neal, and contained a serious omission. In *Bustillos* the defendant *had pled guilty* to the charge against him. By contrast, Pete had always asserted his innocence, both in court and thereafter. What was clearly applicable to O'Neal's petition, though, was the *Bustillos* court's statement that a writ of coram nobis is available to correct errors that resulted in a complete miscarriage of justice, or under circumstances that compelled the use of the writ to achieve justice.[3] We filed O'Neal's petition for a writ of coram nobis to correct errors that resulted in a complete miscarriage of justice under circumstances compelling that action to achieve justice.

Federal and California Law

The US Attorney disputed our presentation of the relationship between the US Gun Control Act and California law, especially as it related to the California Youth Authority. Instead, he reaffirmed Judge Stanley's original interpretation, even though it was based on outdated cases and completely ignored California Youth Authority–related legislation. We responded by repeating the analysis we presented in our petition. We stressed that Section 17 of California's penal code had reduced O'Neal's youthful convictions to misdemeanors punishable by terms of imprisonment of less than two years "for all purposes" and thereby releasing him from "all penalties and disabilities resulting from the offense or crime for which he was committed." The California Supreme Court specifically stated that Section 17 operates both retroactively and prospectively ("for all purposes"), and not only prospectively, as Judge Stanley wrongly held. Consequently, Judge Stanley's conclusion, that O'Neal met the definition of a person eligible for prosecution under the Gun Control Act, misinterpreted California law, federal law, and US congressional intent. Judge Stanley's erroneous interpretation of the law violated O'Neal's Fifth Amendment rights to due process.

Illegal Electronic Surveillance

The US attorney ignored the legal fact that a government's electronic surveillance of American citizens' private conversations without a properly issued judicial warrant is unconstitutional. He also ignored the legal requirement that Judge Stanley should have handed over the fruits of that electronic surveillance to the defendant. Instead, he offered the illogical argument that, somehow, no constitutional violation exists if the defendant cannot show that the electronic surveillance information the court illegally prevented him from seeing contained evidence that could have helped his case! The US attorney did not and could not offer any authorities to support this position.

I pointed out that the electronic surveillance data may have contained information that cast doubt on the government's charge that O'Neal transported the shotgun across the state line. The data may have contained conversations between others who were responsible for the transporting. Or the data might have contained information about O'Neal's absence during the time of the transporting, or information that supported an alibi for O'Neal. O'Neal will never know any of this because the judge erroneously prevented him from exercising his legal right to examine the data.

O'Neal's Fourth Amendment constitutional right against illegal searches and seizures and his Fifth Amendment due process rights were violated. But for these errors O'Neal might not have been convicted. These constitutional violations are of such magnitude that they alone were sufficient reason to vacate the conviction. By wrongfully withholding the electronic surveillance information, the court denied O'Neal "fundamental fairness" (*Murray v. Carrier*).[4]

Insufficient Evidence

The US attorney rejected our claim that Pete was convicted on the basis of insufficient and dubious evidence. As his example of convincing evidence, he recapped (with significant alterations) witness Jean Young's testimony. He wrote: "The lady who had been the manager of the apartment in Kansas City, Missouri, in January 1969 testified the defendant [Pete] had said he had obtained a gun in Kansas, and further stated that he showed *the gun* [*emphasis added*] to her husband and said it was the gun he bought at Sam's Loan."

Jean Young's actual testimony was quite different. She claimed she *had heard* Pete O'Neal (whom she knew as "Gary") tell her ex-husband about purchasing a gun at Sam's Loan. She also said that Pete O'Neal had showed *a gun* (not *the gun* as the US attorney claimed) to her ex-husband, but admitted that she could not identify it, because she did not know one gun from another. Casting doubt on her testimony was the sworn statement of her husband, Harold Young, who maintained that the purported conversation between O'Neal and him never took place. We attached his sworn statement to our response. Importantly, Jean Young was the only witness the US attorney referred to in his response, contending that her testimony was important for the conviction. In a later exchange between us, after Jean Young's credibility had been discredited, he would argue the opposite: that her testimony was only "incidental."

Conclusion

The US attorney summed up his response with the hackneyed charge that Pete O'Neal had made a series of bad choices and "now he tries to blame society, the judiciary and the government for his problems."

I added some additional choices and non-choices that placed O'Neal in his present legal position.

O'Neal chose to become a prominent black civil rights activist during the height of the politically charged civil rights movement in the United States.

He chose to proclaim black pride and to organize a free breakfast program for inner-city children, a free clothing program for inner-city needy, and a free medical clinic for the inner city ill—programs that FBI Director Hoover ordered eliminated and used illegal means to eliminate.

He chose to organize police patrols to follow and monitor Kansas City Police cars in order to prevent the police from exerting excessive force on inner-city citizens—a police practice not uncommon in Kansas City and other American cities.[5]

He did not choose to have the FBI organize COINTELPRO to engage in illegal activities and dirty tricks against black civil rights activists.

He did not choose to have his telephones illegally tapped by federal authorities. (At the same time the FBI even had the audacity to spy illegally on the US Supreme Court.)[6]

He did not choose to have a federal judge (Judge Stanley) declare as legal the unconstitutional electronic surveillance conducted by federal authorities against him without a proper judicial warrant.

He did not choose to have a federal judge (Judge Stanley) erroneously deny him access to the illegal fruits of the government's electronic surveillance and thereby hamper his defense.

He did not choose to have police threaten his life as he walked in and out of the federal courthouse.

He did choose to flee for his life to Africa, where he has lived for the past twenty-eight years.

He did choose to spearhead the creation of the Kansas City—Arusha, Tanzania—Sister City Program so as to promote friendly relations between Tanzania and the United States.

We ended our response with the following statement: "The O'Neal Petition raises serious constitutional questions about fundamental fairness. These issues are not moot, as the Government contends. They address questions crucial to American justice. We urge the Court to exercise its discretion in a positive, humane manner by accepting O'Neal's Petition and deciding whether he received a fair trial." We restated Supreme Court Justice Frank Murphy's eloquent statement in *Eisler v. United States*: "Our country takes pride in requiring of its institutions the examination and correction of alleged injustice whenever it occurs."[7] We submitted our response to Judge Earl E. O'Connor.

Coram Nobis Denied

On July 28, 1998, Judge O'Connor issued his judgment in the form of a memorandum and order. He began by stating: "On September 3, 1970, a jury convicted defendant of transporting a firearm in interstate commerce after having previously been convicted of a crime in violation of 18 U.S.C. § 922(g)(1)." Apparently, Judge O'Connor took no notice of our legal analysis in the petition showing that O'Neal had *not* previously been convicted of a crime in violation of 18 U.S.C. § 922(g)(1).

Judge O'Connor then invoked the fugitive disentitlement doctrine and denied Pete's petition for a writ of coram nobis. The judge reasoned that Pete abandoned his appeal to the Tenth Circuit Court more than twenty-six years ago when he fled the United States. "His counsel represented that defendant fled because he feared for his safety in the United States. . . . [H]is counsel's representations regarding fear for his safety were insufficient to establish cause for defendant's procedural default. Defendant in this case has risked nothing by filing the instant petition: if he prevails on the merits, he can come to the United States as a free man; and if he does not prevail, he simply can remain in Tanzania and escape punishment."

My Motion to Reconsider

In response, I filed a motion to reconsider the judgment as well as a motion requesting oral arguments in order to correct clear error and prevent manifest injustice. My motion responded to Judge O'Connor's rulings in turn.

I began by attempting to correct the Judge's erroneous assumption that Pete had previously been convicted of a crime in violation of the Gun Control Act (18 U.S.C. § 922[g][1]). I again argued that a proper review of California statutes and California case law concerning the California Youth Authority and federal law would have led the presiding judge in Pete's trial to conclude that he was not eligible for conviction under the Gun Control Act.

Fugitive Disentitlement Doctrine

Responding to Judge O'Connor's use of the fugitive disentitlement doctrine, I argued, with the support of numerous federal cases, that the doctrine is not mandatory and should not be invoked when the petitioner has been denied his constitutional protections and due process right to a fair trial. Judges should exercise their discretion in the pursuit of justice. We urged the judge to exercise his discretion in a positive, humane manner and consider O'Neal's petition. We quoted a Supreme Court case that was decided the same year Pete was convicted: "Dismissal of fugitive appeals is always discretionary, in the sense that fugitivity does not 'strip the case of its character as an adjudicable case or controversy.'"[8] Automatic dismissal of a fugitive's appeal "may rest on nothing more than the faulty premise that any act of judicial defiance, whether or not it affects the appellate process, is punishable by appellate dismissal."[9] As US Supreme Court Justice Stewart noted in his dissenting opinion in *Estelle v. Dorrough*, "If an escaped felon has been convicted in violation of law, the loss of his right to appeal results in his serving a sentence that under law was erroneously imposed."[10]

Illegal Government Electronic Surveillance

In addition, I noted once again that Judge Stanley had also misinterpreted federal law when he erroneously ruled that the government's electronic surveillance of O'Neal's apartment was legal, and that he, the judge, was not required by law to turn the illegally obtained surveillance information over to the defendant. These serious errors violated O'Neal's Fourth Amendment constitutional protection against unlawful search and seizure and his Fifth Amendment due process right to fundamental fairness; the Fourth Amendment violation was so egregious that a neighboring federal judge commented negatively on it.[11] Justice Stevens, in the Supreme Court case of *Murray v. Carrier*, wrote that a "constitutional claim that implicates 'fundamental fairness' . . . compels review regardless of possible procedural defaults."[12] Hence, these errors alone are sufficient reasons for a review of O'Neal's 1970 trial.

Threats against Pete

In our response to Judge O'Connor's statement that "Counsel's representations alone that defendant fled because he feared for his safety in the United States are insufficient to establish cause for defendant's procedural default," I asked the judge to examine our original petition carefully. The claim of death threats was not based on "counsel's representations alone." The petition contained an abundance of factual information establishing both the defendant's belief that he was a target of death threats and his reasonable basis for this belief.

Judge O'Connor stated that "Defendant in this case has risked nothing by filing the instant petition: if he prevails on the merits, he can come to the United States as a free man; and if he does not prevail, he simply can remain in Tanzania and escape punishment." We had to refute this statement; it was simply wrong. I responded that the Court had mischaracterized O'Neal's past and future hardships. Because of his unfair trial and the police death threats, O'Neal (a black civil rights leader in the politically charged atmosphere of the time) was wrongfully convicted and forced to leave his homeland and relatives to seek refuge in a foreign country. For the past twenty-eight years, he and his wife, also a US citizen, had struggled against poverty and disease in Tanzania, one of Africa's poorest countries. In 1994 one of the world's worst genocides occurred in Rwanda, a neighbor to Tanzania.

If this Court were to use its discretion in a negative way by simply dismissing O'Neal's petition without fairly and fully considering its merits, many American citizens would continue to regard O'Neal as a political exile and victim of American injustice, who sacrificed his life in his homeland for the cause of racial equality.

In Conclusion

The motion to reconsider ended with the following: "Given the case's historic context, irregularities, and related facts, a denial of Pete O'Neal's petition amounts to a denial of justice. One would not contemplate that a United States Court would deny American justice to a petitioning United States citizen who was forced to seek refuge in a Third World country to save his life from death threats by American law enforcement agents. O'Neal is entitled to the fundamental fairness denied him in his 1970 trial."

Motion for Reconsideration Denied

On September 19, 1998, Judge O'Connor issued his order denying both our motion to reconsider and our motion for oral argument. The judge apparently did not consider any of the constitutional violations in Pete's case. Instead, he focused on a nonconstitutional, judge-made rule—the disentitlement doctrine, which he stated "advances several important principles of the judicial system including deterring escapes and maintaining the dignity and efficiency of the judicial system."

Apparently, Judge O'Connor was claiming that, if someone flees the country after receiving threats by law enforcement agents and enduring an unfair trial and conviction, the individual is insulting the dignity of the judicial system.

A Kansas attorney very familiar with the federal district court and its judges had warned me not to be too optimistic about our petition. Judges Stanley and O'Connor had served together in that court for many years. Judge O'Connor would find it difficult to rule that Judge Stanley, his longtime colleague, had made sufficient errors in O'Neal's 1970 case to warrant a new trial.

12
Evidence of Perjury and a New Petition

In January of 1999, I received a phone call from attorney Kevin L. Jamison of Kansas City, Missouri, asking if I was aware that James Moore, the ATF agent in O'Neal's 1970 trial, had discussed that case in his published memoir. I was not. After some hunting in local bookstores, I managed to secure a copy of Moore's out-of-print book, *Very Special Agents: The Inside Story of America's Most Controversial Law Enforcement Agency—The Bureau of Alcohol, Tobacco and Firearms*. In it, Moore revealed some out-of-court details of the O'Neal case that showed that both he and Jean Young, the prosecution's two key witnesses, lied when testifying.

Consequently, I prepared and filed a new petition coram nobis offering new evidence of false testimony by government witnesses, which deprived Pete O'Neal of a fair trial and constituted grounds for invalidating his 1970 trial and conviction. I also argued, as before, that a petition coram nobis is appropriate where fundamental error and constitutional violations in the 1970 trial are alleged and other remedies are not available.

Before filing the petition I had learned that seventy-six-year-old Judge Earl O'Connor and his sixty-six-year-old wife had been found shot to death in their home, in what the FBI suspected was either a double-suicide or a murder-suicide. The couple had died in their bedroom on November 29, 1998, only two months after he had rejected our petition coram nobis. Each died from a single gunshot wound to the chest from Judge O'Connor's own 38-caliber pistol. He had retrieved the pistol from his office the day before.[1] A local newspaper reported:

U.S. District Judge Thomas Van Bebber, a friend of the O'Connors, said that Jean O'Connor had been in "terrible health" and had been showing no signs of improvement. Van Bebber, who last saw O'Connor a couple of weeks ago, said Jean O'Connor was in pain and suffered from medical problems, including diabetes, several bouts of pneumonia and neurological problems. O'Connor had been depressed recently about his wife's health and he began caring for her almost full time about three weeks ago.[2]

FBI spokesperson Jeff Lanza said there was no evidence that any other person was involved in the killings. He added that O'Connor earned the respect of law enforcement officials. "He was a fine judge and well-respected by the FBI as a fair judge. He will be missed by the law enforcement community."[3]

Republican Governor William H. Avery had named O'Connor to the Kansas Supreme Court in September 1965. He served there until 1971 when then-President Richard Nixon nominated him to the federal district court. O'Connor rose to the post of chief judge before taking on senior status with a lesser workload in 1992.[4]

New Petition

In the new petition, filed on March 1, 2001, I documented the perjury of ATF Agent Moore and apartment manager Jean Young that had been detailed in the *Very Special Agents* book. I also included a sworn affidavit from Pete stating he would appear in court for a new trial should the judge order one. Since the petition was going to Judge G. Thomas Van Bebber, the new judge on the case, I again detailed the other judicial errors and constitutional violations in the 1970 trial. The same US attorney responded, urging the judge to again invoke the disentitlement doctrine. However, Judge Van Bebber showed us a ray of hope when he refused to do so, and instead directed the government to respond "because the present petition appears to raise issues additional to those put forth in Defendant's previous petition." What follows is a description of my final response to the Court, refuting claims made by the US attorney and presenting final arguments supporting a request to vacate Pete O'Neal's 1970 conviction and to order a new trial.

Response to Government and Petition for Writ of Coram Nobis

The US attorney filed his response in opposition to the petition on May 30, 2001. In it, he again misrepresented Jean Young's testimony as to whether she saw "the gun" she had heard Pete say he had bought, or simply "a gun." He again mischaracterized the relationship between the Gun Control Act and California law, especially the California Youth Authority. He again claimed, with support only from dictum, that the writ of coram nobis was "all but extinct." And in his effort to refute our charges of perjury, he produced affidavits that backfired by actually supporting our charges of perjury and prosecutorial misconduct. The next section illustrates our proof that the government witnesses lied under oath.

Perjury by Government Witnesses

Contrary to the government's claim, its two key witnesses against Pete O'Neal unquestionably perjured themselves. In fact, two of the affidavits the government supplied strengthened our claim that: (1) material perjury occurred during O'Neal's 1970 trial; (2) the government was responsible for the perjury; and (3) as a consequence of the perjury O'Neal's constitutional rights were violated, and therefore he did not receive a fair trial.

According to the affidavit provided to the US attorney by ATF Special Agent Dana K. Nichols, the government's key witness—Jean M. Young—had gone by at least seven different surnames: Young, Kilp, Van Duyne, Pierson, Starnes, Uzell, and Walker. According to ATF Agent Nichols, an FBI search showed that Jean M. Young had been arrested three times by the Kansas City, Missouri, Police Department under the name Jean Van Duyne.

According to the affidavit provided to the US attorney by Julie L. Christian, an FBI Criminal Informant Program coordinator, FBI records showed that Mrs. Jean Young had gone by a variety of surnames and that "Jean Marie Young had provided information to the FBI on various violations, including the White Slave Traffic Act, theft of interstate shipments, fugitive cases, and bank robberies." For this information the FBI paid Mrs. Young "from May 17, 1965, to February 6, 1969, . . . a total of 14 times in varying increments from $5.00 to $100.00." ATF Agent Christian stated that Mrs. Young provided information to the FBI concerning Pete O'Neal from March 28, 1969, to August 27, 1970, "at which time she was concerned about having received a federal subpoena to testify at O'Neal's trial on September 1, 1970." ATF Agent Christian maintained that "Ms. Young was never paid by the FBI for any information which she provided concerning O'Neal." However, Jean Young did receive a payment from the FBI on February 6, 1969, which is three days after O'Neal purchased the shotgun involved in the interstate transportation charge against him. Beginning in September 1983, the FBI again began making payments to Jean M. Young.

During cross-examination in the 1970 O'Neal trial, defense counsel Austin Shute had asked Jean Young if she had ever worked for a law enforcement agency.

> Young replied, "No."
> Shute then asked: "Have you ever on any occasion been offered money by anyone connected with any law enforcement agency for testimony or information?"
> Young, in response, shook her head negatively and said "I don't remember of ever being offered money for information, of being offered money for information, no."
>
> (Trial transcript, 122)

Young's replies to these questions while under oath clearly constituted lies and perjury. She had worked for the FBI. FBI Agent Christian's affidavit was specific and unambiguous. Young's last FBI payment occurred less than nineteen months before her testimony quoted above. How could she not remember "ever being offered money [by a law enforcement agency] for information"?

Shute's cross-examination of Jean Young continued:

> Shute: "Do I take it, then, that you have in fact received money for information?"
> Young: "You mean on Pete O'Neal?"
> Shute: "I mean on anybody."
> Young: "No."
>
> (Trial transcript, 122–23)

This reply again constituted perjury. In her affidavit, FBI Agent Christian stated that Young had provided information to the FBI on violations that included human trafficking, theft of interstate shipments, fugitives, and bank robberies. All of these violations involve people. How could Jean Young ever have provided information to the FBI (for which she

was paid) on those crimes without providing information about somebody?

The cross-examination continued:

YOUNG: "Have I ever directly received money for any reason?"
THE JUDGE: "For information, I believe."
SHUTE: "Yes."
THE JUDGE: "Money from a law enforcement agency for informa-
tion, is that the question?"
SHUTE: "Yes, sir."
YOUNG: "*I have but I don't remember on what,* but it was not Pete
O'Neal" [*emphasis added*].

(Trial transcript, 122–23)

Young again perjured herself, this time by claiming that she could not
remember. How could she possibly forget all fourteen FBI payments
(one less than nineteen months before this testimony) for providing information on the serious crimes she had reported on? If she could not
remember these facts, how could she have remembered the details of a
conversation that she later testified took place in the first part of January 1969 (about nineteen months earlier) between Pete O'Neal and her
husband, Harold Young?

According to the affidavit provided by FBI Agent Christian, Jean
Young had received a payment from the FBI on February 6, 1969, and
she had provided information to the FBI concerning Pete O'Neal from
March 28, 1969, to August 27, 1970. In his *Very Special Agents* book, ATF
Agent James Moore wrote that Jean Young had come to him before the
O'Neal trial to tell him that she did not want to be a witness in it. Accord-
ing to Moore, Young told him, "the FBI agent told me that I can't be his
informer any more if I testify. *He'll stop paying me.*"[5] (emphasis added).

Moore admitted the above in his affidavit filed in 2001 responding to our
new petition: In his affidavit, Moore acknowledged that Young told him
that "the FBI would not pay her any more if she testified about O'Neal."
Indeed, during that very time period (from March 28, 1969, to August 27,
1970), Young was providing information on O'Neal to the FBI, and she
was concerned about being paid by the FBI for that information.

The following quotes from ATF Agent Moore's book, *Very Special
Agents,* show that James Moore was well aware that Jean Young was a
paid FBI informant:

[MOORE]: "The next morning an FBI Agent came to my office."

[FBI AGENT]: "We'd prefer you don't use the landlady [*Jean Young*] as a witness."

[MOORE]: "Puzzled, I asked, 'Why not?'"

[FBI AGENT]: "Well, *she's our informant* and we'd rather not have her exposed by testifying" [*emphasis added*]. [*The FBI Agent went on to explain that Young reported regularly to the FBI on the activities of Pete O'Neal and the Black Panther Party, who rented an apartment in her managed complex.*]

. . .

[MOORE]: "What's the goddamned point in paying informers and building files if you won't use the information to put the jerk away?"[6]

If the FBI was not paying or intending to pay Jean Young for providing information on Pete O'Neal, the FBI agent would have corrected Moore and denied that the FBI compensated or intended to compensate Young for information she provided about O'Neal. According to James Moore's account, however, the agent did not correct or deny; he instead accepted Moore's statement and persisted in trying to convince Moore not to call Young as a witness. He was intent on preserving Young as an FBI informant.[7]

Later in O'Neal's 1970 trial the government called Moore to testify. During Shute's cross-examination, Moore falsely denied that he *had ever heard* about Jean M. Young receiving money from a law enforcement agency for information. The following exchange occurred:

SHUTE: "Did you at any time, Mr. Moore, or anyone for you, or any law enforcement agency or individual that you are aware of, ever offer Mrs. Young any money to testify in this case?"

MOORE: "No."

. . .

SHUTE: "You understand I'm not directing that question necessarily to this case."

MOORE: "You said for testimony."

SHUTE: "Information, put it that way."

MOORE: "To my knowledge, not for information either."

SHUTE: "For anything?"

MOORE: *"For nothing except what was said here the other day was the first I had heard of it"* [*emphasis added*].

SHUTE: "And you were here when Mrs. Young testified."
MOORE: "Yes."

(Trial transcript, 180–81)

When ATF Agent Moore replied, "For nothing except what was said here the other day was the first I had heard of it," he was referring to Jean Young's testimony quoted above. Moore's reply constituted perjury. By Moore's own admission, Jean Young had come to him before the trial and told him "the FBI agent told me that I can't be his informer any more if I testify. *He'll stop paying me*" (emphasis added).[8] In his affidavit, Moore admitted that Jean Young told him that "the FBI would not pay her any more if she testified about O'Neal." Consequently, Jean Young's in-court testimony was *not* the first time Moore had heard of Jean Young being paid by a law enforcement agency for providing information. Jean Young had told Moore that she was getting paid by the FBI as an informant. Moore's testimony that he had not heard of this before the trial was simply a lie under oath: perjury.

The government attempted to present Jean Young to the court and jury as just an ordinary apartment manager who was testifying simply to do her duty as a good citizen. In reality, Jean Young was a person of many aliases with an arrest record. She may have even committed perjury when she identified herself in court under oath as Jean Young. She was also a longtime paid FBI informant. Rather than testifying against her interest, as the government maintained in its response, Jean Young had testified in her interest. Because she had been subpoenaed, she had to testify or suffer the legal consequences. In the process of testifying, she persistently lied to cover up her paid FBI informant status, probably with the hope of continuing to work for the FBI for payment in the future. And, in fact, according to the affidavit provided by FBI Agent Christian, Jean Young began receiving FBI payments again in 1983.

Revealing her paid FBI informant status would have negatively affected Jean Young's credibility in the eyes of the judge and the jury. Jean Young and Moore—the case agent who sat next to the prosecuting US attorney throughout the O'Neal trial—perjured themselves to cover up that essential information. The government's action in allowing perjury violated O'Neal's constitutional due process rights to a fair trial, according to the US Supreme Court:

The principle that a State may not knowingly use false evidence, including false testimony, to obtain a tainted conviction, implicit in any concept of ordered liberty, does not cease to apply merely because the false testimony goes only to the credibility of the witness. The jury's estimate of the truthfulness and reliability of a given witness may well be determinative of guilt or innocence, and it is upon such subtle factors as the possible interest of the witness in testifying falsely that a defendant's life or liberty may depend.[9]

The 1970 O'Neal trial resembles the 1972 trial of Black Panther Elmer Geronimo Pratt, who was also convicted on the basis of testimony by an unidentified government informant. In Pratt's 1972 trial, Julius Butler—a prosecution witness, who was also a paid government informant—testified that Pratt had confessed to him that he, Pratt, had committed the 1968 robbery-murder in Santa Monica, California, for which he was being tried. Neither Butler nor the prosecution revealed to Pratt's defense counsel or to the court that Butler had been serving as a paid informant who supplied information about the Black Panther Party to the Los Angeles Police Department, the FBI, and the Los Angeles District Attorney's Office. In that trial, Pratt, who had pleaded not guilty, was convicted of the murder-robbery. After Pratt had served twenty-seven years for these convictions and after numerous appeals, the California Superior Court finally agreed to consider his habeas corpus petition. When the court learned that the government had used a paid informant as a prosecution witness and had withheld knowledge of this witness's paid informant status from the judge and jury, it invalidated Pratt's 1972 conviction and granted him habeas corpus relief.

California Superior Court Judge Everett W. Dickey made clear that he invalidated Pratt's 1972 conviction because the prosecution failed to inform the defense that one of its material witnesses had been a police informant.[10] Judge Dickey explained that both the California Supreme Court (*In Re Ferguson*, 1971) and the US Supreme Court (*Giglio v. United States*, 1972) had held that, when the prosecution suppresses substantial material evidence that would be favorable to the accused—regardless of whether the prosecution does so intentionally and regardless of whether the accused has requested the evidence—the prosecution denies the accused a fair trial, and a resulting conviction must be reversed.[11] Judge Dickey also pointed out that the prosecution's duty to disclose includes "not only evidence which directly relates to the question of guilt, but also to the credibility of a material witness" whose testimony may affect the jury's decision of guilt or innocence.[12]

In the 1970 O'Neal trial, the government's failure to disclose Jean Young's role as a paid informant, and Agent Moore's perjury in claiming not to know Young was a paid informant, fulfilled both options: it concerned the credibility of a material witness whose testimony affected the determination of guilt or innocence, and it aided the government's case. Even more damning to the government's behavior, Judge Dickey went on to note that a prosecutor has a duty to learn of favorable evidence known to law enforcement agencies acting for the government, even if the prosecutor himself is unaware of that information.

In *Kyles v. Whitley* (1995), the Supreme Court held that the petitioner need not prove that the prosecutor was aware of materially important favorable evidence known to law enforcement agencies acting on the government's behalf to meet his burden of showing that the prosecution was at fault. In the O'Neal case, the FBI—a federal law enforcement agency—had information about Jean Young's paid informant status. It is undisputed that Jean Young, a material witness, told ATF Agent James Moore before the trial that she was being paid by the FBI for information. Moore had met with an FBI agent who acknowledged that Young was a paid FBI informant who was supplying the FBI with information about Pete O'Neal. In his affidavit, Moore admitted that he assumed Jean Young was being paid for information by the FBI. Moore acted on behalf of the prosecution in the 1970 O'Neal case. He arranged to have Young subpoenaed to testify. He testified himself and committed perjury when he said he had not previously heard about Jean Young being offered money by a law enforcement agency for information.

It is highly improbable that the government failed to check out Jean Young's legally ambiguous background to assess her credibility before using her as a witness in the O'Neal trial. If it did not check her background, the government, at best, was negligent. Even if the US Attorney's Office was ignorant of Jean Young's background and informer status it was, according to the US Supreme Court in *Kyles*, at fault for failing to discover and reveal to the defense facts about Jean Young (especially her FBI informant status) that reflected on her credibility as a witness and that were known to a law enforcement agency acting on the government's behalf in the trial. Consequently, the government rendered the trial unfair to the defendant, and a reversal is required under *Brady v. Maryland* (1963).

As Judge Dickey explained in the *Pratt* trial, *Brady* (1963) stands for the proposition that, even without a request from the defendant, either intentional or negligent suppression by the prosecution of substantial material evidence favorable to the accused denies the accused a fair trial and requires reversal. *Brady* also made clear that the duty on the part of the prosecution to disclose substantial material evidence favorable to an accused includes not only evidence which directly relates to the question of guilt, but also to the credibility of a material witness whose testimony may be determinative of guilt or innocence.

Judge Dickey further illuminated the logic of the *Brady* rule:

> In *Kyles v. Whitley* the United States Supreme Court recently said: "The individual prosecutor has a duty to learn of any favorable (Brady) evidence known to the others acting on the government's behalf in the case, including the police. But whether the prosecutor succeeds or fails in meeting this obligation (whether, that is, a failure to disclose is in good faith or bad faith)—the prosecution's responsibility for failing to disclose known, favorable evidence rising to a material level of importance is inescapable."
>
> . . .
>
> Since, then, the prosecutor has the means to discharge the government's *Brady* responsibility if he will, any argument for excusing a prosecutor from disclosing what he does not happen to know about boils down to a plea to substitute the police for the prosecutor, and even for the courts themselves, as the final arbiters of the government's obligation to ensure fair trials.
>
> . . .
>
> By failing to disclose to defense counsel the full facts known to law enforcement about [informant] Butler's activities, the prosecution was able to present him to the jury in a much more favorable light then would otherwise be the case.
>
> . . .
>
> Petitioner is not required to demonstrate that with the information about [*informant*] Butler which the prosecution should have disclosed he would more likely than not have been acquitted. He need only show that the cumulative impact of the evidence that should have been disclosed could reasonably be taken to put the whole case in such a different light as to undermine confidence in the verdict.
>
> . . .

The failure of the prosecution to disclose denied Petitioner [Pratt] the fair trial guaranteed by the United States Constitution by impairing defense counsel's ability to fully impeach the credibility of a key prosecution witness (*Kyles v. Whitley*, US Sup. Ct., 1995; *U.S. v. Bagley*, US Sup. Ct. 1985); *U.S. v. Steinberg* (1996); *U.S. v. Smith* (1971).

It is reasonably probable that Petitioner could have obtained a different result in the entire absence of [*informant*] Butler's testimony or had there not been a suppression by the prosecution of the evidence bearing on Butler's credibility to which Petitioner was entitled by the United States Constitution. Confidence in the verdict is undermined, and Petitioner is entitled to habeas corpus relief as requested.

The Government Witnesses' Perjured Testimony Is Grounds for Reversal.

In his response to our petition on behalf of O'Neal, the US attorney maintained that Jean Young's testimony was only "incidental to the case." (In contrast, in his response to our earlier petition, he had argued that Young's testimony was important.) He argued that the jury could have inferred that Pete O'Neal transported a shotgun which he purchased in Kansas to Missouri where he was reportedly photographed with it. However, such inference does not rise to the standard of criminal conviction—beyond a reasonable doubt. The jury had other testimony from which it could have inferred that Archie Weaver (not Pete O'Neal) transported the shotgun across the state line without Pete O'Neal aiding or abetting him. Or it could have inferred that Pete's then-wife, Tilly O'Neal, aided and abetted Weaver in transporting the gun across the state line.

At trial, Tilly O'Neal testified that Pete brought the shotgun home, in Kansas City, Kansas, in January 1969 for her protection. She testified that she was under the impression that he had just purchased it. Pete tried to show Tilly how to operate the shotgun, but could not get it to work. He then put the shotgun in a "little attic like thing, you slide back" in the home. Tilly testified that the shotgun was in the home "maybe about three or four days, something like that, maybe a week." Then Archie Weaver came to the house during Pete's absence. He asked if Tilly knew where Pete was or when he was coming home. Tilly replied "No" to both questions. Tilly testified that Weaver then asked: "Could I get that gun." Tilly testified that she gave Weaver the gun and he left with it. Weaver was subsequently arrested with the gun on February 5, 1969, in Kansas City, Missouri. There was no testimony or evidence that Pete O'Neal directed Weaver to get the gun or aided and abetted him in transporting it. There is no evidence that Pete O'Neal told Weaver about the gun. A number of other people could have informed Weaver.

The jury could have logically inferred from Tilly O'Neal's testimony that Archie Weaver transported the gun from Kansas to Missouri without Pete O'Neal's prior knowledge or help. Hence, reasonable doubt existed as to O'Neal's guilt. Given two equally probable sets of inferences, the government needed FBI informant and perjurer Jean Young's testimony to convict O'Neal. Jean Young testified that she saw and heard Pete O'Neal show her husband—Harold Young—a gun in their Kansas City, Missouri, apartment and supposedly say that he had purchased it in Kansas.

Contrary to the US attorney's claim, Jean Young's testimony was essential to the government's case. At the O'Neal trial the government admitted that it had no eyewitnesses to the gun-transportation charge against O'Neal, the only count of the indictment on which O'Neal was eventually convicted. The government had no direct evidence that Pete O'Neal aided or abetted anyone in the transportation of the gun across the state line.

In his closing statement to the jury, the US attorney alleged, through Jean Young's testimony, that Pete O'Neal admitted buying a gun in Kansas and transporting it to Missouri. Jury members obviously thought that Jean Young's testimony was important because they asked the judge to have it read back to them during their deliberations. The judge did, in fact, have Young's testimony read back to the jury. The jury then convicted O'Neal of the interstate gun-transportation count. Consequently, it is reasonable to conclude that Jean Young's testimony was material, even though it very well may have been false—as were parts of her other testimony.

In fact, in a sworn statement dated January 27, 1970, which we attached to our petition, Harold Young states, "On no occasion did I ever see Pete with a gun and never at any time did I hear him say either to my wife or myself that he had bought a gun in Kansas." Someone—either Harold Young or Jean Young—was lying.

In *Napue v. Illinois* (1959), the Supreme Court stated the following:

> It is of no consequence that the falsehood bore upon the witness' credibility rather than directly upon defendant's guilt. A lie is a lie, no matter what its subject, and, if it is in any way relevant to the case, the district attorney has the responsibility and duty to correct what he knows to be false and elicit the truth. . . . That the district attorney's silence was not the result of guile or a desire to prejudice matters little, for its impact was the same, preventing, as it did, a trial that could in any real sense be termed fair.[13]

We also offered *Giglio v. U.S.* (1972) to support our petition, but the US attorney maintained that *Giglio* could not be used as precedent because it followed O'Neal's 1970 trial. However, had the US attorney actually read *Giglio,* he would have learned that the decision reached there was based on legal principles previously articulated in numerous Supreme Court cases. In *Giglio* the court states that,

> As long ago as *Mooney v. Holohan* (1935), this Court made clear that deliberate deception of a court and jurors by the presentation of known false evidence is incompatible with "rudimentary demands of justice." This was reaffirmed in *Pyle v. Kansas* (1942). In *Napue v. Illinois* (1959), we said, "the same result obtains when the State, although not soliciting false evidence, allows it to go uncorrected when it appears." *Id.*, at 269. Thereafter *Brady v. Maryland* (1963) held that suppression of material evidence justifies a new trial "irrespective of the good faith or bad faith of the prosecution." *Napue v. Illinois* (1959).

Fugitive Disentitlement Doctrine Is Not Justified

We repeated the extensive evidence supporting our earlier argument that the fugitive disentitlement doctrine should not be invoked because Pete O'Neal fled the United States to save himself from threats on his life from both local police and the FBI. We added an affidavit by William Whitfield, a Christian missionary and formerly a civil rights associate of Pete O'Neal in 1969–70, stating that he witnessed police make threats against Pete O'Neal's life.

The Government Mischaracterizes Pete O'Neal

In his response, the US attorney attempted to convince the court that O'Neal was a violent person by quoting some selected general statements concerning the Black Panther Party. However, none of the quoted statements referred to Pete O'Neal or to the Black Panther Party of Kansas City. To characterize anyone as a violent criminal simply because he or she was a member of the Black Panther Party is erroneous and unfair. Many former Black Panthers are outstanding US citizens. For example, former Black Panther Bobby Rush has served in the US Congress as a representative from Illinois. Former Black Panther Kathleen Cleaver (wife of Eldridge Cleaver) completed a law degree at Yale. She then clerked for a federal appellate judge before joining the Emory University law faculty in 1992.

In contrast to the US attorney's misapplication of general statements to O'Neal, several statements made specifically about O'Neal show that, despite his rhetoric, he was a moderate activist who aggressively worked nonviolently for the civil rights of African Americans. Former Kansas City Police Chief Clarence Kelley maintained that Pete O'Neal prevented violence and was "exuberant about the possibility of doing some great things. . . . [The Kansas City Black Panthers] used a lot of language, boasts, and a lot of promises, but there weren't any real bad situations."[14]

In March of 1970 then–US Congressman Richard Ichord of Missouri announced that the House Internal Security Committee, which he chaired, would hold hearings on the Black Panther Party, beginning with the Kansas City Chapter because "the lack of violence here in Kansas City [is] atypical."[15] The news article went on to say that the Kansas City Black Panther Party's lack of violence could be attributed to "the positive influence brought to bear through the ministry of the Methodist leadership of men like Phil Lawson and John Preciphs." Pete O'Neal worked closely with these gentlemen of the church and conducted a free breakfast program for underprivileged inner-city youths in a ministry building.

Prior to submitting this new petition, about four hundred citizens from Kansas City, Missouri, and Kansas City, Kansas, signed a petition asking the government not to oppose the court's consideration of O'Neal's petition on its merits. Would they have done so if they thought O'Neal was a violent criminal? Many of them knew Pete O'Neal and regarded him a good person who put his life on the line to fight discrimination and inequality back in the 1960s.

Conclusion

Pete O'Neal's 1970 trial had serious constitutional defects, including perjured testimony by key prosecution witnesses, the failure of the government to inform the defense that one of its material witnesses was a paid FBI informant, the judge's misapplication of the law, the FBI illegal wiretaps (the fruits of which the judge failed to turn over to the defense), and the insufficiency of evidence. Consequently, O'Neal's trial was neither fair nor just. Given that O'Neal was convicted and sentenced illegally in violation of his Fourth Amendment right and his Fifth Amendment right to due process, and given the other extralegal circumstances surrounding and impinging on his trial, we asked the judge to issue a writ of coram nobis and vacate O'Neal's conviction and order a new trial.

O'Neal had no post-conviction remedies other than the coram nobis petition. Given the case's historic context, irregularities, and related facts, a denial of this petition would amount to a denial of justice. In his affidavit, which we attached to the petition, Pete O'Neal stated: "I would be happy to return to the U.S. for a new trial, if the Court would consider my case on its merits, and not on the bases of the prejudices, COINTELPRO dirty tricks, and perjured testimony by the prosecution that determined the outcome of my first trial." All that O'Neal was asking for is the kind of basic justice that is owed to every American, the kind of basic justice that he was denied in 1970.

The US attorney argued that the judge should invoke the disentitlement doctrine and not spend the court's resources on this case. Such a course would shield the government from facing the consequences of having offered perjured testimony and hidden the FBI informant status of its material witness in order to convict Pete O'Neal. We asked the court not to invoke the disentitlement doctrine in the name of judicial economy and thereby deny justice for Pete O'Neal. We also asked the Court to vacate O'Neal's 1970 conviction and order a new trial on the merits.

13
Justice Denied

On July 24, 2001, Judge G. Thomas Van Bebber issued his order denying our latest petition for a new trial and the vacating of O'Neal's 1970 conviction. He based his decision on the discretionary, judge-made disentitlement doctrine. Judge Van Bebber quoted Judge O'Connor's statement in his earlier denial: "A fugitive should not be able to benefit by a positive adjudication of his claims without submitting himself to the risks of an unfavorable decision." However, Pete had sworn in his affidavit that he would return to the United States for a new trial. Consequently, he would be submitting himself to the risks of an unfavorable decision; Judge Van Bebber's reasoning was spurious.

Judge Van Bebber also quoted from the case of Smith v. United States (1876): "It is clearly within our discretion to refuse to hear a criminal case in error, unless the convicted party suing out the writ, is where he can be made to respond to any judgment we may render." This was another inapplicable statement, because Pete would be in the United States, "where he [could have been] made to respond to any judgment."

But it was Van Bebber's quote from the Molinaro case that was the most revealing: "In Molinaro, the Supreme Court explained: ' . . . While such an escape [by a convicted defendant] does not strip the case of its character as an adjudicable case or controversy, we believe it disentitles the defendant to call upon the *resources* of the Court for determination of his claims'"[1] [*emphasis added*]. Neither in this quote nor in any other quotes or statements made by Judges O'Connor or Van Bebber in their denial motions does the word *justice* appear. Apparently, for them the rationing of court *resources* is more important than justice.

Dignity of the Court

Judge O'Connor's justification for denying O'Neal's petition and invoking the disentitlement doctrine was that it "advances several important principles of the judicial system including deterring escapes and maintaining the dignity and efficiency of the judicial system." There is no mention of justice or of the dignity of the unfairly tried American citizen, who has had to flee the country to avoid police and FBI threats. By his flight Pete did not insult the dignity of the judicial system.

There was no dignity in Pete's trial. The presiding judge failed to competently interpret federal and California state law. He cited clearly outmoded, irrelevant California cases; ignored pertinent US Supreme Court cases; and suspiciously omitted a key, qualifying sentence in his quotation of the California penal code. As a matter of law, Pete should not have been indicted under the Gun Control Act of 1968.

The judge also ignored key Supreme Court decisions stressing the necessity of obtaining a judicial warrant before the FBI invades a citizen's privacy. Instead he endorsed the FBI's illegal wiretap of O'Neal's telephone, privately screened the FBI's illegally obtained surveillance information, and failed to turn that information over to the defense—all in clear violation of Supreme Court precedent. Instead, Judge Stanley sent the information to the attorney general, the very party responsible for violating Pete O'Neal's Fourth Amendment constitutional right.

The prosecution also violated Pete's constitutional right to a fair trial by putting on two witnesses who perjured themselves. One witness, who identified herself as Jean Young, had a criminal record, used as many as seven different surnames, and was a longtime paid FBI informant. None of this was revealed to the judge and jury, as it should have been. The ATF agent in charge of the case, who knew or should have known of Jean Young's paid informant status and shady background, failed in his legal duty to reveal that information to the judge and jury. Both committed perjury when testifying.

That perjury should have resulted in O'Neal's release under our coram nobis petition. In 1997, California Superior Court Judge Everett W. Dickey explained that he invalidated Black Panther Geronimo Pratt's 1972 murder conviction because the prosecution had failed to inform the defense that one of its material witnesses was a police informant. At the time of O'Neal's trial, *Brady v. Maryland* (1963) was well-settled law; it required the prosecutor to find and reveal any material evidence favorable to O'Neal. O'Neal's prosecutor, in contrast, failed to reveal the informant status of Jean Young. This failure was illegal under *Brady*. It denied O'Neal a fair trial and made a mockery of the final judgment. The judge's and the US attorney's claim that Pete could have litigated all of his claims on appeal in 1970 is false. Because Pete's defense became aware of Young's and ATF Agent Moore's perjury after the publication of Moore's 1997 memoir, *Very Special Agents,* the perjury claim could not have been litigated in 1970.

At the sentencing hearing in 1970, Judge Stanley may have openly revealed his bias against O'Neal with his enraged outburst accusing him (without a shred of evidence) of being responsible for placing stickers on the American flag in the witness waiting room. He also threatened to negatively influence Pete's appeal by sending a letter to the circuit (appeals) court containing his unfounded allegation.

The Disentitlement Doctrine as Cover-up

By invoking the disentitlement doctrine and declining to consider the merits of our petitions, the judges found an excuse to ignore the many egregious defects and constitutional violations committed by both judge and prosecution in O'Neal's trial. Pete was simply asking for a fair trial, one he manifestly did not receive in 1970. He swore in an affidavit in 2001 that he would return to the United States to face his accuser. If the judges and prosecutors were primarily concerned about justice, and if they really believed Pete would be found guilty in a fair trial, then the judges only needed to set a date for the trial and make it contingent on Pete's appearance in court thirty days prior. Then their excuse of Pete not being present for a negative judgment would vanish.

The denial of Pete's 1998 petition by Judge O'Connor may have been to protect the reputation of his colleague and friend Judge Stanley, who was still alive at the time. Judge Van Bebber, who succeeded Judge O'Connor as chief judge, may have denied O'Neal's second petition for a similar reason, as it contained devastating evidence of prosecutorially tolerated perjury.

By refusing to examine the merits of Pete's petition, Judges O'Connor and Van Bebber condemned Pete to a life in exile. That is his punishment for fleeing threats from racist policemen after a defective trial that sentenced him to the very prison environment in which the racist policemen's threats could be carried out. Who punished Judge Stanley for ensuring Pete would be tried under misrepresented federal and California law and mishandling FBI illegal wiretaps of Pete's telephone? Who punished the prosecutor and Moore for promoting perjured testimony and not revealing Jean Young's paid informant status and shady background? They, not Pete O'Neal, insulted the American judicial system.

Judges O'Connor and Van Bebber used their discretion to endorse the judicial irregularities and constitutional violations evidenced in Pete's 1970 trial. Invoking the disentitlement doctrine required much less work than seriously examining the petition's merits. The judges efficiently preserved judicial resources.

Ironically, upon entering the Robert J. Dole Federal Courthouse in Kansas City, Kansas, citizens are greeted with the following assuring words by the late Judge Learned Hand: "If we are to keep our democracy, there must be one commandment: Thou Shalt Not Ration Justice." This quotation was chosen by Judge Earl O'Connor.

The disentitlement doctrine is not and should not be automatically invoked. Judges should apply it on a case-by-case basis. When one has credible reasons for leaving a court's jurisdiction and *prima facie* evidence of judicial and prosecutorial irregularities amounting to constitutional law violations, then a reviewing judge is remiss not to examine the fugitive's petition on its merits. Automatic dismissal of a fugitive's appeal "may rest on nothing more than the faulty premise that any act of judicial defiance, whether or not it affects the appellate process, is punishable by appellate dismissal" (*Molinaro v. New Jersey*, 1970). As US Supreme Court Justice Potter Stewart noted in his dissenting opinion in *Estelle v. Dorrough* (1975), "If an escaped felon has been convicted in violation of law, the loss of his right to appeal results in his serving a sentence that under law was erroneously imposed."

As a black civil rights leader and member of the Black Panther Party, Pete was disliked, even hated, by some members of law enforcement. The animus toward Pete was revealed in his 1970 trial and even more recently in the US attorney's responses to Pete's petitions. Most appropriate to Pete's case is Supreme Court Justice Frank Murphy's eloquent statement in *Eisler v. United States* (1949): "Law is at its loftiest when it examines claimed injustice even at the instance of one to whom the public is bitterly hostile."

Pete's Reaction

I notified Pete of Judge Van Bebber's decision. Pete sent me the following email in response.

Date: Fri, 23 Aug 2002
Subject: Re: bad news
Brother Paul, Shikamoo. . . . .

Wow! I have been traveling with Geronimo and Joju Cleaver and was really surprised to find your messages waiting for me. I really expected a different outcome. I could not agree more that we have "fought the good Fight." Particularly you. You have invested a great deal of time and effort and a considerable amount of money in this struggle. Something for which I will always be grateful! For my part, I am more determined than ever to continue the battle. At this point in my life the possibility of my returning to the US has very little appeal for me. I feel that I have created a full and productive life for myself here and I am content. I am however determined to continue my opposition (through the courts) against something I know was not only wrong but illegal. I hope that you are in a position to continue with me, but if not, I will certainly understand. I suppose the circuit court is the route I must follow now. I have not heard from Ramsey Clark but will make every effort to contact him and will give you an update as soon as I know something.

Paul, knowing you and having you for a real friend has reinforced for me the belief that we can indeed build a truly egalitarian society that transcends race, class and nationality. I will never forget what you have taught me through your practice. Let me know your thoughts.

Take care and stay well. . . . . Pete

After conducting research and consulting with colleagues, I concluded that an appeal would be fruitless. I found no case where a federal appellate court had overruled a lower court's invocation of the fugitive disentitlement doctrine. Former US Attorney General Ramsay Clark, who had been briefly in Arusha at the UN Criminal Tribunal for Rwanda, had met with Pete and expressed interest in his case. However, he never offered any concrete help.

PART III

14

The Shakur Proposal

Probably the most famous living American female fugitive is Assata Shakur. A plethora of books, articles, films, songs, and poems have been written about her.[1] Assata Shakur (born JoAnne Deborah Byron in 1947) has been a fugitive living in Cuba since 1984. In the 1960s, she attended City College of New York, where she met and married Louis Chesimard, a fellow student-activist. After divorce and graduation, she briefly joined the Black Panther Party and adopted the name Assata Shakur. Next, she joined the Black Liberation Party (BLP), an offshoot of the BPP devoted to violent revolution against racism, capitalism, and imperialism. She and other BLP members were arrested after a shoot-out on the New Jersey Turnpike in 1973 during which Trooper Werner Foerster was killed with his own gun. Shakur had gunshot wounds in both arms and a shoulder. In a controversial trial, Shakur was convicted of murder and related charges. The prosecution had only to prove that Shakur was an accomplice to murder, not that she fired the shots that killed Trooper Foerster. She was sentenced to life in prison.

On November 2, 1979, three members of the BLP helped Shakur escape from New Jersey's Clinton Correctional Facility for Women. She went into hiding for five years and then surfaced in Cuba, where Fidel Castro granted her political asylum. In 2013 Shakur became the first woman to be placed on the FBI's list of most wanted terrorists. The reward for her capture and return stands at $2 million.[2]

In 2014 US President Barack Obama and Cuban President Raúl Castro agreed to a process of normalizing relations between their two countries.

Three years later, Donald Trump cancelled the so-called Cuban Thaw and demanded that Cuba extradite all American fugitives there, especially "the cop-killer Jo Anne Chesimard."[3]

During the 1960s and 1970s, the FBI, through its COINTELPRO operation, had bribed informants, agent provocateurs, and conspirators to assist the bureau in its efforts to destroy the Black Panther Party. In 2014 an attempt was made to bribe Pete O'Neal.

FBI Attempt to Bribe O'Neal

Paul Magnarella's email to Pete O'Neal, March 4, 2014:

> Marahaba Brother Pete,
>
> Hope you, Sister Charlotte, members of the UAACC, and the children are all well. I have some interesting news to convey to you.
> A few days ago the Federal Prosecutor, with whom I had locked horns back in the late 1990s, called my office and left a message on the answering machine, asking me to call him back. I did so, and we conversed.
>
> He told me that he had been contacted by New Jersey law enforcement wanting to know if you would be willing to help with the arrest of a fugitive. The fugitive is Assata Shakur. She had been convicted of murdering a NJ State Trooper and subsequently fled to Cuba. He said if you helped, your sentence "would be looked at."
> I pressed him on this point, and he said that his office would file a motion asking that your sentence be reduced, potentially to zero years. He also said there is a $2 million reward for the arrest of Shakur.
>
> I asked what you would be expected to do, since Shakur is in Cuba. He explained that because US-Cuban relations may normalize, fugitives there might be planning to leave. He said if you invited her to visit you in Tanzania and called authorities once she was there, then she could be arrested. Tanzania and the US have an extradition treaty covering major offenses, like murder.
> I agreed to convey this information to you, and your reply to him.
> I look forward to hearing from you.
> Brother Paul

Reply from Pete O'Neal to Paul J. Magnarella, March 6, 2014:

Warm greetings Mzee Paul and Shikamoo!

I hope this message finds you well!

Man, Talk about a bombshell!! I cannot for the life of me figure why they would approach me with a crazy proposition like that!! My answer is NO, absolutely NOT, irrevocably NO, in this life or the next, if such a thing exists. . . . . . NO!!! I will not in any way aid and abet their efforts to entrap Ms. Shakur. I am offended that they could entertain making that proposal to me.

The mentioning of a two million dollar reward is a ridiculous insult. Anyone that knows me is aware that in my past I have done things that I profoundly regret, things that cause me on occasion to wake at 2 AM filled with remorse for deeds that cannot be erased or undone. You will not however, find among those misdeeds an instance where I betrayed a compatriot, not one! That I have never done, and I do not intend to start now. Reflecting on this "proposal" I'm beginning to wonder if all is not as it initially appears. They SAY they want Ms. Shakur to respond to an invitation from me, someone she has never met, and based only on that invitation come to Tanzania. I doubt that she would be that foolish.

I have absolutely no intentions of colluding with them on anything!!! Tell them in the strongest terms that I am not interested in their proposals now or ever!!! What I can state categorically is I will not be their Judas or a pawn in their Machiavellian machinations! Paul, I thank you for your continued support. I know that as my legal representative you are morally obligated to inform me of any and all developments such as this. I am grateful, but I would like to think that you knew before hand what my response would be! Keep well and be blessed, Pete

15
Life Then and Now

In 1972, Pete and Charlotte O'Neal migrated to Tanzania, eventually settling in the WaMeru tribe's homeland, about eighteen miles outside of Arusha and sixty miles from Mount Kilimanjaro. They built their home in the wilderness, over two miles from an all-weather road. When the O'Neals first arrived at their present home site in Imbaseni Village, it was wild bush without access to electricity or water. They had to contend with wild animals, including snakes and malaria mosquitoes. They became African American pioneers in their ancestral homeland, learning about windmills, farming, raising livestock, and appropriate technology. The O'Neals made bricks to build their home, installed over a mile of poles and wire to bring electricity, and laid over a mile of pipe for water.

In 1991, as a continuation of the Black Panther–inspired community programs, the O'Neals founded the United African American Community Center (UAACC), a nonprofit NGO with programs designed to enrich the Arusha area community, both urban and rural, and to promote closer cultural ties with the United States. They later changed its name to United African Alliance Community Center[1] to reflect its wider international focus. Through the UAACC the O'Neals organized free workshops and classes dealing with health and nutrition, conservation, AIDS education, writing, art appreciation, crafts, history, and computer skills to well over one hundred Tanzanian youths annually. The center also facilitates the involvement of international volunteers in its many educational and health programs. The O'Neals established a student-exchange program

with De LaSalle Academy in Kansas City as well as a Sister City relationship between Arusha and Kansas City. Supporters of this Sister City program, friends and contacts of the O'Neals have donated needed medical
supplies and equipment (including two cardiac defibrillators) to Arusha
hospitals. Pete arranged for the defibrillators by contacting Dr. Gary
Morsch, president and founder of Heart to Heart, an American organization that supplies donated medicines and equipment, often through
emergency airlifts, to countries in crisis around the world.

My Arrival

On a dark, rainy night in May of 1997, my KLM flight from Amsterdam
landed at the Mount Kilimanjaro Airport, 52 kilometers (32.3 miles) from
Arusha, Tanzania. Charlotte O'Neal had arranged for her husband, Pete,
to meet me. After a protracted effort to locate my suitcase among the
many that had been scattered across the floor in the dimly lit termi-
nal, I exited the luggage area to find Pete and Sterling Hill (Charlotte's
father) patiently waiting for me. After greetings and introductions, we
boarded Pete's aging Isuzu and traveled slowly and carefully along a
two-lane hard-surface road to Majiachai Village. From there, we turned
onto a two-mile, muddy, pothole-adorned road that eventually would
take us to the O'Neal homestead. Along the way we passed a number of
dark shacks that served as homes for some MaMeru people. I jokingly
asked if a stream gushing across the road was the local Usa River. "No,"
Pete laughingly replied, "that's just rain water." When we arrived at the
O'Neal home, I was amazed to find a fine structure with electricity, running water, glass windows, shower and toilet, interior walls paneled with
banana-tree wood, and a solid roof. I felt like I had arrived at a haven in a
bleak jungle. Charlotte's warm welcome coupled with her prepared meal
put me completely at ease.

The next morning the O'Neal compound of five buildings came alive
as Tanzanian girls and boys arrived. Some went to work in the kitchen
to learn food preparation with Charlotte; others joined Pete and Christopher (Pete's "Tanzanian son") to work on construction and maintenance
projects. At some points during the day, all attended art, crafts, and English classes taught by Charlotte and volunteers.

My second day I adjusted to the new time zone and got some exercise
pushing the Isuzu out of a muddy ditch. That night Pete explained that

he earned some income by making and selling mustard to safari outfitters in Arusha. However, his blender stopped working and he needed to find a small part to repair it. So he handed me a flashlight and a thick stick (to fight off the snakes) and off we went into the dark night to hunt for a blender part in a storage shed on his property. Somehow we discovered the tiny part in one of the shed's many boxes containing large assortments of odds and ends. "It was like finding a needle in a haystack!" Pete exclaimed.

I soon learned that, despite his many years in the remote bush, Pete was computer savvy. When he got his first computer, he immediately opened it, examined its insides, and concluded that he understood how it operated. Soon the overworked and sole computer technician in Arusha was hiring Pete to deal with some of his clients' smaller repair jobs. Pete loves electronics. If he ever got back to the States, he told me, he would immediately go to a Radio Shack to examine all of its products.

At this point, his father and mother were still alive and they along with his and Charlotte's two adult children were living in Kansas City. Although the community work Pete and Charlotte were doing in Tanzania was socially and spiritually fulfilling, Pete occasionally revealed a reserved desire to return to his native home. He asked me about the American home-mortgage system, national politics, and race relations.

The UAACC's Expanded Mission

The UAACC has established linkages with several study-abroad programs in the United States, including the School for International Training in Brattleboro, Vermont; the State University of New York at Stony Brook; Bridgewater State University in Massachusetts; and the University of Oregon in Eugene. Students from these institutions lodge at the O'Neal compound for a week or two and experience Tanzania through cultural and educational programs, including village and museum visits, safari trips, and mountain climbing arranged by Pete and Charlotte. Some of these visiting American students return to the O'Neal compound as volunteer teachers.

During a week in April 1999, Pete, Charlotte, and crew took a large group of students from the Tanzanian branch of the School for International Training on safari to the world-famous Serengeti Plains and to Ngorongoro Crater. Pete had been asked to manage the operational activities of the safari and, despite all the work and time that involved, he managed to keep a journal of the unique experiences. Here is one excerpt from his fascinating journal.

1:00 a.m. Friday Morning, Ngorongoro Crater, Simba campsite

Charlotte's asleep and the students are in their tents. I am typing by flashlight and thinking how blessed we are to live a life that has not lost its excitement and sense of adventure. Living as we do, in a developing country, we don't enjoy the economic and social security that many in the West have, but our lives are refreshed each day as we confront the challenges and newness of our pioneer-like existence.

We're camping at Ngorongoro for the night. This place is awesome! We're right on the rim of the vastly huge Crater that many consider the "eighth wonder of the world." Ngorongoro is a 20-mile diameter crater that is the result of the ancient implosion of a huge mountain that was much higher than Mount Kilimanjaro. The Crater developed into a complete eco-system that supports varied forms of wildlife including large numbers of prey and predators. As I type I can hear the roar of a pride of lions in the distance. Last night a hyena came into camp right up to the kitchen tent, grabbed a 50 pound sack of potatoes and proceeded to drag it into the bush. Christopher raised the alarm and the animal abandoned its booty and scampered off angrily into the night.

I heard the roar of a lion in the not far distance and put my hand on Charlotte's arm to waken her when I heard the answering roar of a male lion right outside our camp. I'm talking 30 feet from our tent!! I have never heard anything like that in my life! The sheer volume of his roar was unbelievable! Our entire camp was instantly still and became one fearful, cautious entity. I am sure we were collectively experiencing the response of a herd of prey to the presence of marauding predators. Not a sound came from any tent. We could hear the regal and graceful movement of the beast as he moved through our camp. Totally unafraid, it roared again as if to say, "Yes I'm here, and if anyone has a problem with that come forward!!" Needless to say, no one moved. Charlotte and I flattened ourselves on our mattresses when we saw its huge, lantern cast silhouette fall on our tent as it moved silently through the grass behind us. After a few minutes of inspecting our camp he apparently gave it his royal approval, and with one last ear-shattering roar he slipped back into

238   Black Panther in Exile

the bush and back into the night. You could "feel" the collective sigh of relief from those in our camp. Their excited, muted voices indicated that they were preparing the stories they would tell once they returned home.

The UAACC and the Kuji Foundation, created by Geronimo Ji Jaga Pratt, hired a South African company to drill a very deep well for the village community. Now village women no longer have to walk long distances carrying water jugs on their heads for their basic family needs. Geronimo's Kuji foundation also donated a "spirit of the panther" ambulance truck to the UAACC, which is used to transport ill or injured villagers to hospital for treatment. In 2008, with support from the Kuji Foundation, the center trained several young, mixed-gender Tanzanian teams to install solar panels in eighty-five village homes that had no electricity.

Pete was overjoyed to be reunited with his old friend and fellow Panther Geronimo Ji Jaga Pratt. On August 22, 2003 Pete sent me the following email.

Hello big Brother Paul and Shikamoo!
All is well here. Our work and Center has grown a great deal. Our computer classes, English and empowerment through the arts classes now have a combined student body of over 200! I surely must have told you about Geronimo coming out here and donating money for us to dig a water borehole and how his organization (the Kuji Foundation) and UAACC joined forces to start a village water supply project and we are continuing to collaborate on HIV/AIDS and other relevant efforts. Geronimo and his wife the former Joju Cleaver (Eldridge and Kathleen's daughter) moved to Arusha and their Son Kayode (to whom Charlotte and I are Godparents) burst into the world on the 17th of Feb. and has his parents overwhelmed with joy and pride!!! I'll send you some photos!
At present they are in the US securing medical supplies for donations we want to make to Arusha later this year. Geronimo is returning here the middle of next month with Johnnie Cochran.[2] We are planning to organize a day climb of Kili [*Mount Kilimanjaro*] and other activities for him. I have no idea if he will express an interest in my legal situation or not (Geronimo seems to think he will) but if he does I was thinking of suggesting that he contact you if that's alright.

Charlotte and I continue to prosper and to feel blessed with our lot in life. Once again I want to thank you from the bottom of my heart for all the kindness you have shown us and all the effort you made on our behalf. Stay well. . . . . Pete

I would have been more than happy to work with Johnnie Cochran. However, he never contacted me, and my attempts to contact him were unsuccessful. Cochran died on March 29, 2005, less than two years after the above email.

Through time, the O'Neals built a computer lab, music studio, radio station, classrooms, dormitories for overseas visitors, a basketball court, a vegetable garden, and a corral for their pet horse, Bullet. The walls around the compound are adorned with brightly colored murals with civil rights and African animal themes.

In 2008 the O'Neals added the Leaders of Tomorrow Children's Home to their compound. They admitted over twenty young children, some being orphans, others from families too poor to raise them. In every case, the child's parent or relatives pleaded with Pete to accept their child. The center provides the children (free of charge) with housing, clothing, meals, education, health care, and a warm extended family environment. The children attend local schools and have private tutoring on a daily basis. Mwajabu Sadiki Sikukuu, a local woman who has been with the O'Neals since she was fifteen, directs the school and cares for the children as would a loving mother. "I learned everything here," Sadiki says, "how to speak English, clothing design, sewing, computers, even yoga. Now I teach it all to the children." Nine years after the program's inception, the children have shown exceptional scholastic achievement, with many finishing at the head of their classes. Some have been offered internships with local businesses.

On October 10, 2017, Pete sent me the following email:

Warm greetings Brother Paul and Shikamoo!
We are all well here, my kids from our "Leaders of Tomorrow Children's Home" have somehow morphed into young teenagers and as a father you know that is a totally different ball game! They are all healthy and happy and I'm completely enjoying being a fussy but doting grandfather! I have raised these 21 children for almost 10 years and for me it has been a labor of love!

Just last night I received a message from a supporter in New York stating that she is sending 4 sewing machines to my son Malcolm in KC. Charlotte is there for a short visit on her way to Venezuela to attend an Eco-socialism conference and when she and her 90 year old father, Sterling, return next month they will move heaven and hell to bring the sewing machines with them!

In December 2017 Pete wrote: "We will be inaugurating the ONE WORLD VOCATIONAL TRAINING WORKSHOP building which will be the site of Electric & Electronic Workshop: Sewing & Tailoring Workshop and Woodworking & Cabinet Making Workshops! Wow! We also have a newly built pizza and bread oven; a pizza chef volunteered to teach our kids the fine art of cooking in a brick, wood fired oven."

The Emergence of Charlotte

Charlotte Hill O'Neal, also known as Mama C, has become an international celebrity, spreading her message of peace, love, and African culture around the world. Having no outstanding warrants against her, she can travel freely to the United States and internationally. Along with being codirector of UAACC, she is a visual and spoken-word artist, musician, and filmmaker. Back during her teen years, Kansas City's famous jazz, blues, and gospel music touched Charlotte deeply. She explained, "When in Kansas City, I always visit Strangers Rest Baptist Church, the foundation of my spiritual path that has led me to the exploration of our African traditional religions. I love seeing the elders that I've known since I was a baby and getting filled with the spirit from the voices of the choir." Charlotte showed me an old photograph. "This is me at 18 years old in my West African lace gown and real stick earrings and sandals and close cut natural . . . my outfit for the prom! I was the only one at the prom dressed in traditional African clothes in 1969 at Wyandotte High School in Kansas City, Kansas. Wow! That was a while ago." Charlotte now integrates elements of those influences into her music, the rhythm of her poetry combined with African beats and the vibe of her own spirit.

Charlotte's artwork has been featured in art books and magazines, galleries, museums, and traveling exhibitions. For about twenty years she has been making guest presentations in Africa, Asia, and South America and at colleges and universities across the United States during Black

History Month (February) and International Women's Month (March). She speaks about the UAACC's Heal the Community Program and the Leaders of Tomorrow Children's Home. She describes the life that she and Pete have built in Tanzania during their more than four decades of exile. Charlotte's appearances often include the screening of two documentary films: *Panther in Africa*, about the life of Pete O'Neal, and *Mama C: Urban Warrior in the African Bush*, which depicts Charlotte's years as an artist activist. The 2004 documentary *Panther* by Aaron Mathews was selected as best documentary at the St. Louis International Film Festival and winner of the Cine Golden Eagle Award. The film *Mama C* by Joanne Hershfield premiered at the 2013 Pan African Film and Arts Festival in Los Angeles.

Charlotte also offers readings from her poetry books: *Warrior Woman of Peace* (2008) and *Life Slices . . . a Taste of My Heaven* (2013). In these she explores the reality of her existence as a Diaspora-born African who has lived most of her years in Tanzania. Charlotte can be seen reading one of her famous poems, "I Almost Lost Myself," on YouTube.[3] She performed several of her poems during the 2010 Poetry Africa Tour which took her to Cape Town, South Africa; Harare, Zimbabwe; and Blantyre, Malawi. She also participated in the Fourteenth Annual Poetry Africa Festival sponsored by the Creative Arts Center at the University of KwaZulu-Natal.

As a musician, Charlotte performs on two of tribal Kenya's traditional eight-string lyres: the *obokano*, played by the Gusii people, and the *Nyatiti*, unique to the Luo. With the Peace Power Productions studio at UAACC she created *nyatiti/obokano*, a musical album featuring these two instruments.

The following description of Charlotte's appearance at Laney College in Oakland, California, is typical of the enthusiastic reception she receives on tour:

> On Wednesday, Feb.13, 2013, for over three hours, the Laney College Forum rang with the sounds that only an evening spent with artist, musician, activist Charlotte Hill O'Neal, affectionately known as "Mama C," could produce: the sounds of love, laughter, awe and welcome of a community embracing one of its own. And the next day, on Feb. 14, the CSU Diversity Center in conjunction with the CSU Ethnic Studies and History Departments proudly presented "An afternoon with Charlotte Hill O'Neal."

"Mama C" is poet, musician, visual and spoken-word artist, African woman of the world. She is touring the world in her annual UAACC Heal the Community Tour and debuting her new documentary about her life, "Mama C: Urban Spirit in the African Bush."[4]

Recognitions

Pete and Charlotte's community work has been widely recognized, as evidenced by the many plaques adorning the walls of their home. Some of the more significant ones are:

- The "Malcolm X Recognition Award to Pete O'Neal for Outstanding Commitment and Service to African People," presented by the Kansas City Black United Front, May 21, 1993.
- "Certificate of Appreciation to Pete O'Neal for developing the Heal the Community Foundation in recognition of your dedication and commitment to the quality of life in Kansas City, Missouri," presented by Mayor Emanuel Cleaver II,[5] July 1996.
- The "People's Lifetime Commitment Award to Black Panther Party Freedom Fighters Pete O'Neal and Charlotte 'Mama C' O'Neal for your enormous example of commitment to the cause of Black Liberation and Revolution and for the enduring challenge of exile!" Presented by the People's Organization for Progress,[6] September 29, 2016.
- Certificate of Appreciation to Mama Charlotte O'Neal, presented by the African Student Association of Indiana University, September 19, 2006.
- The Bob Marley Peace Award to "Charlotte 'Mama C' O'Neal and Pete O'Neal, Panthers in Africa." Presented by the World Beat Center, April 4, 2017.
- On African Liberation Day 2017, the All-African People's Revolutionary Party[7] presented the Daughters of Africa Award to Charlotte Mama C. O'Neal. The beautiful award was constructed by the Ras Mzizi's collective of artists from bark cloth and beads and framed with dhow wood. It was presented by the international women's wing of the party.
- The Black Panther Party Alumni's Legacy Award presented to Pete O'Neal "for exemplary community spirit and excellence as a role model for youth." Awarded during the Black Panther Legacy Celebration in Kansas City, October 2014, in conjunction with Bobby Seale's eightieth birthday party.

Charlotte and Pete are proud of all of these recognitions, but especially of the last one. Mama C sent me the following message: "What an honor to have received on behalf of Brother Pete O'Neal, the UAACC Family and the KC BPP Chapter the Black Panther Party Legacy Award at the Bobby Seale 80th Birthday Party with Sister Kathleen Cleaver; Congresswoman Sister Barbara Lee; Brother Chairman Bobby Seale and Brother Omar Barbour in attendance. Receiving this Award from my Panther comrades was one of the highlights of the BPP 50th Anniversary celebrations for me and spurs me on to keep doing what we do . . . Service . . . spreading love and inspiration."

A number of internationally known personalities have visited the O'Neals at their home in Imbaseni Village. Among them are the actors Sean Penn and Jude Law and their wives, for whom Pete arranged Serengeti safaris. Mr. Mater Diop, a judge at the UN Criminal Tribunal for Rwanda, located in Arusha, visits Pete. The two men share their love of jazz. Former US Attorney General Ramsey Clark, who spent time in Arusha while defending a Hutu at the UN Criminal Tribunal, spent an afternoon with the O'Neals. Pete was excited about his visit and sent me the following email:

May 14, 2002.

Greetings Brother Paul, I hope you and your family are well. Charlotte and I just had a wonderful afternoon with the former US Attorney General Ramsey Clark. Wonderful man! As gracious and gentlemanly as he is progressive and knowledgeable. I gave him a brief over-view of the case. He indicated that he had heard of me and our efforts and said that it would be "exciting" to offer some assistance. I asked this of him but only after "bragging" about you and stating that I was well represented! Bottom-line, I'm for whatever you think is best. I think however that his involvement couldn't do anything but help. Your call. As I said before he is an inspiring human being! The only downside is that he labors under the misconception that Texas (where he's from) has bar-b-que on a par with Kansas City. Poor man! I intend to work with him on that point and set him straight! Let me know your thinking about his assistance. Much Love from here. . . . . Pete

I replied that I welcomed Ramsey Clark's involvement, and I offered to send him copies of my petitions. Unfortunately, Clark never responded.

Pete and Charlotte's mutual love and commitment to community service and their international message of justice and respect for all have remained strong, even strengthened over the years. Pete told me, "We are a loving and happy couple that have been together for what will be 50 years in 2019. Our present day community outreach service continues to be informed by our time as Black Panthers. My exile has indeed been a blessing in disguise. Who would have thought that when Judge Stanley sentenced me to prison he was in fact doing me a great service!"

Despite this euphoric statement, Pete and Charlotte have experienced serious health challenges in Tanzania; among them are periodic debilitating bouts of malaria. With these and other health problems in mind, I had wanted to add a humanitarian appeal to my court petitions. Pete, however, strictly forbade me from doing so. He wanted justice, not sympathy.

There have been some changes. I jokingly told Pete how some of his requests from me over the years have been revealing. Prior to my 1997 visit, he asked me to bring him twelve large Butterfinger candy bars and six bags of Fritos. Before my 2012 visit, Pete requested five tubes of Poligrip dental adhesive and two bottles of Pepto-Bismol! Pete's dear mother, Florene, whom he loved and admired greatly, died on February 26, 2018. He had told me that one of the main reasons why he wanted to get back to the States was to spend time with her before she passed on.

One evening during my 2012 visit I joined Pete in his audio-visual room. He was seated in an easy chair surrounded by about a dozen of his children from the Leadership of Tomorrow Children's Home. They address Pete affectionately as *babu* (grandfather). The children were silently watching a PBS *Nature* video on a large screen and enjoying a treat that Pete had gotten for them in Arusha. I apologized to Pete for delaying the writing of a book about his legal case. My excuse, I told him, was that I had been hoping for a positive legal outcome, a happy ending. Pete spread his arms out, as if to embrace the children seated around him, and replied, "Paul, this is my happy ending!"

Notes

INTRODUCTION

1. For the history of the Black Panther Party, the reader can choose from a large number of informative books, including: Hilliard, *This Side of Paradise*; Seale, *Seize the Time*; Kathleen Cleaver and Katsiaficas, eds., *Liberation, Imagination, and the Black Panther Party*; Jones, ed., *The Black Panther Party Reconsidered*; Austin, *Up Against the Wall*; Murch, *Living for the City*; Spencer, *The Revolution Has Come*; Bloom and Martin, *Black against Empire*.

2. The Lowndes County Freedom Organization was an independent political party in rural Alabama, one of whose organizers was Stokely Carmichael, a former Howard University student civil rights activist, who had been involved in Mississippi voter registration activities as a member of the Student Non-violent Coordinating Committee (SNCC). The Deacons for Defense and Justice had been established in Jonesboro, Louisiana, on July 10, 1964, by a group of African American men who were mostly veterans of World War II and the Korean War. Their goal was to combat Ku Klux Klan violence against Congress of Racial Equality (CORE) volunteers who were promoting voter registration. Their stance stood in opposition to Martin L. King's nonviolent philosophy.

3. The Black Panther Party Platform is available at http://history.hanover. edu/courses/excerpts/111bppp.html.

4. Since the early 1970s, the prison and jail populations in the United States have increased at unprecedented rates, with more than a 500 percent rise in the number of people incarcerated. The growing imprisoned population exhibits an increasingly disproportionate racial composition. African Americans have been incarcerated at 5.6 times the rate of whites. See Bonczar, "Prevalence of Imprisonment in the U.S. Population, 1974–2001," and Harrison and Beck, "Prison and Jail Inmates at Midyear 2005." An analysis conducted by researchers at Harvard's School of Public Health found that in the United States between 1960 and

2010, black men were always more than 2.5 times as likely to die due to enforcement actions, termed "legal intervention," than white men. The ratio for black vs. white men for death due to legal intervention was 10 to 1 in 1969. See Krieger et al., "Trends in US Deaths Due to Legal Intervention Among Black and White Men, Age 15–34 Years, by County Income Level: 1960–2010."

5. Rhonda Williams, *Concrete Demands*.

6. Witt, *The Black Panthers in the Midwest*; Tyson, *Radio Free Dixie*.

7. Monaghan, "New Views of The Black Panthers."

8. Smith, *An International History of the Black Panther Party*, 68.

9. Eldridge Cleaver, *On the Ideology of the Black Panther Party*.

10. Eldridge Cleaver, "Eldridge Cleaver Discusses Revolution," 112.

11. Newton, *Huey P. Newton Reader*, 184.

12. Newton wrote: "Bobby [Seale] had collected all of Malcolm X's speeches and ideas from papers like *The Militant* and *Muhammad Speaks*. These we studied carefully" (*Huey P. Newton Reader*, 50).

13. Newton, *Huey P. Newton Reader*, 185.

14. Hilliard, *This Side of Paradise*, 238.

15. Hilliard, *This Side of Paradise*, 163.

16. Newton, *Huey P. Newton Reader*, 148.

17. Seale, *Seize the Time*, 60.

18. Newton, *Huey P. Newton Reader*, 50.

19. Newton, *Huey P. Newton Reader*, 152.

20. Newton, *Revolutionary Suicide*, 195.

21. Newton, *Revolutionary Suicide*. 195.

22. Newton, *Revolutionary Suicide*. 195.

23. Newton, *Huey P. Newton Reader*, 185.

24. Seale, *Seize the Time*, 25–26.

25. Hilliard, "If You Want Peace," 128.

26. Hilliard, "If You Want Peace." 128.

27. Kathleen Cleaver, "Back to Africa," 230.

28. Eldridge Cleaver, "Eldridge Cleaver Discusses Revolution," 110.

29. Newton, *Huey P. Newton Reader*, 187.

30. Newton, *Huey P. Newton Reader*, 298–99.

31. Newton, *Huey P. Newton Reader*, 253.

32. Newton, *Revolutionary Suicide*, 167.

33. Eldridge Cleaver, *Soul on Fire*, 139.

34. Newton, *Revolutionary Suicide*, 167.

35. Newton, *Huey P. Newton Reader*, 148.

36. Hilliard, *This Side of Paradise*, 121.

37. Newton, *Huey P. Newton Reader*, 198.

38. Eldridge Cleaver, *On the Ideology*, 7.

39. Eldridge Cleaver, *On the Ideology*, 7.

40. Eldridge Cleaver, *On the Ideology*, 7.

41. Seale, *Seize the Time*, 64.

42. Booker, "Lumpenization," 147–53.

43. Newton, *Huey P. Newton Reader*, 216.

44. Newton, *Huey P. Newton Reader*, 216–17.

45. Newton, *Huey P. Newton Reader*, 229.

46. The statistics in this section come from *Kansas City Star* and *Kansas City Times, Our City in Racial Ferment* (reprint series), September 21–27, 1968.

47. The information in this section comes from "Reflections on the Kansas City Riot of 1968," video transcript, Missouri State Archives (n.d., 2008?). http://www.sos.mo.gov/archives/presentations/ap_transcripts/kcriot.

CHAPTER 1. GROWING UP

1. This and the following chapters are based on Pete O'Neal's recollections as told to me, Paul J. Magnarella, in June 1998 at Pete's home in Embaseni Village, Tanzania. My additions to Pete's narratives are generally italicized and enclosed in brackets.

CHAPTER 2. LIFE'S TRANSITIONS TO THE BLACK PANTHER PARTY

1. Information about this hearing comes from "Hearings before the Committee on Internal Security House of Representatives," 91st Congress.

2. "Hearings before the Committee on Internal Security House of Representatives," 91st Congress, 2674.

3. Messman, "Rev. Phil Lawson."

4. Hammer, "Lawson's Church Loses Funding."

CHAPTER 3. BLACK PANTHER PARTY–COMMUNITY RELATIONS

1. Nazaryan, "National Park Service Refuses to Honor Black Panthers."

2. McCorkle, "Police Arrest Four at Rally."

3. "Pete O'Neal Fined $25."

4. "Key Man System in Jails."

5. "Jail Overcrowded, Underfunded."

6. "Jail Overcrowded, Underfunded."

7. "Pageant Fracas."

8. Penn. *Case for a Pardon*, 35.

9. Hammer, "Arrest of Church Trainees Is Protested."

10. Fisher, "Church Melee with Activists."

11. Information in this section comes from the author's personal communications with Pete O'Neal, *Kansas City Star* articles from June 1 to 2 and June 26 to 27, 1970, and court documents submitted by defense attorney Austin Shute in the author's possession.

12. "O'Neal Guilty in Disruption."

13. Attorney Austin Shute defended O'Neal in this and many other trials. Shute (1926–2007) was born in Salem, Massachusetts, of an Irish Catholic mother and a Penobscot father. After being honorably discharged from the US Navy in 1942, he joined a VFW post and a yacht club in Massachusetts. When he learned that neither admitted blacks, he quit both. Later, when he moved to Missouri, he witnessed racial segregation that shocked him. "Blacks couldn't get a meal downtown, couldn't go to the bathroom, couldn't get a hotel room" (Shute "A Conversation," 12). Shute earned a JD at the University of Missouri in 1952. He was admitted to practice before the Missouri Supreme Court in 1952 and the US Supreme Court in 1989. For most of his career he served as a criminal defense attorney and as a civil rights advocate. He had a reputation for never turning away any client who could not pay a fee. His many diverse clients included the original flower children, hippies, yuppies, motorcycle clubs, and the Black Panthers of Kansas City. He always represented the Panthers *pro bono*. See Shute, "A Conversation," 12–13.

14. Fisher, "Church Melee with Activists."

15. Undated joint statement in the possession of the author.

16. Fisher, "Church Melee with Activists."

17. *Batson v. Kentucky* (476 US 79).

Chapter 4. Police and US Government Relations

1. Harry Jones, "Police, Negroes, Move for Accord."

2. Harry Jones, "Police, Negroes, Move for Accord."

3. Harry Jones, "Police, Negroes, Move for Accord."

4. Affidavit in the possession of the author.

5. Rowan, "Black Panther Raids Disturbing."

6. Weatherby, "Kansas City Fascist Pig." See also Weatherby, "Off-Duty Pig's Last Act of Terror"; and Harry Jones, "Panther View of Dacy Death."

7. Statement in the possession of the author.

8. Stout, "Clarence M. Kelley."

9. "Servicemen's Clubs, Black-Marketeering Investigated."

10. "General in Service Club Pleads Guilty."

11. "Panthers and Police Battle."

12. Statement in the possession of the author.

13. "Police Reject Blacks' Plan."

14. Pruitt and Lewis, Complaint #Supp. #A408, A409.

15. Smith, Complaint #Supp. #A408, A409.

16. "Police Arrest Panther Chief."

17. "Panther Leader Is Freed."

18. Unless otherwise noted, the information in this section comes from "Hearings before the Committee on Internal Security House of Representatives."

19. Harry Jones, "Panther Rise Linked to Ills."

20. The O'Neal federal case, to be discussed below, involved an almost identical set of laws and facts. Attorney Shute made the same motion for dismissal, but Judge Arthur Stanley rejected it.

21. Harry Jones, "Panther Rise Linked to Ills."

22. Harry Jones, "Panther Rise Linked to Ills."

CHAPTER 5. ARREST, TRIAL, ESCAPE

1. A CIA document described Charles Garry as a "fifth amendment communist," a label that goes back to the hysteria of McCarthyism (CIA Report).

2. "Flag Is Defaced."

3. The US District Court of Kansas appointed attorney Michael Lerner to represent Pete on appeal. However, Pete fled the United States while out on bail before the appeal could be heard. Lerner was later disbarred for reasons unrelated to Pete's case.

CHAPTER 6. FLEEING TO SWEDEN AND ALGERIA

1. For excellent discussions of the Panthers in Algeria, see Kathleen Cleaver, "Back to Africa," and Mokhtefi, *Algiers, Third World Capital.*

2. Kathleen Cleaver, "Back to Africa," 229.

3. Mokhtefi, "Diary," 34.

4. Mokhtefi, *Algiers, Third World Capital,* 109.

5. Hersch, "C.I.A. Reportedly Recruited Blacks for Surveillance of Panther Party."

6. In a US Department of State Memorandum of Conversation dated July 31, 1972, David D. Newsom, US assistant secretary for African affairs, advised Abdel Kader Bousselham, chief of the Algerian Interests Section, that the United States expected Algeria to follow international law with respect to hijacked aircraft by freeing the plane and its crew, returning any ransom money, and either denying the hijackers asylum or prosecuting them.

7. "Black Panther Villa in Algeria Sealed Off After Raid."

8. Mokhtefi, *Algiers, Third World Capital,* 165.

9. On January 18, 1972, Miss Denise Oliver, spokesperson for the Revolutionary People's Communication Network, announced in New York that Eldridge Cleaver had stepped down as head of the International Section of the Black Panther Party and was replaced by Pete O'Neal ("O'Neal to Cleaver Post").

10. Kathleen Cleaver, "Back to Africa," 250.

11. Angelo, "We All Became Black."

12. Kathleen Cleaver, "Back to Africa," 249.

13. Allmanjan, "The 'Rebirth' of Eldridge Cleaver."

14. Mansnerus, "Timothy Leary, Pied Piper of Psychedelic 60's Dies at 75."

15. Mokhtefi, *Algiers, Third World Capital,* 115.

CHAPTER 7. LEAVING ALGERIA AND LIVING IN TANZANIA

1. The *Kansas City Times* reported that David McMahon, the vice consul at the US Embassy in Tanzania, acknowledged that Pete O'Neal and some other African Americans had been arrested by Tanzanian authorities. The initial arrest occurred on May 28, 1974, after Tanzanian officials found a small number of undeclared firearms in a shipment of household goods sent to the African Americans from the United States. O'Neal was later arrested for possessing a walkie-talkie (Harry Jones, "Tanzania Arrests O'Neal, Kansans").

CHAPTER 8. SETTLING IN IMBASENI VILLAGE

1. Stormy's namesake, Ann Wood, was a heroine who led a group of escaping teenaged slaves from Loudon County, Virginia, to Philadelphia in 1855 (Still, *The Underground Railroad*).

2. Charlotte's poems can be found in her two publications, *Warrior Woman of Peace* and *Life Slices . . . a Taste of My Heaven*.

CHAPTER 9. FROM THE HAGUE TO ARUSHA TO KANSAS FEDERAL COURT

1. Judge Stanley's biographical information comes from *United States District Court for the District of Kansas*.

2. *United States District Court for the District of Kansas*; Dauner and Fitzpatrick, "Arthur J. Stanley Jr., Longtime Judge, Dies."

3. Unless otherwise stated, the information and quotations in this section come from *Gessner v. United States* (1965).

4. Criminal Docket, *U.S. vs Gessner*.

5. *Ex parte Milligan* (1886).

6. *United States District Court for the District of Kansas*.

7. "Conviction Nullified."

CHAPTER 10. FIRST PETITION

1. *United States v. Felix Lindsey O'Neal* (1970).

2. *United States v. Williamson* (1986).

3. *Pyles v. Boles* (1966).

4. *United States v. Wainwright* (1991).

5. "Dismiss Woman in Name Calling Case," *Kansas City Times,* December 23, 1968, 3A.

6. Affidavit in possession of the author.

7. US Senate Select Committee to Study Government Operations with Respect to Intelligence Activities, 1976. Also see US Senate, Committee on the Judiciary, Subcommittee on Constitutional Rights, 1974.

8. Books based on these and other government and court documents include: Swearingen, *FBI Secrets*; Perkus, ed., *COINTELPRO*; Theoharis, *Spying on*

Americans; David J. Garrow, *The FBI and Martin Luther King, Jr.*; Churchill and Vander Wall, *The FBI's Secret Wars against the Black Panther Party and the American Indian Movement* and *The COINTELPRO Papers*.

9. *Hampton v. Hanrahan* (1979), 613–15.
10. *Hampton v. Hanrahan* (1979) 621–22.
11. *Hampton v. Hanrahan* (1979), 609–10.
12. *Hampton v. Hanrahan* (1979), 641.
13. *Hampton v. Hanrahan* (1979), 642.
14. O'Reilly, *Racial Matters,* 315; Churchill and Vander Wall, *The COINTELPRO Papers*.
15. Pearson, *Shadow of the Panther,* 110–11.
16. Smith, *An International History of the Black Panther Party,* 68.
17. "Hearings before the Committee on Internal Security House of Representatives," 2966.
18. US 1975.
19. US 1949.
20. CA3 NJ 1963.
21. 133 P. 2d 818.
22. 24 P.2d 766 (1933).
23. 330 P. 2d 894.
24. 7 Cal. 3d 248.
25. 5 Cal. 3d 330.
26. 1997 US 7th Cir.
27. 899 F.2d 543, 6th Cir. 1990.
28. 993 F.2d 686, 691, 9th Cir. 1993.
29. Trial transcript, 3–4.
30. 321 F. Supp. 1074 (1971).
31. Criminal No. KC-CR-1204 (D.C. Kan., September 1, 1970).
32. That is, *Weeks v. United States,* 232 US 383 (1914); *Mapp v. Ohio,* 367 US 643 (1961); *Silverthorne Lumber Co. v. United States,* 251 US 385 (1920); *Silverman v. United States,* 365 US 505 (1961); *Katz v. United States,* 389 US 347 (1967).
33. 321 F. Supp. 424 (C.D. Cal. 1971).
34. 407 US 297; 92 S. Ct. 2125 (1972).
35. 394 US 165 (1969).
36. Indictment, filed October 29, 1969.
37. Trial transcript, 66, emphasis added.
38. "Los Angeles Confronts a Bitter Racial Legacy."
39. Penn, "Ex-Panther Hopes Exile Will End."

CHAPTER 11. SUBMISSION, RESPONSES, AND FINAL ORDERS

1. *Carlisle v. United States* (1996).
2. *United States v. Bustillos* (1994).

3. 10th Cir. 934.

4. *Murray v. Carrier* (1986)

5. See Kansas City Star and Kansas City Times, *Our City in Racial Ferment.*

6. See Charns, *Cloak and Gavel.*

7. 338 US 189 (1949).

8. *Ortega-Rodrigues v. United States* (1993), quoting *Molinaro v. New Jersey* (1970).

9. *Ortega-Rodrigues v. United States* (1993).

10. *Estelle v. Dorrough* (1975).

11. See *United States v. Sinclair* (1971).

12. *Murray v. Carrier* (1986).

CHAPTER 12. EVIDENCE OF PERJURY AND A NEW PETITION

1. Espinoza, "Notes Found in House."

2. Crayton and Dauner, "Judge, Wife Found Dead."

3. Crayton and Dauner, "Judge, Wife Found Dead."

4. Crayton and Dauner, "Judge, Wife Found Dead."

5. Moore, *Very Special Agents,* 97.

6. Moore, *Very Special Agents,* 96.

7. Moore, *Very Special Agents,* 96–97.

8. Moore, *Very Special Agents,* 97.

9. *Napue v. Illinois* (1959).

10. *In Re Elmer Geronimo Pratt* (1997).

11. *In Re Elmer Geronimo Pratt* (1997); *Brady v. Maryland* (1963).

12. *In Re Elmer Geronimo Pratt* (1997).

13. *Napue v. Illinois* (1959), quoting New York Court of Appeals, *People v. Savvides,* (1956).

14. Penn, "Ex-Panther Hopes Exile Will End."

15. "House Committee to Investigate Panthers."

CHAPTER 13. JUSTICE DENIED

1. *Molinaro v. New Jersey* (1970).

CHAPTER 14. THE SHAKUR PROPOSAL

1. For a list of these films and publications see: Cultural Influence, Assata Shakur.

2. Griego, "Cuba Still Harbors One of America's Most Wanted Fugitives."

3. "Trump Calls on Cuba to Return U.S. Fugitives."

CHAPTER 15. LIFE THEN AND NOW

1. United African.

2. Johnnie Lee Cochran Jr. was an American lawyer best known for his role

in the 1995 defense and criminal acquittal of O. J. Simpson for the murder of his former wife, Nicole Brown Simpson, and her friend Ron Goldman. Cochran had represented Geronimo Pratt in his 1972 murder conviction trial. Pratt's conviction was vacated in 1997 because the prosecution in his 1972 trial had failed to inform the court that its key witness was an FBI and Los Angeles Police Department informant. In 1998, Cochran represented Pratt in a civil lawsuit against the FBI and the LAPD, accusing them of malicious prosecution and false imprisonment. The suit was settled for $4.5 million. Pratt established the Kuji Foundation with his share of the settlement. Cochran died on March 29, 2005.

3. Charlotte O'Neal, "'Mama C,' I Almost Lost Myself."

4. *Francisco Bay View*, April 5, 2013.

5. Emanuel Cleaver II is a distant cousin of Pete O'Neal and a member of the Democratic Party. He served as Mayor of Kansas City, Missouri, from 1991 to 1999. In 2004, Cleaver was elected to represent Missouri's Fifth Congressional District in the US House of Representatives.

6. The People's Organization for Progress (POP) is a New Jersey–based, independent, politically progressive association of citizens working for racial, social, and economic justice. Founded in 1983, POP grew out of the struggles of the African American community for justice during the late sixties and seventies. It has awarded similar recognitions to Malcolm X and scholar-activist W. E. B. DuBois.

7. The All-African People's Revolutionary Party is an Africa-based organization founded in 1968 by Dr. Kwame Nkrumah, Ghana's first president. It has promoted Pan-Africanism: the total liberation and unification of Africa under scientific socialism. Kwame Toure (Stokely Carmichael) was one of the party's leaders from the 1970s until his death in 1998.

Bibliography

PRIMARY SOURCES

FEDERAL CASES

Alderman v. United States. 394 US 165 (1969).

Batson v. Kentucky. 476 US 79 (1986).

Beecham v. United States. 511 US 368 (1993).

Brady v. Maryland. 373 US 83 (1963).

Brown v. Board of Education. 347 US 483 (1954).

Brown v. Board of Education. 349 US 294 (1955).

Carlisle v. United States. 517 US 416, 429 (1996).

Citronelle-Mobile Gathering, Inc. v. Watkins. 943 F.2d 1297, 1034 n. 5 (11th Cir. 1991).

Eisler v. United States. 338 US 189 (1949).

Estelle v. Dorrough. 420 US 534, 544 (1975).

Ex parte Milligan. 71 US (4 Wall.) 2 (1866).

Gagnon v. Scarpelli. 411 US 778, 782, 36 L. Ed. 2d 656, 93 S. Ct. 1756 (1973).

Garrison v United States. 154 F.2d 106 (5th Cir. 1946).

George John Gessner, Appellant, v. United States of America, Appellee. US Court of Appeals Tenth Circuit. 354 F.2d 726 (1965).

Giglio v. United States. 405 US 150, 31 L.Ed 2d 104, 108, 92 S. Ct. 763 (1972).

Goldstein v United States Parole Comm'n (1996, CD Cal). 940 F Supp 1505.

Hampton v. Hanrahan. 600 F.2d 600 (7th Cir. 1979).

Kagen v. United States. 360 F.2d 30 (10th Cir. 1966).

Katz v. United States. 389 US 347 (1967).

Kiger v. United States. 315 F.2d 778 (7th Cir. 1963).

Korematsu v. United States. 584 F. Supp. 1406 (N.D.Cal. 1984).

Kyles v. Whitley. 514 US 419, 131 L. Ed 2d 490, 508–10, 115 S. Ct. 1555 (1995).

Loving v. Virginia. 388 US 1 (1967).

Mapp v. Ohio. 367 US 643 (1961).

Molinaro v. New Jersey. 396 US 365 (1970).

Mooney v. Holohan. 294 US 103 (1935).

Morgan v. United States. 222 F.2d 673, 674 (2d Cir. 1955).

Murray v. Carrier. 477 US 487 (1986).

Napue v. Illinois. 360 US 264 (1959).

Ortega-Rodrigues v. United States. 507 US 234 (1993).

Pyle v. Kansas. 317 US 213 (1942).

Pyles v. Boles. 250 F. Supp. 285 *N.D.W.Va.* (1966).

Silverman v. United States. 365 US 505 (1961).

Silverthorne Lumber Co. v. United States. 251 US 385 (1920).

Smith v. Secretary of New Mexico Dept. Of Corrections. 50 Fed. 3d 801, 824–26, certiorari denied 116 S. Ct. 272, 133 L.Ed. 2d 193 (1995).

Smith v. United States. 94 US 97 (1876).

United States v. Bagley 473 US 667, 87 L.Ed. 2d 481, 105 S.Ct. 3375 (1985).

United States v. Bustillos (10th Cir. 1994).

United States v. Cariola. 323 F.2d 180 (CA3 NJ 1963).

United States v. Cassidy. 899 F.2d 543 (6th Cir. 1990).

United States v. Felix Lindsey O'Neal. Criminal No. KC-CR-1204 (D.C. Kan., September 1, 1970).

United States v. Fuller. 938 F. Supp. 731 (US Dist., KS 1996).

United States v. Holmes. 680 F.2d 1372 (11th Cir. 1982).

United States v. Liska. 409 F Supp 1405 (ED Wisc. 1976).

United States v. Lupino. 505 F.2d 643 (8th Cir. 1974).

United States v. McClelland. 941 F.2d 999 (9th Cir. 1991).

United States v. Morgan. 346 US 502, 98 L.Ed 248, 74 S Ct 247 (1954).

United States v. Ransom. 985 F. Supp. 1017 (US Dist. KS 1997).

United States v. Romero. 642 F.2d 392 (10th Cir. 1981).

United States v. Sinclair. 321 F. Supp. 1074 (1971).

United States v. Smith. 321 F. Supp. 424 (C.D. Cal. 1971).

United States v. Steinberg. 99 Fed.3d 1486 (1996).

United States v. Strother (1970, CA5 Miss). 434 F2d 1292, later app (CA5 Miss) 458 F2d 424, cert den 409 US 1011, 34 L Ed 2d 305, 93 S Ct 456.

United States v. Taylor. 648 F.2d 565 (9th Cir. 1981).

United States v. Thompson. 117 F.3d 1033, 1034 (7th Cir. 1997).

United States v. U.S. District Court for the Eastern District of Michigan. 407 US 297; 92 S. Ct. 2125 (1972).

United States v. Varela. 993 F.2d 686, 691 (9th Cir. 1993).

United States v. Wainwright. 938 F.2d 1096 (10th Cir. 1991).

United States v. Wickham. 474 F Supp 113 (CD Cal. 1979).

United States v. Williamson. 806 F.2d 216 (1986).

Weeks v. United States. 232 US 383 (1914).

CALIFORNIA STATE CASES

Ex parte Miller. 24 P.2d 766 (1933).
In Re Elmer Geronimo Pratt. Memorandum of Decision. Superior Ct. CA, A 267020 (May 29, 1997).
In Re Ferguson. 5 Cal. 3d 525 (1971).
In Re Herrera. 23 Cal.2d 206 [143 P.2d 345] (1943).
People v. Hannon. 5 Cal. 3d 330 [96 Cal. Rptr. 35, 486 P.2d] (1971).
People v. Johnson. 330 P.2d 894 (1958).
People v. Navarro. 7 Cal. 3d 248 (1972).
People v. Weaver. 133 P.2d 818 (1943).

NEW YORK CASE

People v. Savvides. 1 N.Y.2nd 554 (1956).

STATUTES AND US CONSTITUTION

18 USC 921(a)(20). Definitions (1970).
18 USC 922(g)(1). Unlawful Acts (1970).
18 USC § 927. Effect on State law.
28 USCS § 1651 (1997), § 1651. Writs.
California Penal Code. Sections 17, 496, and 4532(a).
California Welfare and Institutions Code. Section 1772.
US Constitution. First, Fourth, Fifth, Thirteenth, and Fourteenth Amendments.

US CONGRESSIONAL AND GOVERNMENT PUBLICATIONS

Bonczar, Thomas P. "Prevalence of Imprisonment in the U.S. Population, 1974–2001." *Bureau of Justice Statistics*, 2003.
CIA Report. "Black Panther Party." Date redacted, MORI DocID:22138.
Criminal Docket, *United States v. Gessner.* US District Court of Kansas, May 29, 1963.
Harrison, Paige M., and Allen J. Beck. "Prison and Jail Inmates at Midyear 2005." *Bureau of Justice Statistics, 2006.*
"Hearings before the Committee on Internal Security House of Representatives." 91st Cong., 2nd Sess. Black Panther Party. Part 1, Investigation of Kansas City Chapter; National Organization Data. March 4, 5, 6, and 10, 1970. Washington, DC: US Government Printing Office.
Kerner Report (National Advisory Commission on Civil Disorders). 1968. http://www.archive.org/stream/kernerreportrevio00asse/kernerreportrevio00asse_djvu.txt.
Pruitt, William, and Larry Lewis. Complaint #Supp. #A408, A409. Kansas City Missouri Police Department, 27th St. Station, January 2, 1970. Investigation arrest and recovery property. Copy in author's possession.

Senate Select Committee to Study Governmental Operations with Respect to Intelligence Activities. *The FBI's Covert Action Program to Destroy the Black Panther Party*. S.Rep. No. 94–755, 94th Cong., 2d Sess., 187 (1976).

"Servicemen's Clubs, Black-Marketeering Investigated." *Congressional Quarterly Almanac 1969*, 25th ed., 902–6. Washington, DC: Congressional Quarterly, 1970.

Smith, F. Complaint #Supp. #A408, A409. Kansas City Missouri Police Department, 27th St. Station, February 3, 1970. Arraignment of prisoners. Copy in author's possession.

US Department of State. Memorandum of Conversation, July 31, 1972.

United States District Court for the District of Kansas. 1990–2014. https://static1.squarespace.com/static/54170cd0e4b00eba52a2db00/t/56993fdfbfe873c77d04e200/1452883948069/DistrictOfKansas_1990-2014.pdf.

US Senate, Committee on the Judiciary, Subcommittee on Constitutional Rights, 93rd Cong., 2nd Sess. *Hearings on FBI Counterintelligence Programs* (Washington, DC: US Government Printing Office, 1974).

US Senate, Select Committee to Study Government Operations with Respect to Intelligence Activities. 94th Cong., 1st Sess. Vol. 6: *The Federal Bureau of Investigation*. Washington, DC:, US Printing Office, 1976.

SECONDARY SOURCES AND NEWSPAPER ARTICLES

Abu-Jamal, M. *We Want Freedom: A Life in the Black Panther Party*. Cambridge, MA: South End Press, 2004.

Acoli, Sundiata. *A Brief History of the Black Panther Party: Its Place in the Black Liberation Movement*. 1995. http://www.hartford-hwp.com/archives/45a/004.html.

Allmanjan, T. D. "The 'Rebirth' of Eldridge Cleaver: The Old Cleaver Wanted to Overthrow the 'American Nightmare.' The New Cleaver Is Promoting the 'American Dream.' Is He a Convert or an Opportunist?" *New York Times*, January 16, 1977.

Angelo, Anne-Marie. "We All Became Black: Tony Soares, African-American Internationalists, and Anti-Imperialism." In *Other Special Relationship: Race, Rights, and Riots in Britain and the United States*, ed. Robin D. G. Kelley and Stephen Tuck, 95–102. London: Palgrave Macmillan, 2015.

Atiba, Phillip et al. "The Science of Justice: Race, Arrests, and Police Use of Force." Center for Policing Equality, July 2016. http://policingequity.org/wp-content/uploads/2016/07/CPE_SoJ_Race-Arrests-UoF_2016-07-08-1130.pdf.

Austin, Curtis J. *Up against the Wall: Violence in the Making and Unmaking of the Black Panther Party*. Fayetteville: University of Arkansas Press, 2008.

"Black Panther Party Ten Point Program." http://history.hanover.edu/courses/excerpts/111bppp.html.

"Black Panther Villa in Algeria Sealed Off After Raid by Police." *New York Times,* August 12, 1972, 6. https://www.nytimes.com/1972/08/12/archives/black-panther-villa-in-algeria-sealed-off-after-raid-by-police.html.

"Black Panthers Become Sons of Malcolm." *The Call,* May 8, 1970.

Bloom, Joshua, and Waldo E. Martin Jr. *Black against Empire: The History and Politics of the Black Panther Party.* Los Angeles: University of California Press, 2016.

Booker, Chris. "Lumpenization: A Critical Error of the Black Panther Party." In *The Panther Party Reconsidered,* ed. Charles E. Jones, 147–53. Baltimore: Black Classic Press, 1998.

Charns, Alexander. *Cloak and Gavel: FBI Wiretaps. Bugs, Informers, and the Supreme Court.* Urbana: University of Illinois Press, 1992.

Churchill, Ward, and Jim Vander Wall. *The COINTELPRO Papers: Documents from the FBI's Secret Wars against Domestic Dissent.* Boston: South End Press, 1990.

———. *The FBI's Secret Wars against the Black Panther Party and the American Indian Movement.* Boston: South End Press, 1990.

Cleaver, Eldridge. "Eldridge Cleaver Discusses Revolution: An Interview from Exile." In *The Black Panthers Speak,* ed. Philip S. Foner, 108–16. New York, J. B. Lippincott, 2014.

———. *On the Ideology of the Black Panther Party.* Pamphlet, 1970. http://www.etext.org/Politics/MIM/bpp/bppideology1970.html.

———. *Soul on Fire.* 1968. New York: Word Books, 1978.

Cleaver, Kathleen Neal. "Back to Africa: The Evolution of the International Section of the Black Panther Party (1969–1972)." In *The Black Panther Party Reconsidered,* ed. Charles E. Jones, 211–54. Baltimore: Black Classic Press, 1998.

———, and George Katsiaficas, eds. *Liberation, Imagination, and the Black Panther Party.* New York: Routledge, 2001.

"Conviction Nullified: Freed Prisoner Flays Injustice." *Ogden Standard-Examiner,* March 9, 1966, 7A.

Crayton, Rasheeda, and John T. Dauner. "Judge, Wife Found Dead. Murder-Suicide Suspected in Death of Mission Couple." *Kansas City Star,* November 30, 1998, 1A.

Cultural Influence, Assata Shakur. https://en.wikipedia.org/wiki/Assata_Shakur#Cultural_influence.

Dauner, John T., and James C. Fitzpatrick. "Arthur J. Stanley Jr., Longtime Judge, Dies." *Kansas City Star,* January 31, 2001, B3.

Espinoza, Richard. "Notes Found in House. Only Judge, Wife Were Involved in Deaths, Police Say." *Kansas City Star,* December 5, 1998, B1.

Fanon, Frantz. *The Wretched of the Earth.* New York: Grove, 1968.

Fisher, Brenda. "Church Melee with Activists." *Kansas City Star,* June 2, 1970, 1.

"Flag Is Defaced." *Kansas City Star,* September 3, 1970.

Foner, Philip S., ed. *The Black Panthers Speak.* New York, J. B. Lippincott, 1970.

Garrow, David J. *The FBI and Martin Luther King, Jr.: From "Solo" to Memphis.* New York: W. W. Norton, 1981.

"General in Service Club Pleads Guilty." *New York Times*, April 4, 1971. http://www.nytimes.com/1971/04/10/archives/general-in-service-club-inquiry-pleads-guilty-to-gun-charges.html.

Griego, Tina. "Cuba Still Harbors One of America's Most Wanted Fugitives. What Happens to Assata Shakur Now?" *Washington Post,* December 20, 2014.

Hammer, Charles. "Arrest of Church Trainees Is Protested." *Kansas City Star,* June 2, 1970.

———. "Lawson's Church Loses Funding." *Kansas City Star,* November 8, 1970, 1A.

Hass, Jeffrey. *The Assassination of Fred Hampton: How the FBI and the Chicago Police Murdered a Black Panther.* Chicago: Chicago Review Press, 2011.

Hersch, Seymour. "C.I.A. Reportedly Recruited Blacks for Surveillance of Panther Party." *New York Times*, March 17, 1978, 15.

Hilliard, David. *This Side of Paradise: The Autobiography of David Hilliard and the Story of the Black Panther Party.* Boston: Little Brown, 1993.

———. "If You Want Peace You Got To Fight for It." In *The Black Panthers Speak*, ed. Philip S. Foner, 128–29. New York, J. B. Lippincott, 1970.

"House Committee to Investigate Panthers." *Kansas City Star*, March 4, 1970, 1A.

"Jail Overcrowded, Underfunded." *Kansas City Times,* January 13, 1970.

Jeffries, Judson L., ed. *Comrades: A Local History of the Black Panther Party.* Bloomington: Indiana University Press, 2007.

Jones, Charles E., ed. *The Black Panther Party Reconsidered.* Baltimore: Black Classic Press, 1998.

Jones, Harry. "Panther Rise Linked to Ills: Rep. Herman Johnson Says Kansas City Officials Over-React." *Kansas City Star*, March 7, 1970.

———. "Panther View of Dacy Death." *Kansas City Star*, August 2, 1969.

———. "Police, Negroes, Move for Accord." *Kansas City Star*. February 16, 1969, 1A.

———. "Tanzania Arrests O'Neal, Kansans." *Kansas City Times*, July 19, 1974, 4.

Kansas City Star and Kansas City Times. *Our City in Racial Ferment.* Reprint series, September 21–27, 1968.

"Key Man System in Jails." *Kansas City Times*, January 9, 1970.

Krieger, Nancy, et al. "Trends in US Deaths Due to Legal Intervention Among Black and White Men, Age 15–34 Years, by County Income Level: 1960–2010." *Harvard Public Health Review* 3 (2015). http://harvardpublichealthreview.org/190/.

"Los Angeles Confronts a Bitter Racial Legacy in a Black Panther Case." *New York Times,* July 20, 1971.

Mansnerus, Laura. "Timothy Leary, Pied Piper of Psychedelic 60's Dies at 75."

New York Times, June 1, 1996. https://www.nytimes.com/1996/06/01/us/
timothy-leary-pied-piper-of-psychedelic-60-s-dies-at-75.html?mtrref.

Mauer, Marc, and Ryan S. King. "Uneven Justice: State Rates of Incarceration
by Race and Ethnicity." *The Sentencing Project.* Washington, DC, July 2007.
http://www.sentencingproject.org/publications/uneven-justice-state-rates-
of-incarceration-by-race-and-ethnicity/.

McCorkle, William L. "Police Arrest Four at Rally: Negro Leaders Taken into
Custody at Trash Protest." *Kansas City Star,* June 14, 1969.

Messman, Terry. "Rev. Phil Lawson: Building the 'Beloved Community." *Street
Spirit,* Aug. 9, 2013. http://www.thestreetspirit.org/rev-phil-lawson-build-
ing-the-beloved-community.

Mokhtefi, Elaine. *Algiers, Third World Capital: Freedom Fighters, Revolutionaries,
Black Panthers.* New York: Verso, 2018.

———. "Diary." *London Review of Books* 39, no. 11 (June 1, 2017): 34–35.

Monaghan, Peter. "New Views of the Black Panthers Paint Shades of Gray."
Chronicle of Higher Education 53 (March 2, 2007). http://chronicle.com/week-
ly/v53/i26/26a01201.htm.

Moore, James. *Very Special Agents: The Inside Story of America's Most Controversial Law Enforcement Agency—The Bureau of Alcohol, Tobacco, and Firearms.*
New York: Pocket Books, 1997.

Murch, Donna Jean. *Living for the City: Migration, Education, and the Rise of the
Black Panther Party in Oakland.* Chapel Hill: University of North Carolina
Press, 2010.

Nazaryan, Alexander. "National Park Service Refuses to Honor Black Panthers
after Police Union Complains." *Newsweek,* November 6, 2017. http://www.
newsweek.com/national-park-service-refuses-honor-black-panthers-after-
police-union-702730.

Newton, Huey P. *The Huey P. Newton Reader.* New York: Seven Stories Press,
2002.

———. *Revolutionary Suicide.* New York: Harcourt Brace Jovanovich, 1973.

Olsen, Jack. *Last Man Standing: The Tragedy and Triumph of Geronimo Pratt.* New
York: Doubleday, 2000.

O'Neal, Charlotte. *Life Slices . . . a Taste of My Heaven.* Kansas City: Pennbooks,
2013.

———. "'Mama C,' I Almost Lost Myself." https://www.youtube.com/
watch?v=gTbVJiw9Kf8.

———. *Warrior Woman of Peace.* Kansas City: Pennbooks, 2008.

"O'Neal Guilty in Disruption." *Kansas City Star,* June 26, 1970, 1, 2.

"O'Neal to Cleaver Post." *Kansas City Star,* January 18, 1972.

O'Reilly, Kenneth. *Racial Matters: The FBI's Secret File on Black America 1960–
1972.* New York: Free Press, 1989.

"Pageant Fracas." *Kansas City Star,* June 9–10, 1970.

"Panther Leader Is Freed; Magistrate Says State Failed to Make Case against O'Neal." *Kansas City Star,* January 8, 1970.

"Panthers and Police Battle." *Kansas City Star,* December 6, 1969.

Pearson, Hugh. *Shadow of the Panther.* Boston: Da Capo Press, 1994.

Penn, Steve. *Case for a Pardon.* Kansas City: Pennbooks, 2013.

———. "Ex-Panther Hopes Exile Will End; Mayor Cleaver Leading Effort for a Pardon from Clinton Administration." *Kansas City Star,* February 20, 1993.

Perkus, Cathy, ed. *COINTELPRO: The FBI's Secret War on Political Freedom.* New York: Monad Press, 1975.

"Pete O'Neal Fined $25; Black Panther Leader Guilty of Disorderly Conduct." *Kansas City Star,* January 8, 1970.

"Police Arrest Panther Chief; Pete O'Neal Is Charged with Common Assault." *Kansas City Times,* January 3, 1970, 3A.

"Police Reject Blacks' Plan." *Kansas City Times,* December 20, 1969, 1A, 8A.

Rowan, Carl T. "Black Panther Raids Disturbing." *Scrantonian,* December 28, 1969, 28.

Seale, Bobby. *Seize the Time: The Story of the Black Panther Party and Huey P. Newton.* Baltimore: Black Classic Press, 1991.

Shute, Austin. "A Conversation with Austin F. Shute." *KC Counselor* 5, no. 4 (1966).

Sikora, Andrew G. and Michael Mulvihill. "Trends in Mortality Due to Legal Intervention in the United States, 1979 through 1997." *American Journal of Public Health* 92, no. 5 (2002): 841–43.

Smith, Jennifer B. *An International History of the Black Panther Party.* New York: Garland, 1968.

Spencer, Robyn C. *The Revolution Has Come: Black Power, Gender, and the Black Panther Party in Oakland.* Durham, NC: Duke University Press, 2016.

Still, William. *The Underground Railroad.* Philadelphia: Porter and Coates, 1872.

Stout, David. "Clarence M. Kelley, Director of F.B.I. in the 70s, Dies at 85." *New York Times,* August 6, 1997. http://www.nytimes.com/1997/08/06/us/clarence-m-kelley-director-of-fbi-in-the-70-s-dies-at-85.html?mcubz=3.

Swearingen, M. Wesley. *FBI Secrets: An Agent's Exposé.* Boston: South End Press, 1995.

Theoharis, Athan. *Spying on Americans: Political Surveillance from Hoover to the Houston Plan.* Philadelphia: Temple University Press, 1978.

"Trump Calls on Cuba to Return U.S. Fugitives, Including Cop-Killer Chesimard." *Washington Times,* June 16, 2017. https://www.washingtontimes.com/news/2017/jun/16/donald-trump-calls-cuba-return-us-fugitives/.

Tyson, Tim. *Radio Free Dixie: Robert F. Williams and the Roots of Black Power.* Chapel Hill: University of North Carolina Press, 1999.

"United African." https://www.uaacc.net.

Weatherby, Andre. "Kansas City Fascist Pig Performing His Final Duty." *Black Panther*, August 8, 1969.

———. "Off-Duty Pig's Last Act of Terror." *Black Panther*, August 2, 1969.

Williams, Jakobi. *From the Bullet to the Ballot: The Illinois Chapter of the Black Panther Party and Racial Coalition Politics in Chicago*. Chapel Hill: University of North Carolina Press, 2015.

Williams, Rhonda Y. *Concrete Demands: The Search for Black Power in the 20th Century*. New York: Routledge, 2014.

Witt, Andrew R. *The Black Panthers in the Midwest*. New York: Routledge, 2007.

Zukerman, Michael. "Criminal Injustice: Alec Karakatsanis Puts 'Human Caging' and 'Wealth-Based Detention' in America on Trial." *Harvard Magazine* 120, no. 1 (2017): 44–51.

Index

PAUL J. MAGNARELLA has held various academic positions at the University of Florida. He was a professor in the Department of Anthropology and in the Department of Criminology, Law and Society. He was also an affiliate professor of African studies, European studies, and law. Most recently, he served as an adjunct professor of law. During a ten-year period away from the university, he founded and directed the Peace and Justice Studies Program at Warren Wilson College in Asheville, North Carolina. He holds the PhD, Harvard University, and the JD with honors, University of Florida College of Law. He sits on the editorial boards of several journals, including the *Journal of Social Justice* and the *Journal of Global South Studies*. He has served as expert-on-mission to the UN Criminal Tribunal for the Former Yugoslavia and as legal counsel to the American Anthropological Association's Human Rights Committee and the Association of Third World Studies (ATWS). Paul is a past president of ATWS and a recipient of that association's Presidential Award. He has authored over one hundred academic articles and seven books. His book *Justice in Africa: Rwanda's Genocide, Its National Courts, and the UN Criminal Tribunal* received ATWS's Book of the Year Award and was nominated for the Raphael Lemkin Book Award. Paul also served as pro bono attorney for Black Panther Pete O'Neal, who is exiled in Tanzania.

Printed in the United States
By Bookmasters